LEARNING TO LIVE

RACHELLE R. GREEN

LEARNING TO LIVE

PRISONS, PEDAGOGY, AND THEOLOGICAL EDUCATION

BAYLOR UNIVERSITY PRESS

© 2024 by Baylor University Press
Waco, Texas 76798

All Rights Reserved. No part of this publication may be reproduced, stored in a retrieval system, or transmitted, in any form or by any means, electronic, mechanical, photocopying, recording, or otherwise, without the prior permission in writing of Baylor University Press.

Cover and book design by Elyxandra Encarnación
Cover photo: Xiaoyi/Pexels

Library of Congress Cataloging-in-Publication Data
Names: Green, Rachelle R., 1982- author.
Title: Learning to live : prisons, pedagogy, and theological education / Rachelle R. Green.
Description: Waco, Texas : Baylor University Press, [2024] | Includes bibliographical references and index. | Summary: "Uses ethnographic research to bring the standpoints of women surviving incarceration to conversations about a good life and the purposes of theological education"-- Provided by publisher.
Identifiers: LCCN 2024021070 (print) | LCCN 2024021071 (ebook) | ISBN 9781481320719 (paperback) | ISBN 9781481320740 (adobe pdf) | ISBN 9781481320733 (epub)
Subjects: LCSH: Women prisoners--Religious life. | Theology--Study and teaching.
Classification: LCC BV4595 .G73 2024 (print) | LCC BV4595 (ebook) | DDC 230.071/5--dc23/eng/20240610
LC record available at https://lccn.loc.gov/2024021070
LC ebook record available at https://lccn.loc.gov/2024021071

For the people in Theology

CONTENTS

Preface ix
Acknowledgments xv

    Introduction: A Matter of Life and Death   1

1   Learning in a Place that Feels like Dying   19

2   Imagining Your Good Life   49

3   Is Your Good Life Possible Here?   95

4   What Theology Makes Possible   123

5   Fostering Life-Affirming Praxis in Theology   173

6   Nurturing Life-Affirming Futures through Theological Education   197

Notes 207
Bibliography 229
Index 237

PREFACE

The first time I stand in the classroom, I fidget. The room is tense, yet I am the only one in it. White cinder block walls surround me. The wall to my right is lined with windows, the glass clouded with the passage of time. I open the white blinds covering the windows to admit what little light I can. The room faces a small cement courtyard. Several feet away is another brick wall. The room smells of age and disinfectant. On the wall to my left is a chalkboard flanked by two steel doors that automatically lock when closed. At this point, they are propped open, but once I close them, no one can get inside without a key. In a few minutes, I will be in here with twenty-five incarcerated students. I walk between the tables and chairs, hoping that my prayer-filled promenade will release the knots tightening in my stomach.

You do not want to be flashy or parade your aesthetic choices before these women. I remember this from the volunteer training offered by the Department of Corrections. *Do not tempt them with jewelry or incite them with your appearance. Remember, they are in prison for a reason*, the trainer said with utmost seriousness. *They will try to manipulate you.* Internally, I protested the comments when they were made, but here I stand—in simple black pants. A gray top. Simple pearl stud earrings. Like the room, I tried to make myself as plain as possible. I am not sure whether I should sit or stand. How should I greet the students? What will they be like? Will I be safe in this room alone? Will this class be meaningful here? I wait at the front of the room.

Before I see them, I hear them. Laughter. Chatter. Intermittent greetings. It sounds like joy. And then they enter. Bright purples, blues, and pinks of various saturations are painted on eyes, nails, and lips. Intricate braids, twists, and plaits adorn the kinky, coily, straight, and curly hair. Buzz cuts and fades from dusty blonde to deep brunette. And there is jewelry—rings and earrings. They come into the class full of laughter and color, and life.

That was 2012, the first time I stepped inside a state prison for women in Georgia to teach in the Certificate in Theological Studies program. It was the middle of the fall semester of my second year of seminary, and I was teaching a course on the theological contributions of women in the eighteenth, nineteenth, and twentieth centuries. For twelve weeks, I came to class each Friday, my wardrobe and outlook becoming more colorful with each trip. Students came eager to discuss the letters, prayers, poems, speeches, interviews, and writings I presented from thinkers like Sojourner Truth, Elizabeth Cady Stanton, Delores Williams, Ada María Isasi-Díaz, and Barbara Brown Taylor, among others. Students wrote weekly in their theological reflection journals, exploring their responses to the material and making connections to contemporary challenges. Often in class, we investigated texts by reading and enacting them aloud. We modeled debates about women preaching and feminism. We wrote twenty-first-century versions of *The Declaration of Sentiments* from prison. We challenged the theologians on the page and those sitting next to us in the room. The atmosphere was charged. Having read other women diagnose and navigate the social challenges of their day, students in this class did the same as they named the inhumane conditions they faced daily in prison and the ones their loved ones faced outside. They expressed their hopes for a future better than the present.

I knew that this would not be the last time I would step inside this prison.

Five years later, after completing my MDiv and beginning my doctoral work in practical theology and religious education, after teaching courses in prison on Theology and Black Women's Literature, Biblical Foundations, The Art of Spiritual Writing, Theology and Film, and Theology and Literature, I became the program director. For years, I watched as new students desired to enroll in Theology and as alumni students returned quarter after quarter to take classes. I also witnessed students face depression, chronic illness, and violent attacks. I witnessed people denied the opportunity to learn, people denied work because there was no job available. I listened as students compared prison to dying.

For seven years, I taught theology in a place of literal and symbolic death, a place governed by the logic of death and domination. I cultivated classrooms with people who knew first-hand the anxiety, fear, and hopelessness of death but did not let the threat of death stop them from living. For over a decade, I have been asking: *Why do people participate in a theology program when they live in a place that feels like dying? What good is theological education for people trying to make a life in a death-dealing institution? What kind of life does theological education make possible in prison?*

I set out to investigate why students participate in the Theology program and what it means for someone surviving incarceration. I formed a research group with two scholars of theological ethics. We used ethnographic practices of participant observation, interviews, and focus groups to embark on a research project of deep listening to students in Theology. We began with the premise that good theological education contributes meaningfully to the lives of people pursuing it and should be life-affirming and life-enhancing. And we proceeded to listen to students describe the kinds of life they want for themselves while incarcerated; what kind of life is possible in prison. We listened as they discussed what theological education has to do with cultivating meaningful living while incarcerated. This book intends to share what I learned from people studying theology in prison—through their conversations, classroom participation, and artifacts of wisdom, even as I share my reflections on how their wisdom shapes my approach to theological education.

I wrestled with pursuing this research project. I did not want the practice of research to make my long participation in Theology feel instrumental. I was nervous and honest about my feelings with students. Nevertheless, nearly every student encouraged me to proceed and agreed to participate. I am forever grateful to them and hope this book will contribute to more life-affirming futures for them and many others trying to live and learn against the grain of death-dealing forces.

Ethnographic Research in Prison

Over the last several decades, there has been growing interest in the qualitative study of women's carceral experiences and the impact and analysis of prison ministry and prison education in the United States.[1] While there are texts that study religious programming in prison and some that study theological education in men's prisons, scant give focused attention to theological education programs in women's prisons and what they have to do with surviving incarceration.

Doing research in prison is hard. To learn formally about the lives, hopes, and experiences of students in Theology, I knew I wanted to employ ethnographic methods of participant-observation and qualitative research. This required gaining approval from the warden, the Department of Corrections, and the institutional review board (IRB) to work with vulnerable populations. I was not allowed any recording devices and had to schedule interviews and groups in advance with prison staff. I also knew that such research was best done collaboratively. Researching in a team became essential for this learning to occur.

As a research team, we commissioned the first IRB-approved in-prison qualitative research project of the Theology program. We called our research *Good Life* because we wanted to understand what kind of lives our students imagined for themselves, what was possible and made difficult in prison, and what the Theology program means for their ability to live while incarcerated. For my work in practical theology and religious education, I wanted to know how we might practice theological education better in this prison and elsewhere.

Gathering the wisdom of Theology students required a variety of ethnographic methods: semi-structured focus groups, individual interviews, artifact analysis (drawings, homework assignments, and other relevant creative expressions including music and performance), and participant observation to capture the essence of prison from classroom conversations about everyday life to sounds and smells.[2]

Our primary mode of information gathering occurred in focus groups. For several months, we met with students in groups of four to six and followed a semi-structured discussion guide. We chose groups deliberately to ensure a representative sample of the diversity of the program, including diversity of age, sentence length, time in the program, and religious affiliation. The stories I share in this book are both aggregation and interpretation of data, allowing me to offer a depiction of the Theology program using individual stories and communal conversations.[3]

Knowing that ethnographic research can harm even as it seeks to do good, we insisted that our prison research not cause undue stress for the students. We wanted this experience to be enjoyable mainly because so many experiences in prison are not. We wanted the research to *feel* life-giving in a place that feels like dying. The dialogue in qualitative research requires contexts of mutual trust, hope, and critical thinking. Students shared that in prison, "nobody cares what we think," so the practice of gathering students to talk about their opinions and experiences was an act of humanizing praxis. Research and dialogue became an "act of creation" as I tried and hoped to keep it from serving "as a crafty instrument for the domination of one person by another."[4] This research sought to create conditions where students could name their experiences for themselves and (re)locate their hope in the process.

Good ethnographic research is deeply relational work. Research that seeks to liberate must also be loving. I have long admired the relationship that educator Paulo Freire maintains exists between love, freedom, and dialogue:

> As an act of bravery, love cannot be sentimental; as an act of freedom, it must not serve as a pretext for manipulation. It must generate other acts of freedom; otherwise, it is not love. Only by abolishing the situation of oppression is it possible to restore the love which that situation made impossible. If I do not love the world—if I do not love life—if I do not love people—I cannot enter into dialogue.[5]

I hoped that this summer of research functioned as loving dialogue—a form of research that not only seeks information and knowledge but ultimately or most importantly seeks to generate other acts of freedom in the process. To use a definition of love offered by bell hooks in her book *All about Love*, when research is loving, it nurtures the spiritual growth of all involved. Research as loving dialogue requires the virtues that hooks espouses: "care, affection, responsibility, respect, commitment, and trust."[6] As an act of faith, research as loving dialogue requires me to believe in humankind's ability to create and re-create even in death-dealing environments. It requires me to have faith in students' "vocation to be more fully human," which compels me to listen intently for the wisdom that will guide us to more hopeful futures.[7]

I could not have written this book without the long relationship I have had with these students even as I recognize how my relationship with them is a complicated one. I am not an insider. I do not know the experience of incarceration the way they do. I also do not know the experience of the Theology program the way they do. They are students in the program; I have facilitated and directed the program. I operate in multiple worlds, as an ally with them in the program, an advocate for them to the outside world, and a complicated and often conflicted liaison between the prison and the students. Nevertheless, my long-term relationship with the students governs my concern and commitment to their liberation—to their pursuit of their good lives.

ACKNOWLEDGMENTS

> "Thank you" is the best prayer that anyone could say. I say that one a lot. Thank you expresses extreme gratitude, humility, understanding.
>
> Alice Walker

At last. Through graduations and new beginnings, relocations, pandemics, deaths of beloved family members, and births of new ones. It is with utmost gratitude that I release this book into the world. Whatever is good, truthful, and valuable in what follows is because of the many villages and voices that have shaped this project and supported me along the way.

First and foremost, to the Theology students in prison who taught me about friendship, joy, perseverance, forgiveness, and courage. Your brilliance and generosity never ceased to amaze and inspire me. Thank you for teaching me how to listen and reimagine the work of theological education, for sharing your lives and dreams with me, and for teaching me how to teach. Thank you for trusting me with these stories. I am better because I spent Fridays with all of you.

To Elizabeth Bounds. I do not have words adequate to thank you for your vision, care, and perseverance. You have modeled for me what it means to be faithful and committed to the lives of your students, those in prison and those outside. Whatever good Theology has been and whatever positive impact it has had on students like me, it is because of you. Partnering with you and Cara Curtis on this project is a highlight of my graduate studies. Without you both, I could not have written this work or completed this project—thank you. And to all who transcribed for us, we are indebted to you.

To Michael Yandell and the community of teachers and volunteers in Theology, thank you for being companions in this work, for the long car rides, short lunches, and invaluable conversations. I also thank those wardens, chaplains, officers, and staff who supported this program and assisted us in and out of locked gates and around problematic policies. I especially thank Susan Bishop, Cathy Zappa, Thomas Fabisiak, and Wende Ballew.

To Jennifer Ayres and Joy McDougall, I am deeply grateful for your years of support and encouragement and for nurturing early iterations of this project. To the many mentors, friends, and colleagues at Emory University, thank you for your guidance, leadership, and friendship; special thanks to the PCRL faculty, to Sarah Farmer, and to the best e-crew ever: Courtney Buggs, Hyemin Na, and Joi Orr.

To the many institutions who supported my development as a scholar-writer-teacher-colleague: Forum for Theological Exploration (FTE), Louisville Institute, Wabash Center for Teaching and Learning, and Religious Education Association, thank you.

To the Theological Education Between the Times (TEBT) twelve, under the leadership of Ted Smith, thank you all for being the grace-filled community I needed to deepen my hopes for theological education, remove the veil on the writing process, and welcome me as a colleague. And a distinctive thank you to Uli Guthrie for your editing genius and generosity and for encouraging me to trust myself.

To my colleagues and students at Fordham University, thank you for listening to later versions of this project and helping me to refine my thoughts. To our dearly departed Steffano Montano, thank you for encouraging me to write and teach "my way."

To my family—the living and the ancestors—who support me in all things, thank you for unconditional love and fervent prayers and for reminding me of my gifts when the world makes me doubt them. To my grandmother, Joan Carol, who did not live to see the publication of this book—when dementia increased your forgetting, you always remembered to ask me about the "women at the prison." Thank you for so many memories.

To my husband, Mario, I could not ask for a better partner in life and love. Thank you for everything you do to make this life possible. And to our son, thank you for giving everything new significance.

Finally, I am grateful to and for the Spirit of God at work in this project, the Divine giver of words worth writing. I pray I have heard well.

INTRODUCTION
A Matter of Life and Death

> Theology is more than something to do on Fridays. It is a matter of life and death.
>
> **Theology student**

"Listen. Prison is like bearing witness to your *own* death. Think about it. People fear dying because they have no control over it, right? And they fear death because they have no idea what it will be like. Coming to prison is a lot like dying. You watch the world close in on you and you watch as your family fills the gap at home that your absence creates. It's like being dead—*and knowing that you're dead.*"[1]

The words caught me by surprise. I was substitute teaching in the Pastoral Perspectives on Death and Dying class in the Certificate in Theological Studies program at a state prison for women, and the topic was coping with the physical loss of loved ones. A student named Cate took the conversation in a different direction. She wanted to talk about a form of dying she believed everyone in the class knew well—a type of dying she experiences as an incarcerated woman. For Cate, both dying and coming to prison are experiences characterized by a lack of control and deep uncertainty, where your world collapses, and loved ones are forced to reconstruct their lives without you. To feel like you have died is to feel powerless and expendable.

Cate is one of hundreds of students studying theology in this prison, and I cannot begin to count the number of times, over seven years, that I heard students describe experiences of incarceration. However, something about the way Cate strung her words together that day unsettled me, preoccupying me long after the class ended. They crawled into my consciousness and refused to leave. For days, I kept hearing them. On the hour and a half drive home from the prison. While I sipped coffee the next morning. As I returned books to the Emory library. As I walked the aisles of the grocery store in Southwest Atlanta.

It's like being dead and knowing that you're dead.

I kept turning over Cate's words in my mind, connecting them to similar themes I'd encountered while teaching in and researching about prison. Literature abounds that explores the inner workings of incarceration and the US criminal punishment system as a totalizing, death-dealing institution.[2] I thought about the time I heard a student describe prison as "one step away from death." I thought about Gregory Ellison's book, *Cut Dead but Still Alive*, in which he describes how young African American men are "cut dead"—deliberately ignored as a form of punishment; categorically unseen and unheard, invisibilized and muted.[3] I thought about Kaia Stern's research into prison education with incarcerated men in New York whom she describes as *socially dead*, "no longer belonging to civic community, [with] minimal social existence outside of the totalizing institution of the prison." Cate's words were consistent with other prison testimonies and scholarship—death is a pervasive theme of incarceration. But Cate's words encouraged me to consider something more—how prison functions as death's *teacher*.

For Cate and many people surviving carceral experiences, the *knowledge* of death is especially cruel. The practices and procedures used in incarceration function to remind people of their status as socially expendable persons without dignity. To go along with Cate's analogy, the death felt by incarceration is not a one-time occurrence but an ongoing reality. A state of being. A way of knowing. The world outside keeps moving; keeps changing. And as another student put it, the world inside stops turning and life is on infinite pause. *It's a lot like dying.* Much has been written to document the deleterious and negative effects of incarceration. The stories in this book will add to that account. But negative stories alone never move us toward better practice.

As a researcher of long-term imprisonment contends, "highlighting the negative dimensions of prison helps us to understand what *not to do*, but it does not inform our next steps. . . . We will never learn how to do things better if we only focus on highlighting ineffective and damaging practices."⁴

The reality of premature death by incarceration is real, but people like Cate are not dead. In fact, they are very much alive and have hopes and dreams of lives better than the ones prescribed for them by a death-dealing punishment system. Hopes that compel them in prison to make friends, get jobs, get an education, and for some, study theology. This book is about living, *how people in a US prison for women imagine good lives for themselves amid death-dealing realities, and how they actualize those desires in a theological education program*. I intend to move beyond merely critiquing the punitive pedagogies of the penal system and construct a life-affirming pedagogical vision for those called to the work of teaching in carceral spaces.

Over the course of a summer, I embarked on a journey of listening to student conversations and testimonies about the relationship between living a good life and learning in prison. I wanted to better understand how a theological education program could contribute meaningfully to the lives students wanted for themselves—good lives. *Learning to Live* shares the stories entrusted to me—stories about the death-dealing reality of women's incarceration, the visions of a good life that sustain students against death's threats, and the ways students use a theological education program to embody, practice, and live into their hopes for creating a life that matters. Informed by the perspectives of people studying theology in a US prison for women, I ultimately contend that especially in a place governed by pedagogies and practices of death and domination, theological education should affirm and actualize God's vision and students' hopes for a good life.

Theological Concerns and Practical Aims

What does God require of us when we encounter people like Cate who are trying to make a life in (social) death-dealing contexts? As a liberationist practical theologian, I am concerned with asking questions about how people understand, question, and/or doubt God's activity in contexts of confinement and domination. Moreover, I am interested in questions of human responsibility; how we respond to and participate with God's activity in prison.

My primary concern in this project is how, through the practice of theological education, humans participate with God to bring about meaningful life in death-dealing spaces. The theological task is to discern where God is calling back to life people counted as dead, people like Cate, and to understand what is required from a (learning) community to help them live more fully. I believe that wherever God calls people back to life, there is human work to be done to participate with God in this redemptive project—and I believe this is, in part, the work of education.

Three times in the New Testament Gospels, before Jesus' death and resurrection, we find Jesus calling everyday people back to life from experience with death. One is the son of a widow. Another is the daughter of a religious leader. And the third is an old friend. When Jesus calls these people into life, he calls them from isolation into community (belonging), from stagnancy to mobility (growth), and from being bound to being boundless (freedom). I became captivated by these stories during the summer of these prison conversation groups, reading them as parables against the death-dealing reality of imprisonment. Although miraculous, I am less focused on the divine work of Jesus calling people from death to life. I am most intrigued by what Jesus requires of the everyday people standing around witnessing the restorations. I am intrigued by the work that Jesus assigns to human beings to participate in the life force of others—the collaborative work of restoring and redeeming life. Guided by student perspectives and narratives, this book argues that a learning community in prison can actively participate in this redemptive project.

This book has three overlapping aims. The first aim is to understand how students in Theology define and pursue their ideas of a good life through theological study in prison. I intend for this investigation to contribute to the growing scholarly collection of qualitative research with people surviving women's carceral institutions. In addition to women's pathways and desistance contributions, this book builds on knowledge of intersectional, gender-based carceral experience by focusing on a different set of questions, questions related to how people live *while* incarcerated. A harmful stereotype about incarcerated people is that they either lack the moral fortitude to know what is good or their visions of life are fundamentally corrupt to begin with. This book demonstrates that despite what brought them to prison and even in constraint and under domination, ideas of a good life remain, and they are ideas that, I suspect, will resonate with many of us.

As a practical theological project, *Learning to Live* not only *describes* how students engage theological study to make a life for themselves, but it also *constructs* a life-affirming vision for theological education in prisons and beyond. As such, the second aim of this book is to identify the pedagogical commitments and practices that support and affirm life in a prison classroom and allow those practices and dispositions to inspire more life-affirming futures for theological education in prison and other death-dealing environments. Our educational task is to better understand how and why people *feel alive* in a prison theology program and to name the pedagogical practices that contribute to life and not death.

Finally, the third aim is to encourage reflective practice for those who continue to work inside prisons as faith-based educators. Cultivating learning communities that affirm life in death-dealing institutions weighs heavily on all involved. It takes habitual reflection to resist slipping into pedagogies of domination, pedagogies that support prison's death-dealing lessons. I trust that as you read students' hopes for their good lives and their perspectives on participating in a theological education program, your hope in the transformative potential of theological education might be refreshed and reenergized as well.

The Certificate in Theological Studies Program

For years, a prison chaplain and a university-based theological school professor dreamed of a postsecondary education program in which incarcerated women could earn a college degree. They knew the wide-reaching literature and statistics that contend higher education programs in prison increased feelings of positive achievement, gave people constructive outlets to spend their time, and lessened the likelihood that someone would return to prison once released.[5] They also knew that it was less likely for women in prison to experience these opportunities because it was customary for the US correctional system to extend educational opportunities to men more than women, despite the growing numbers of women in prison.

The United States has only 4% of the world's population of women, but accounts for more than 30% of the world's incarcerated women. In 2019 in the United States, nearly 1.2 million women were under the control of the correctional system, of whom about 250,000 were incarcerated.[6] According to the latest Sentencing Project report, 2020 saw a substantial downsizing due to the COVID-19 pandemic, but the trend reversed with a 10% increase in 2021.[7] Women account for just 10% of the total prison population; however, women's state prison populations have grown 834% over nearly forty years—more than double the pace of the growth among men. Despite the significant growth, media, documentaries, literature, and criminological studies often leave out or gloss over the concerns and conditions of women.[8] Prisons are deeply gendered organizations and failing to consider conditions in women's institutions risks missing and neglecting the intersectional inequalities and disadvantages unique to this population.[9] Owen et al. state the significance this way: "For women whose pathways lead them to prison, such disadvantages are replicated and often magnified inside prison, which, in turn, increases the threats to their already tenuous sense of safety and well-being."[10] Furthermore, prisons reflect what Beth Richie calls the most "concentrated disadvantage based on racial, class and gender inequality in the country:"

> There, behind the razor wire fences, concrete barricade, steel doors, metal bars, and thick plexiglass windows, nearly all the manifestations of gender domination that feminist scholars and activists have traditionally concerned themselves

with—exploited labor, inadequate healthcare, dangerous living conditions, physical violence, and sexual assault are revealed at once. That gender oppression is significantly furthered by racism and poverty is undeniable from this point of view. Women's correctional facilities constitute nearly perfect examples of the consequences of the multiple subjugation and the compounding impact of various stigmatized identities. The convergence of disadvantage, discrimination, and despair is staggering. In fact, it could be argued that prisons incarcerate a population of women who have experienced such a profound concentration of the most vicious forms of economic marginalization, institutionalized racism, and victimization that it can almost seem intentional or mundane.[11]

The growth of women's involvement in the justice system is mainly due to changes in law enforcement, harsher sentencing under the "War on Drugs" and the "tough on crime" political climate of the 1980s and 1990s. Nearly thirty years ago, scholars proclaimed that the war on drugs was a war on women.[12] Little did we know just how true their statement would become. Laws meant for drug kingpins—mandatory sentencing and Three Strikes—disproportionately impacted women involved in low-level offenses. Women of color were exceptionally and unreasonably affected.

The rise in women's incarceration also reflects a long history of the criminalization of women's survival behaviors with disproportionate impact to communities of color, working-class communities, and nonconforming individuals.[13] According to a report by Wendy Sawyer published in 2018, states continue to "widen the net" of criminal justice involvement by criminalizing women's responses to gender-based abuse and discrimination.[14] The phrase "carceral feminism" was coined to categorize reliance on police, punishment policies, and carceral procedures to respond to gender-based violence and harm. Policies that were designed to support women have led to increased justice involvement, particularly for women of color and nonconforming groups. Examples include mandatory or "dual" arrests for fighting back against domestic violence, increasing criminalization of school-aged girls' misbehavior, including survival efforts like running away, and the criminalization of women who support themselves through sex work.

Consequently, the most common pathways to prison for women are related to the survival of abuse, poverty, addiction, and exposure to trauma.[15] According to national statistics, justice-involved women, when compared to male offenders, have experienced higher rates of childhood victimization, sexual and physical abuse.[16] They are also more likely to be drug abusers, suffer from infectious diseases, and require mental health services. While women in prison are more likely than their male counterparts to have a high school diploma, they are more likely to be underemployed or unemployed than their male counterparts. Statistics in the state of Georgia follow this pattern. At the time of writing, 73% of incarcerated women in Georgia reported having some mental health condition requiring at minimum outpatient treatment (compared to only 36% of men). Of the 73% of women, three-quarters also met the criteria for substance dependence or abuse, and more than two-thirds (68%) had a history of physical or sexual abuse.[17] Despite the data documenting the overwhelming need for resources, treatment for the wide range of trauma and mental health concerns and access to educational and vocational programming is often inadequate or unavailable for women.

The chaplain and professor sought to intervene in the lack of resources with a postsecondary educational program, but the obstacles proved too great to overcome. They faced challenges finding a college or university that would offer educational credit to inmate populations, especially at that time, without access to federal Pell Grants that funded most in-prison educational programs.

The federal Pell Grant program, authorized by Title IV of the Higher Education Act of 1965, as amended (HEA; P.L. 89–329), is the single largest source of federal grant aid supporting postsecondary education students and was the primary funding source for people seeking degrees in prison. Pell Grants for incarcerated people, which accounted for less than 1% of all Pell spending, led to a steady increase in college-in-prison programs offered by secular and religious universities and colleges throughout the twentieth century.[18] By 1973, data collectors could identify 182 programs nationwide; by 1976, there were 237; and by 1982, there were 350 with 27,000 incarcerated people enrolled in classes.[19] By the 1982 count, college-in-prison programs—both public and private, religious and secular, through universities and community colleges—could be identified in forty-five states and involved 10% of the incarcerated population. In the early '90s, the number of college-in-prison programs on record peaked at 772 in more than 1,280 correctional facilities.[20] However, two actions in the early '90s decimated college-in-prison programming.

In 1992, the Amendment of Higher Education Act prohibited prisoners serving life, life without parole, or death sentences from using Pell Grants. Then, in 1994, the Violent Crime and Law Enforcement Act banned all prisoners from receiving Pell aid.[21] As funding ceased, all but eight of the publicly funded credit-bearing college prison programs ended by 1995. As a result, publicly accessible higher education programs in prisons have been scarce, except for programs offered by privately funded institutions like colleges and universities. Thus, as women's prison populations were rising exponentially in the '90s, access to higher educational funding and resources came to a screeching halt.

Funding was just one hurdle preventing a postsecondary degree program. The standards of admission at many schools the chaplain and professor contacted were believed "too high a hurdle" for many incarcerated students to clear. According to a Prison Policy Initiative report, inequalities between the general public and formerly incarcerated people begin early and accumulate at each level of education.[22] Formerly incarcerated people are nearly twice as likely to have no high school credentials. More than half hold only a high school diploma or GED. Unlike the general public, people who have been to prison are more likely to have GEDs than to have a traditional high school diploma and three-quarters of those GEDs are earned in prison—credentials that may seem less valuable to a college admission committee. In fact, the Prison Policy Initiative analysis shows that GEDs earned in prison do not yield the same benefits as those earned outside:

> For formerly incarcerated people, a GED earned in prison is almost never a stepping-stone to higher education. Of all formerly incarcerated people with in-prison GEDs, less than 10% go on to take any college coursework, and less than 1% attain college degrees. In contrast, nearly half of GED holders in the general public go on to complete at least some college. These results point to a vast system of barriers to entry into higher education . . . including in-prison GED programs that, without supplemental educational experiences, are insufficient to prepare students for further education.[23]

The report goes on to suggest that incarcerated people are often relegated to the "lowest rungs of the educational ladder" and rarely get the chance to make up for the educational opportunities from which they have been excluded.

With a spirit of administrative imagination, the chaplain and professor suggested they try a certificate program in theology instead. A certificate program could provide higher academic engagement without the strict requirements of a degree-granting program. Furthermore, as a continuing education model, it would enable many incarcerated women with no post-secondary education to participate. In its pragmatism, the Theology program created a pathway for the participation of a wider array of students who otherwise would not have been eligible. With only a high school diploma or GED, students without a negative disciplinary record could complete an application to study theology in prison.

A certificate program in theology in a prison for women was novel at the time. Religious institutions had long been active developers and funders of college-in-prison programs, but little is known of any explicitly religious higher education programs in women's prisons during this time. While religious programming such as Kairos Prison Ministry and Prison Fellowship were offered, neither of these programs culminated in degrees or certificates in academic theological education, nor were they traditionally led by seminaries or divinity schools.

New York Theological Seminary (NYTS) was the first to bring formal, accredited theological higher education into prison in the 1980s with the development of the Master of Professional Studies (MPS) program at Sing Sing Prison in Ossining, New York.[24] Additional religious higher education programs emerged in prisons thereafter, bringing opportunities for incarcerated students to obtain bachelor's and associate degrees in Christian ministry and certificates in pastoral leadership.[25] Most of the programs attest to an intentional desire to equip students to provide professional Christian service inside the prison for personal and communal transformation. Almost all were offered in male institutions.

In 2007, the chaplain and professor visited NYTS as well as the BA program at Bedford Hills Correctional Facility for Women in New York. The chaplain also visited the New Orleans Baptist Theological Seminary program in Louisiana. They garnered the support and involvement of a consortium of local seminaries to secure funding and volunteers for their vision. For two years, these women planned and envisioned, and in January 2009, seventeen women formed the inaugural class of students in the Certificate in Theological Studies program, known by students simply as *Theology*.

Hundreds of students have completed an application of a written essay and a recommendation from prison staff to enroll in Theology. Applicants are interviewed by the Theology director(s). Twenty-five students can be admitted each year into the program. To receive a certificate in theological studies, students complete one year of course work, which includes two foundation courses: one in Bible and one in Theology, three elective courses, and a capstone or cumulative project. After meeting all requirements, students, in cap and gown, and to the sound of "Pomp and Circumstance," graduate in front of family and teachers with a certificate in theological studies. And for some students, it is the first graduation ceremony they ever attend.

Since its inception, the Theology program has graduated more than 190 students. But the demand to keep taking classes was so great that it developed another program, the Advanced

Certificate in Theological Studies (ACTS). Students complete an additional year of electives for this second certificate, including advanced research and writing courses. The culminating project is an in-depth research paper. As I write this manuscript, more than thirty students have completed the advanced program. And still, students continue to take classes. One student who has been in the program since it began has received both certificates and continues to take classes. To date, she has completed more than sixty courses in theological studies, and at the time of writing, she is still signing up for classes.

The Theology program began with a goal of preparing students to become leaders in prison.[26] The program's stated aim was to educate students to act as lay leaders in and outside of prison. Another goal was to help students get jobs upon release, though the program was not explicit about how this would happen. Students, however, state their original goals for enrolling in Theology quite simply: they want to learn more about the Bible and God, they want to remain mentally active, better themselves, and "make something" of their time. As they participate in Theology, their reasons for remaining take a different tone. "Theology is not just something to do on a Friday," one student remarked. "It is a matter of life and death."

The People in Theology

I made decisions worth mentioning here about how I speak collectively about the participants in Theology. First, I am choosing to refer to them as people or students to be as inclusive as possible with my use of language. Though the Theology program is housed in a prison for women, not all participants of the program identify as women. Second, I am choosing not to focus on details of individual's crime.[27] Except for distinguishing between short-term and long-term sentences, I do not identify persons by what brought them to prison. Instead, I am choosing to highlight student perspectives on prison, living, and learning. Finally, I am choosing to highlight specific race, class, and gender categories in my descriptions of students to broaden our perceptions of who resides in a state prison for women. Here is why.

One November, during a large, annual conference, I shared a story about an experience I had teaching in prison. At the end, a white, male spectator commended my presentation, stating how moved he was by the stories I shared about Black women in prison. I gave him a perplexed look and responded that, on this occasion, I did not tell a story about a Black woman in prison. When he heard me speak about a woman incarcerated, he imagined the body as Black. In fact, many people imagine Black bodies when they imagine carceral bodies and with some understanding. According to a 2023 Prison Policy Initiative report, Black people in the United States account for 13% of the general population and 38% of the prison population whereas white people comprise 60% of the general population and 38% of the prison population. The same remains true in women's prisons, but not to the same degree. The Bureau of Justice Statistics report that in state and federal prisons in 2021, 47% of women were white (vs 54% of general population), 17% Black (vs. 14% of general population), 19% Hispanic (vs. 21% of general population), 2.5% American Indian or Alaska Native, 0.75% Asian/Pacific Islander, and 13.3% "other" (women reporting two or more races and other groups not broken out).

The same trend is true among women in Georgia. Black women in Georgia are incarcerated at rates higher than those for white women[28] (40% of women in prison versus 32% of Georgia population[29]). However, white women account for the majority of women in Georgia prisons (58%) with Hispanic women (1.4%) and the remaining combination of Asian, Native American, Native Hawaiian, and other or unknown categories (0.6%) comprising the rest of the population.[30] Black people and Black women *are* overrepresented in carceral populations. That only tells part of the story.

On average, a person[31] is young when they arrive in a Georgia prison for women, most often just twenty-four years old.[32] Once incarcerated, their time in prison will not be short. On average, they will spend twenty-three years there. They are likely imprisoned for a violent crime (45%), a property crime (25%), or a drug crime (21%), but even these categories are so broad as to be misleading. A violent crime may include drug use, and a drug crime may include property crime. They were likely employed before becoming incarcerated (48%), and their education varies (44% with some high school education, 36% HS graduate/GED, 13% with some college education). They likely have children. Though over 65% of people in Georgia prisons for women report having children, chaplains who work in the prisons claim that this reported number is lower than the reality. One chaplain estimates the number to be closer to 80%.[33] Though Georgia does not report this statistic, national data suggest (and personal experience in prison confirms) that a person in a prison for women in Georgia is more likely than her male-identified counterparts to identify as lesbian or bisexual. A 2017 national study revealed that one-third of incarcerated women identify as lesbian or bisexual, compared to less than 10% of men. The same study found that lesbian and bisexual women are likely to receive longer sentences than their heterosexual peers.[34]

Statistics are helpful in painting a general picture. But individual stories offer a more nuanced perspective. Through the narratives shared in this text, I hope to convey that not every person in prison is Black just as not every person in prison is poor or comes from a broken home or is addicted to drugs or uneducated, and so on. These factors *are* overrepresented among carceral populations, but they do not and cannot tell everyone's story. In this text, you will hear from thirty students in Theology representing a diverse mix of ages, races, gender expressions, social classes, sexualities, and religious perspectives.

Prison populations are diverse, and structural inequalities exist as much inside prison as outside. Theology students commonly express that Black, queer, and non-Christian women are less likely to gain access to prison education and other resources than white and Christian women. The people in Theology are Christian, Muslim, Jehovah's Witness, Agnostic, and Atheist. They are heterosexual, homosexual, queer, transgender, and those who reject labels. They come from middle-class families in suburban neighborhoods, working-class farm communities, and low-income urban environments. They are high school and college graduates, and some have master's degrees. They are preacher's kids and foster kids. Their realities are varied and distinct. What they have in common is an experience with incarceration and a desire to give meaning to their lives. Through drawn images, group conversations, classroom debates, and individual interviews, diverse student perspectives show us what makes life and theological education good and help us shape a more life-nurturing vision for the practice of education in prison and elsewhere.

Social Death, a Good Life, and Theological Education

This book is an invitation to hear stories—stories about dying, domination, and constraint, and stories about life, freedom, and possibility—and to allow these stories to form and re-form our practice of theological education. It is an invitation to consider the work and shape of theological education in prison; an invitation to name and ponder what theological education becomes in the hands and hearts of people surviving incarceration and what more it might become for others living in death-dealing contexts.

This book begins by exploring the context of incarceration through students' claims that prison is a lot like dying. Chapter 1 takes you inside prison and offers a first glimpse into the complicated process of trying to teach and learn in prison. After presenting a scene from a Theology class and a homework assignment from a student named Claira, I expound on the claim that prison is death's teacher. Using Orlando Patterson's social death theory as a theoretical frame, I name prison's formational practices as a form of social death education. Social death education, I assert, uses ritualized practices of degradation and debasement that have as their goal the formation of people without honor—people without a future—people without a good life. I argue that prisons, by design, train and mold human bodies and minds into receiving objects whose creative power is intentionally inhibited and whose thinking and action, and senses of identity and community, are shaped and defined by an institution of domination, cultivating learners to become radically dependent, uncritically obedient, and disconnected from sources of life-giving meaning.

Scholar Lisa Marie Cacho in her assessment of the nature of social death asserts, "For the most part, value is not ascribed to living life in meaningful ways, and it also means that those who are socially devalued do not get to decide what makes a life meaningful or the terms by which their lives are evaluated as meaningful or meaningless, as valuable or valueless. . . . A meaningful life is not a luxury but rather the purpose of the struggle itself, the difference between surviving and living."[35] In a social death institution like a US prison for women, there is no perceived meaningful future for people like Cate, no social imagination that supports the idea of her good life. But Cate and her colleagues do know what gives life meaning; they know what gives their life value.

Chapters 2, 3, and 4 present dialogue from group conversations and individual interviews as we explore three questions at the heart of this project: What is your idea of a good life? (chapter 2), Is your good life possible in prison? (chapter 3), and Why do you study theology here? (chapter 4). While much has been written in academic texts attempting to define *a* good life, chapter 2 explores how students in prison define and enact *their* good life for themselves. Thirty students across six focus groups imagine that someone took a picture of their good life. I share some of their drawings in this text. Together, we analyzed the images as we questioned if and how their hoped-for good lives were possible in prison. In my dialogue with students, a working conception of a good life emerges. A good life is many things, but commonly, it involves what I label as belonging, dynamism, and freedom.

Chapter 3 asks if students' images of a good life are possible in prison. While not undisputed, most students suggest that features of their good life are attainable through mundane, practical actions—some of these actions they practice in a theological education program. Chapter 4, thereby, connects students' ideas about their good life to their participation in the Certificate in Theological Studies program, allowing me to discern how this learning community allows students to affirm and actualize elements of their desired good lives (belonging, dynamism, and freedom) over and against a life-negating prison culture.

Building on empirical insights, chapter 5 illuminates how a learning community affirms life using life-affirming practices that encourages students to experience a way of life that liberates from the burden of shame, frees from the degradation of dehumanization, and creates space for people to live into a vision of life beyond the confines and constraints of social death. I highlight six life-affirming pedagogical practices used to nurture life in this theological learning community: coming together (cultivating community), choosing names (claiming identity), considering one another (listening and perspective-sharing), critical questioning (deconstructive analysis), creating theology (constructive embodiment), and celebrating life (practicing joy). I name these practices as *redemptive* because they momentarily liberate from present conditions of bondage and mediate traces of God's affirming presence in contexts of death-dealing carcerality.

I conclude in chapter 6 with a theological reflection on life-affirming educational praxis and the implications for theological education in contexts of domination and constraint, both in carceral and noncarceral settings. This life-affirming vision for theological education is rooted in the perspectives of incarcerated students and modeled after the ministry of Jesus of Nazareth.

The Hope

I write out of concern for students trying to imagine and enact a meaningful life in and against systems trying to annihilate it. I also write for theological educators who are, as I was, entering prisons as acts of social justice and Christian ministry and who desperately want their pedagogy to be a lived-out theology of liberation and hope. I write for educators who want to cultivate learning communities that are life-affirming, life-honoring, and life-navigating in prisons and elsewhere.

I experienced *Learning to Live* as a gift—an offering—from the students in Theology to our understanding of meaningful living in contexts of constraint and how theological education can be life-nurturing for themselves and others. It is a gift that has enlarged my hopes and imagination for a theological education that matters. This book is my effort to share what I learned from these students about a more expansive purpose for theological education, one that participates in God's work to redeem life in and against death-dealing systems.

Though I am focused on prison as my context of immediate concern, I suspect that you will find yourself drawing parallels to other institutions that practice similar types of death-dealing education. Prisons are not the only institutions that practice carceral pedagogy, drawing on beliefs and practices of carcerality—surveillance, punishment, dominance, and control—to render people as objects and exercise control over them.[36] Carceral pedagogy is pervasive. We should investigate all oppressive methods and techniques used in learning spaces. It is possible that your educational institution, school, or church, exists on a carceral spectrum and needs redeeming. I invite you to name those institutions and how it feels to teach and learn in their midst.

Ultimately, I hope that *Learning to Live* offers educators pragmatic hope—habits of resourcefulness, persistence, and courage—for teaching and learning in the face of death-dealing forces.

1
LEARNING IN A PLACE THAT FEELS LIKE DYING

> They don't care about our humanity here, but we do.[1]

I never sleep well on Thursday nights—fear of missing the alarm, mostly—and this time is no different. I look at my phone and it reads 5:25 a.m. I sigh at the futility of five remaining minutes; there is no need to attempt more sleep. But who wants to get out of bed *before* the alarm? So I lay and allow my mind to run over the list of things I need to do today for the Certificate in Theological Studies program. In addition to normal activities such as returning homework and handling individual requests for materials, I must confirm an available classroom for our research. Today will be our initial day of qualitative research for the first IRB-approved in-prison research project of the state's first theological education program in a women's prison.

I get up quietly so as not to wake my husband, dress, and grab the clear backpack filled with homework papers and reading assignments. I make the thirty-minute drive to our carpool location. The first to arrive, I park my car and make my way inside the coffee shop for a small cup of dark roast, a weekly ritual for nearly a year now. I take a seat near the door and eavesdrop on the boisterous debate from a group of elderly men I have grown accustomed to seeing every Friday morning just before 6:30 a.m. I smile, hoping to have those sorts of friends when I am their age. I take another sip of my coffee when headlights beckon me to look up as my carpool companions arrive. The faculty director of the program arrives followed by a doctoral student who codirects with me and an MDiv student who is teaching with us for the first time. The other graduate student teachers will meet us at the prison. I walk outside, wading through the humidity to greet them. As the sun brightens the sky, we load into the car and make the almost one-hour drive to the prison for Theology.

As we journey from I-85 N to I-985 N, the scene shifts from the buzz of metro-Atlanta to the quieter pace of the North Georgia mountains. Little by little, the six-lane highway becomes a two-lane thoroughfare bringing us nearer to one of the largest prisons for women in the state. We drive past familiar landmarks: the gas station on the right, the farm that sells boiled peanuts and fresh strawberry ice cream, and finally the school bus graveyard before we make our turn. I remember the street name because it is the same name as the Baptist church in Ohio in which my grandmother grew up: Mt. Zion. As we make our way down the street, I glance at the other familiar landmarks: the church with a cemetery on the corner to the left, and signs for the equestrian center to the right. We are too early to see children getting on the bus, but later this afternoon, I am sure we will see them: mainly Hispanic elementary-aged children getting off the buses to head home. The homes are small near the prison. Other than the children and the neighborhood dogs, I seldom see anyone walking around. As we turn the bend, small homes give way to barbed wire fence. And we see the chapel. The chapel always stands out to me, a large building behind the wire fence with a cross up top. It is one signal that we are nearing the prison: the cross behind the barbed wire fence. We enter the parking lot just as I finish my coffee. We park the car, stash our cell phones and belongings in the trunk, gather our clear backpacks, and make our way inside.

We line up outside the front entrance and are asked to wait. There are three tracks or class times for Fridays: the first track begins at 7:40 a.m., the second at 9:50 a.m., and the third at 1:30 p.m. Customarily, employees who need to clock-in are ushered in ahead of us. It is 7:50 a.m. before we finally make it to the security desk. We remove our shoes and jackets and place them along with our clear backpacks on a conveyor belt as if we are at the airport preparing for travel. Our destination this morning, however, is the school hall in the state prison, and it is proving as cumbersome to navigate as a trip out of the country. The officer opens my backpack full of graded papers, freshly copied articles for next week's homework and sundry other items needed for teaching. I hold my breath as I have done countless times before, praying that this officer will not look too closely at the reading assignments or examine the texts. I can never predict with assurance what they will deem "unacceptable" reading for the prison. By this point, I know enough about the culture here not to bring in articles with words like *queer* or *sexuality* in the title. I know enough to obscure the title of Marcella Althaus-Reid's *Indecent Theology* when it is assigned as a reading for Theological Foundations. But there are other times when I am simply surprised. Like the time we brought in the movie *Black Panther* for our Theology and Film class and the officer held it up and warned us that it was inappropriate because there were images of "men with their shirts off." So I always hold my breath when they are going through our bags. It is one of my many times of prayer in prison.

As we walk through the metal detectors and reassemble ourselves, we are finally inside. We proceed through no fewer than eight locked gates and doors, the sounds of jangling keys and clacking iron forming the soundtrack to our journey inside. We are late.

It is after 8:00 a.m. when we finally get to the school hall, but it is silent. No one is here. We walk down the corridor where our classrooms are located, but there are no students waiting. The school hall is empty. We open our classrooms and prepare the space for learning, not knowing with any certainty when or if students might arrive. The faculty director learns from an education staff member that there was a fire in the kitchen this morning. We also learn that people have struggled all week to gain access to the store and get in and out of dorms for their work details, let alone educational classes. Any of these problems alone would derail a typical Friday. This morning, we encounter a trifecta of complications.

We soon learn that there is even more to the delay. More than thirty minutes after we arrived in an empty hall, a few students from the nearby honors dorm show up. Their agitation is evident. They tell us more of the story.

More than three hours prior, they were awakened at 5:30 a.m. with a surprise inspection. After they dressed, they waited and watched as officers came through each room rummaging through their belongings, looking for contraband and violations—drugs, weapons, or one too many water bottles or T-shirts. Whether they found anything or not, officers left each room in disarray, each person's belongings scattered across the concrete floor. When the inspection cleared, each resident moved quickly to reassemble their room, making sure to gather their belongings before they were stolen by an opportunistic bystander. With rooms reassembled, students in Theology waited to be called out for their 7:40 a.m. class, but when the time came, the dorm officer did not release them. "Are we ever getting out of here?" asked one person, exasperated. The dorm officer looked up slowly from his reading material and snips, "Y'all just gotta wait." So they waited. After twenty minutes, another student asked, "Are we having Theology today?" There was no response.

Eventually, the officer's radio crackled with an announcement, "School hall is open. Release offenders." Some officers relayed the message to students, others did not. Students who did not lose hope and go back to bed were finally, almost three hours after they arose, released to come to class.

As we listened, other students began to arrive, filling the school hall with sounds of chatter, laughter, and greetings from people happy to be free to come to class. Nearly twenty students enter the second classroom on the left for Biblical Foundations, the first class they are taking as Theology students. They are relieved if not exhausted by the journey, and it is only 8:30 in the morning. Class can now begin.

Theology Class

As students settle into their seats, we get started the way we always do—with one word. "When I call your name, please share one word that describes how you are feeling, how you are entering the space, or a hope for our time today."

Fly: *Energized*
Storm: *Tired*

Baldwin: *Curious*
Fierce: *Just-trying-to-make-it*
"Tonia?"

I call Tonia's name already knowing that she is not in the room. "Has anyone seen or talked to Tonia?" I ask.

"What dorm is she in?" I ask. Someone responds—F2.

Scanning the room, my eyes find Sue. "Sue, you're in F2, right?" Sue, who just entered class responds, "Yes, T has a medical appointment this morning. She will be here second track, but she gave me her homework to turn in."

"Monica?"

I likewise call Monica's name knowing she is not in the room. "What about Monica? Has anyone talked to her this week?" No one seems to know where Monica is this morning. "Will anyone see Monica this week?" I ask. Students look around the room at each other. I add, "Who can *make it a point* to see her this week?"

"I should," someone remarks. "I'll make sure she gets the homework and stuff for the week."

"Thank you, and let her know we missed her today." I then ask the other instructor in the room how he feels. "Accomplished! After the obstacles it seems like we all went through to get in today, I'd say we're winning already." We all laugh agreeably. He then asks the same question of me.

"Hopeful," I reply.

"Alright," I transition, "let's start in groups of three. Each person should share highlights from the essay you wrote for homework. After each person has shared, take notes on similarities and distinctions. We will come back together in twenty minutes as a larger group to discuss." The homework assignment was to write a reflection on the topic "What the Bible means to me."[2] Students come to theological study familiar, at least nominally, with the Bible. They either have memories of it from growing up in church or because they recall it gracing the mantel of their grandparents' home. Some utilize it in Bible studies in prison. Whatever the case, almost everyone, regardless of their religious affiliation, has experienced the Bible throughout the process of incarceration. Whether it is family quoting scripture or volunteers who come to share the gospel in jail, Bible talk is familiar, if not understood.

After listening to one another's stories, finding commonalities, and pointing out differences, I ask for a volunteer to help me write on the board all the ways the Bible is understood in this learning community. We write: the Word of God, a tool used for control, instruction for living, history, fiction, and hope. We leave these words on the board to remind us throughout class that the Bible means different things to each of us. It is with respect for these differences and a curiosity about how they function in our lives that we proceed with the next activity for the day.

The focus for today's class is the book of Genesis. Instead of reading the text aloud, I invite students to act out the text.[3] We split the class into two groups and assign each the task of enacting one of the creation stories. What we thought was going to be a quick activity turned into a pseudo-stage production. Students ask us to wait in the hall so they can prepare their performance. I hear movement in the classroom and watch as people run in and out to find props and make impromptu costumes out of whatever they can find nearby: garbage bags, toilet paper, extra head scarfs from a few Muslim women down the hall. After twenty minutes, we are finally invited back into the room.

The tables and chairs have been pushed to the sides of the room transforming the center into a stage. Each group offers an interpretation of creation based on the text they were assigned. They have taken on the roles of God, darkness, light, wind, water, various animals, and finally, humans. We learn not just with our ears but with our eyes and our whole bodies what it feels like to create.[4] We watch, listen, and laugh while appreciating the scenes before us.

After the appropriate time for applause and celebration at the end of each presentation, we discuss similarities and differences between the narratives. We critically reflect on what it might mean to have two creation stories in Genesis—why the original authors may have crafted these stories, why the choosers of the biblical canon kept them, how they might have been received by the original audiences, and what they might mean for us today.[5] I interject the topic of myth into the discussion, reminding students of their previous reading on ancient mythological texts where they learned about other creation stories like the Babylonian myth Enūma Eliš. We talk about one of our readings that suggests the creation narratives to be myth and not *factual accounts*.

"This is really interesting," one student remarks. "If we had talked about this in church growing up, I may never have left," she laughs. She is drawn to the idea that the biblical text might be more complicated and nuanced than the text she encountered growing up. She finds the investigation and possibilities intriguing.

There is another student, however, who is seated on the edge of her chair with crossed arms and a scrunched-up face. She sits tall in her chair and intervenes. "I don't know about all of this creation myth stuff. I still believe the Bible is God's Word and cannot be wrong." She sits back in her chair, satisfied with her declaration.

"Why is naming the Bible as God's word important to you . . . or to anyone else here who holds this commitment?" I ask while pointing back to the board listing the many ways the Bible is understood in this community. "Why is it important that the Bible never be *wrong*?" I follow.

Several students begin to share memories of parents and pastors who told them the Bible was the word of God and never wrong. They share stories about "the big, old Bible" that stays open to the twenty-third psalm in their grandparents' house; stories of Sunday school lessons where they sang "B-I-B-L-E, That's the Book for Me." They share stories about their experiences with the Bible in county jail where "well-meaning" volunteers would give them a Bible and tell them to just "follow everything in it and it will get your life on track" or "everything you need for life is right in this book."[6]

Sitting straight in her chair again, our intervener adds, "If you start picking apart pieces of the Bible, then the whole thing would fall apart. Then what would we have left?" Several heads nod along while others sit pondering.

Our curious investigator counters, "You would still have a really interesting piece of history that you can still learn from, that people can still use to motivate their lives. . . . I don't think it's all or nothing."

At this point, my co-instructor interjects with more questions. "Can a story be true and not factual? Must a story have happened exactly as it was written for it to be theologically meaningful?"

To encourage additional perspective sharing from those less likely to interject into the ongoing debate between colleagues, I invite students to discuss these questions in relation to the two creation stories and their homework essays in small groups at their tables.

Not ten minutes into the engaged table discussions does a voice emerge from the hall—"EMERGENCY COUNT! EVERYONE TO THE GYM!" The sound startles us, calling us back from whatever this room has become. The officer pokes his head in the door and yells, "To the gym!" leaving quickly to tell the next room.

"So much for the rest of that discussion!" someone remarks. I agree but hope it will continue in the dorms between roommates and friends. Some students wonder if they can leave their belongings in class, hoping against hope that they might be able to return. Most know better and take their materials with them, making their way to the gym. I can overhear the officers bellow "Offenders, you know what to do." Without missing a beat, students line up in rows to be counted. The counting of bodies takes precedence over anything else we were going to do in Theology today. Class begins late and ends early without explanation and leaves the conversation about truth, myth, story, and the Bible unsatisfyingly unfinished.

The juxtaposition between creative expression, critical debate, and count is not lost on me. For decades, educational prophet bell hooks counseled us about the power and promise of the classroom.

> The academy is not paradise. But learning is a place where paradise can be created. The classroom, with all its limitations, remains a location of possibility. In that field of possibility, we

have the opportunity to labor for freedom, to demand of ourselves and our comrades, an openness of mind and heart that allows us to face reality even as we collectively imagine ways to move beyond boundaries, to transgress. This is education as the practice of freedom.[7]

For hooks, the classroom is a place of power and subversion in death-dealing educational institutions and cultures. It is an otherworld where possibilities for moving boundaries exist and learning communities can lean into the power of life over death. But what happens when the classroom is subject to count?

Prison has lessons of its own. Count is the practice of counting human bodies as a protocol of safety. Several times a day, people incarcerated must line up in silence and be counted. Count is said to clear if the numbers reported by officers matches the numbers of people on record. If there is an incident or suspicion of an incident, an emergency or unscheduled count is called, and the prison is locked down until every inmate is counted. Count is a reminder of control, surveillance, and required obedience. While count is a frequent and common prison practice, students suggest emergency count is something more. They suggest that random emergency counts, like inspections, are at times used as deterrence; intentional acts to prevent students from positive activities and dissuade volunteers from showing up. But this is what it is like to learn here, to try to make a life—one step forward and two steps back.

There is perhaps no better illustration of the frustration students face trying to live in the face of prison's lessons than what I encountered in a student's homework assignment.

Claira's Homework

On the first page, there was only one word in large, bold print: **SHAME**. I turn the page and see a clean and crisp image of a prison drawn in black ink on white paper. This is someone's homework from the class Art and Public Narrative. The assignment was to write and illustrate a story about one of your most transformative life moments. The sharpness of the images, the style of prose—I know whose work it is before I read the name: Claira.[8] Claira and I are about the same age. But the year that I graduated college and moved to southern Ohio to begin my professional career, Claira left behind her infant daughter for a life sentence in prison. Like others I have read from incarcerated students over the years, her homework wrestles with the complicated and frustrating reality of trying to make a life in prison.

SHAME

At first it was really hard.

There was hard labor and a lot of isolation. I struggled to believe I was really there. It was like I had died in a little courtroom. Yet, I was still breathing; a shell of myself.

It was like the weight of my sentence had buried me alive and, in the aftermath, I was shredded and suspended in time. The prison was another universe where the Earth had stopped turning and the grass didn't grow. I was lost. I was certain my life was over or at least on some infinite pause.

Years went by.

Eventually, it occurred to me that time was still moving, and I was actually alive; that these awful days full of grief and gruel were *still* days, days that *had* to matter in the grander scheme of things. My life SUCKED! but it was still a life I had to learn to live.

I made some friends. I went to school. I got a better job.

Responsibility gave me a sense of purpose. The higher the quality of my performance, the more responsibility I was given. I helped with recreation, the paint detail, and programs in the gym.

For these events, we cleaned from top to bottom. When the gym was ready, we would take breaks in the sanitation closet.

We would sneak and use the microwave to heat up water and drink instant coffee we had bought with the little money our friends and relatives had sent us. We would listen to the radio and talk.

"Do you guys ever feel like time has stopped? Like we're in some other dimension where there are no weeks or years? Like its ONE really long day?"

"I don't feel like I'm getting older, if that's what you mean. I'll be 19 years old . . . forever? It's creepy."

"I think it's awesome! Like some Peter Pan shit. Who wants to get old?! Gross!!"

"I don't think we're talking about the fountain of youth here! There is evidence of time. I have wrinkles around my eyes and gray in my hair. That wasn't there 10 years ago."

"So you're saying . . . it's like a gap in psychological development?"

"How are we gonna deal with that?"

It is phenomenal that after so much oppression and loss I could get comfortable in the routine of things. Being in prison was always awful. But it had gotten easier. I felt like I belonged to a community, in a world I cared about. I felt respected and loved.

But it's as if some cosmic force never fails to swoop down and remind me of some bigger truth . . .

I had to pee.

Which was usually no big deal, but on one particular afternoon, the bathroom I would normally have used was occupied.

[Approaching another door labeled bathroom, an officer's

voice bellows out] *"Hold it right there! What do you think you're doing? You know you don't use this bathroom!!"*

I had forgotten about the other inmate bathroom because we didn't use it much . . . due to its condition.

As I opened the door I could feel the pieces of my shattered perception fall back into their respective place. I must remember that I am being punished, perpetually. Punished for riding in cars with boys, for being addicted to crack, for what *he* did, for not really knowing *him*, for what *he* didn't even know *he* was capable of. For two decades there will be punishment and if I, for even a moment forget, I will be reminded. . . . Shame is what they're after. It has sunk down into the very core of my being. It hangs in my clothes. It sleeps in my body. I am wholly defined by guilt and shame. The system pivots between being punitive and restorative and for the sake of rehabilitation inundates me with words like Character, Integrity, and Valor! . . . but never utters a thing about Dignity.

Figures 1.1 and 1.2. Illustrations from Claira's Art and Public Narrative Assignment

Claira's story raises several themes echoed throughout other autobiographical prison writings, themes of trauma, turning points, and growth. If we read her narrative through the frameworks offered by criminological scholarship, we will note the extraordinary nature of her story. Lila Kazemian, in her book *Positive Growth and Redemption in Prison*, describes adversarial growth as a framework that "highlights the positive changes that result from exposure to and recovery from trauma and hardship."[9] Claira's narrative chronicles her positive transformation, her "series of cognitive and emotional changes that eventually result in less suffering."[10] She has what desistance scholars call a turning point in her narrative where she makes a conscious decision to live a life that matters. Kazemian argues that individuals like Claira "who succeed in achieving transformation in prison have made the conscious decision to extract some positive outcome out of highly painful and traumatic experiences."[11] Claira's narrative is notable because the positive growth she narrates "is only possible with extraordinary motivation, determination, and resilience."[12]

But Claira's story illustrates how, beyond what most volunteers can see, prison teaches tireless lessons of shame and degradation that work against her positive efforts. The traumatic experiences of incarceration go beyond initial incarceration; they are inherent to living in prison. The feelings Claira describes when she arrives in prison—a shell, buried alive, shredded, suspended in time, infinite pause—are consistent with what one returning citizen calls the trauma of incarceration:

> Living in prison is what I imagine living in suspended animation would be like. I imagined my existence as a being on ice, frozen in time. "On ice" carries the connotation of being dead. When sentenced to a term of life in prison, one is considered civilly dead. Knowing that I was perceived as being dead, regardless of how it was phrased, was psychologically disturbing.[13]

Criminologist Dyan McGuire argues that deleterious prison conditions, such as those represented by the inmate bathroom, are an intentional part of the US punishment philosophy and pose serious challenges to agency and psychological well-being:

> After all, an institution whose purpose is to warehouse society's "trash" and to punish its miscreants is *supposed* to be bleak, harsh and unpleasant. Scarcity of material resources, degradation of the person and an almost complete deprivation of privacy are inherent to its penological approach.[14]

How is a person supposed to muster the agency to change, to make a life that matters, if the purpose of the prison is to teach a different, more death-loving lesson?

The Educational Project of Incarceration

From its earliest design, prisons have operated on an instructive logic of death and domination, leading millions of people throughout history to agree with Claira's assessment that a prison sentence feels like dying. According to a historical account from a nineteenth-century New York penitentiary, prisons were designed to be an educational experience in death, a death that ostracizes persons from broader social connections and *teaches* people inside to consider themselves dead:

> Convicts were to "receive no letter or intelligence from or concerning their friends, or any information on any subject out of

prison." Relatives were not permitted to visit with an inmate and he, in turn, was not allowed to correspond with them. "The prisoner," a Sing-Sing chaplain of this period recalled, "was taught to consider himself dead to all without the prison walls." And the warden himself repeated this analogy when instructing new convicts on their situation. "It is true," he told them in 1826, "that while confined here you can have no intelligence concerning relatives or friends. . . . You are to be literally buried from the world."[15]

In 1982, sociologist Orlando Patterson published *Slavery and Social Death*, where he studied features of slavery across more than sixty societies.[16] He observed three principal practices used to maintain and enforce domination: the forceful use of power to coerce, natal alienation, and continual dishonoring of the enslaved.[17]

The coercive use of power, whether real or symbolic, refers to methods used to strong-arm people into submission. In slavery, humans justified a free license to dictate who lives and dies, exercising the absolute power over the life and death of one person over another. Natal alienation refers to the disruption and attempted destruction of the transmission of cultural and communal knowledge and belonging. Natal alienation is one practice that differentiates the enslaved from other human beings "in that they were not allowed freely to integrate the experience of their ancestors into their lives, to inform understanding of social reality with the inherited meanings of their forebearers, or to anchor the living present in any conscious community of memory."[18] Finally, Patterson observed that people enduring enslavement were constantly and intentionally treated as persons without honor—despised and degraded through practices that communicate powerlessness. Patterson associates honor with dignity, freedom, and personhood. As such, the work of slavery was to perpetually remind the enslaved of their inability to claim honor for themselves. Through brutal and mundane practices of coercive power, natal alienation, and dishonor, enslavement methods attempted to *teach* people to consider themselves socially dead.

The term "social death" first appeared in social science in 1967. It was later adopted in carceral studies to connect the depth of loss associated with incarceration to larger legacies of human dignity-denying practices in studies of enslavement, genocide, and gerontology. Social death describes when living people are treated as if they have already died—*it's like being dead*—and occurs through systematic and persistent processes of exclusion, rejection, degradation, and neglect with internal and external effects, impacting how people view themselves and how society views them—*like knowing that you're dead*. Social death functions through a set of practices that shape human behavior toward a desired end—it is something humans *perform* and *experience*. Modern prisons are social death institutions because they *teach* social death as their curriculum.

People like Claira and Cate, while they may not refer to Orlando Patterson or use the term "social death" to describe prison practices, can name how those practices make them feel in their bodies—"It feels like dying. . . . I was shredded and suspended in time. . . . I had to learn to live." As I listened to Theology students describe what prison feels like, I joined the ranks of scholars of prison studies and mass incarceration who see similarities between Patterson's portrayal of the process of social death in slavery and that same process in incarceration.[19] As an educator, I began to see social death as more than a state of being. Social death is a form of pedagogy.

Pedagogy is a theologically significant political, ethical, and moral practice, and it concerns more than methods and techniques in a classroom.[20] Pedagogy refers to the practice and study of how knowledge, skills, and values are imparted, passed on, embodied, and adapted. To be concerned with pedagogy is to be concerned with individual and institutional practices, dispositions, and commitments that shape and influence human formation and development. To be concerned with pedagogy is to be concerned with how prison teaches people to feel like they have died—how prisons practice a form of social death education.

Claira's story demonstrates the impact that a social death-dealing system can have on people's ability to imagine and enact the life they want for themselves and helped me to name how a social death education attempts to form human bodies toward irrelevance. Social death is an educational process and goal that *teaches* bodies (and communities) to become and accept themselves as socially insignificant, alienated, and powerless. If I wanted to better understand how students live and learn in prison, I first had to understand that social death education functions as the dominant process trying to educate people in prison; the dominant process that we must engage with and resist if we seek life-enhancing educational practice.

Social Death as Pedagogy

Social death is a formation process that requires consistent practices to teach its message of irrelevance. Through ritualized practices of degradation and debasement, the process of social death attempts to form its subjects into people without honor, people without a future. Social death requires the use of lessons in dying.

Lessons in dying are small doses or micro-rituals of abusive power used to discipline bodies and attenuate agency. Lessons in dying teach shame and indignity. They are reminders of powerlessness, designed to punish and curtail any growing perception of purpose, worthiness, and value. In prison, death-dealing practices masquerade as standard protocol, but the nature of these quotidian and mundane practices is to punish, degrade, dehumanize, control, and ultimately, shame. These mediated messages are not unique to the prison where Claira resides but are pervasive throughout the US prison punishment complex:

> The Department of Corrections is what sociologists refer to as a "total institution." The goal of this kind of institution is to control most aspects of the incarcerated citizen's life. As a total institution, therefore, the DOC is rule-oriented. It deemphasizes choice, offers no explanation for orders barked, rigidly applies its rules, will not keep incarcerated residents in the loop, and requires residents to just "do as you're told." We are stripped of all meaningful identity, reduced to a number, and stamped with the non-authoritative label "felon." Moreover, it is no secret that one goal of the system is to perpetuate the existence of a non-dominant group. Prison is a dehumanizing environment.[21]

Lessons in dying occur through exposing people to what philosopher Achille Mbembe calls "small doses" of death that structure everyday life.[22] In prison, small doses of death range from daily humiliations, hyper-surveillance, symbolic violence, surprise transfers, and other forms of psychosocial destruction and abasement. They function to teach toward submission slowly but consistently. To live in prison is to encounter small doses of death every day.[23]

Small doses of death are corrosive; the "cumulative exposure to stressors, to the attritions of time, to the emotional and psychological consequences of structural conditions, erodes body and soul."[24] The small doses of death incurred through regular but unpredictable acts of random inspections, contingent access to care, or the use of decrepit facilities normalize disruption and inconsistency in students' lives. These practices are just some of the many lessons that shape human bodies into objects to be disciplined, controlled, and contained. These everyday lessons teach students that their lives and livelihood are unimportant and that their development and growth are insignificant. Daily lessons in dying are the teaching mechanisms of social death education.

To practice social death as an educational strategy is to enact a pedagogy of corrosion that persistently weakens and degrades self-worth, hope, and dignity. It is to commit oneself or an institution to teach toward irrelevance, a form of necropedagogy. Necropedagogy is a pedagogical ideology of an *education for extinction*. To be educated for extinction is, at best, to be tolerated—to be left alone to exist. No vision of a meaningful life undergirds necropedagogy, no goal or imagination of possibility. There is nothing life-enhancing or life-nurturing in an education for extinction. It is merely a warehousing technique, a confinement or containment strategy.

As a pedagogical commitment, social death justifies meaninglessness for certain bodies over and against others. Its practices distort identity, dismember community, and destroy hope for a meaningful present and future. These are not merely pedagogical problems; they are theological as well. Social death attempts to preclude the possibility of redemption for some people, to cut off an imagination for a future. Social death makes the idea of a good life for people like Claira seem absurd.

The pedagogic value of social death theory and its import to those teaching and learning inside death-dealing institutions lies in its conception as a process of formation and not just as a state of being.[25] In slavery, incarceration, and education, social death is something humans do to one another. It is an intentional education, a purposeful denial of another person's humanity, and the systematic degradation of dignity for power and punishment. Social death as a strategy and commitment is operationalized through behaviors and practices.

Social Death Education

Social death education (SDE), as one form of death-dealing education, is the training and molding of human bodies and minds into receiving objects whose creative power is intentionally inhibited and whose thinking and action, and senses of identity and community, are shaped and defined by an institution of domination, cultivating learners to become radically dependent, uncritically obedient, and disconnected from sources of life-giving meaning. Social death education distorts, diminishes, and degrades the imagination of and ability to enact a meaningful life with other living beings. Social death education is institutionally sanctioned disenfranchisement.

The goal of social death education is a relative sense of aimlessness, carelessness, and thoughtlessness regarding one's life and the life of others; a resignation to accept a bare life as it presents itself. An education in social death is an education in despondency, joylessness, and overall apathy about life. The heart of this death-dealing education is a desire to form human bodies, minds, and spirits toward insignificance. There is no upward mobility in a death-dealing education. It is an education not for transformation but for preserving dominator culture.

Learning Outcomes of Social Death Education

I draw on Claira's narrative to help me name some of the learning outcomes of prison's death-dealing education, to expose the knowledge or skills prison practices seek to cultivate in people and how they impact the ability to enact and imagine a meaningful life. Inspired by Claira, I identify five areas of impact on identity formation, imagination, relationality, dignity, and vocation.

Outcome 1: Disidentification

Who am I? is a fundamental question of identity and human development, and instances of trauma or radical disruption such as coming to prison can generate an existential crisis to reconsider this question. According to Claira, carceral practices teach people to answer this identity question with the word: inmate. Consider Claira's confession after entering the inmate bathroom: *As I opened the door I could feel the pieces of my shattered perception fall back into their respective place. I must remember that I am being punished, perpetually. . . . I am wholly defined by guilt and shame.* Despite her efforts to make her days matter and demonstrate growing responsibility and relationality, shame is the message Claira hears loudly from the inmate bathroom. Whatever she is trying to become, punishment, guilt, and shame are what the prison offers.

Claira's essay demonstrates how prison cultivates malignant disidentification, the distortion, and disfiguration of one's sense of self. The inmate bathroom functions to remind her of who she is in the eyes of the prison: an inmate. The word "inmate" is intentional; language impacts self-perception and the ability to change. There are movements among formerly incarcerated people against using words like "inmate," "criminal," and "convict" as labels for people in prison. About the use of words such as "inmate," the Vera Institute of Justice writes:

> Calling a person who was convicted of a crime a "criminal," "felon," or "offender" defines them only by a past act and does not account for their full humanity or leave space for growth.

These words also promote dangerous stereotypes and stoke fear, which stigmatizes people convicted of crimes and makes it harder for them to thrive.[26]

Students in Theology are hyperaware of the stereotypes associated with the words "inmate," "offender," and "felon." Many fear no longer knowing who they are in relation to the "real world" and wonder if they will be conceived as "normal" when released. They fear that the identity of a felon will supersede all other ways of being known, fundamentally defining them in perpetuity. They fear incarceration will preclude their ability to shape new perceptions of who they are and what they can become.

Criminologist Timothy Flanagan reports that incarcerated people "hope that the day would never arrive when they would stop questioning the rules and regulations that are perceived as petty."[27] A paramount fear, according to Flanagan's sources, is that threats to their fundamental humanity will prevail, rendering them an object of the prison; that a day will come when they accept the identification of prisoner without protest, and they will lose themselves. "To lose yourself" in prison is to become who and what the prison says you are; it is to lose the ability or desire to self-actualize and self-define.

In more ways than the physical body, the mind is where students in prison believe they exercise autonomy to (re)construct and maintain their identity. They feel in control of how they can use their minds to grow, learn, and accomplish, and they fear what would happen if they lost this ability. Nevertheless, the inmate bathroom scene is emblematic of how lessons in dying contribute to the work of identity destruction. As Claira attempts to learn to live a life possible to her in prison, she is confronted with the reality that in prison, inmate is the identity offered to her.

Outcome 2: Disimagination

What kind of life will I have now? Social death education not only distorts identity but also alters the ability to dream and imagine. In a conversation with colleagues, Claira confesses that *"even our dreams are plagued by prison."* As she spoke, I thought about the depths that a death-dealing institution deforms, impacting even the ability to dream. In a 1978 publication, Sam Keen and James Fowler reflect on what kind of education a healthy society needs.[28] Keen argues that education for a healthy society needs more affective dimensions and that we must teach people to stay in touch with their dreams and physical bodies. A death-dealing education does the opposite. It distorts and deforms dreams; it detaches people from their bodies (*it feels like dying*). Social death education makes a meaningful life difficult to imagine.

Claira's story navigates her attempt to construct a life that matters in prison, but lessons in dying attempt to constrain her ability to envision any form of life beyond that determined by the death-dealing institution. For Claira, the enduring lesson of prison was that the only life possible for her was a life without dignity—a life where her past would always determine her present and leave no room for growth or transformation. This second learning outcome of social death education is what I refer to as *disimagination*—the inability to imagine a meaningful conception of a good life.

> I must remember that I am being punished, perpetually. . . .
> For two decades there will be punishment and if I,
> for even a moment forget, I will be reminded. . . .
> Shame is what they're after.

Theologian and religious educator Mai-Anh Le Tran writes about the pedagogic power of disimagination. Disimagination is a form of miseducation that "distorts the long arc of historical memory; it suffocates critical thinking and critical self-reflection; it paralyzes difficult, dissenting, divergent dialogue; it chips away moral courage and social agency; it debilitates strategies of political resistance, thereby snuffing out possibilities for 'educated hope.'"[29] Le Tran retrieves the language of disimagination from Henry Giroux and Georges Didi-Huberman, who define imagination as "the capacity of individuals to bear witness to a different and critical sense of remembering, agency, ethics, and collective resistance."[30] They assert that disimagination undermines "the ability of individuals to think critically, imagine the unimaginable, and engage in thoughtful and critical dialogue."[31]

Disimagination is an acquired capacity. It is a way of thinking that is enforced and encoded. The inability or constrained ability to believe another way is possible results from intentional deformation and erosion. In educational systems, disimagination manifests as despondency and despair.

Outcome 3: Disconnection

Who are my people? Where do I belong? A third learning outcome conveyed in Claira's narrative is social disconnection. Practices that promote social and communal disconnection are practices that communicate that a person does not belong. The juxtaposition of the "good bathroom" and the inmate bathroom exemplifies how physical space can signal where one belongs. In Claira's story, the bathroom scene comes after the scene in the gym where she is laughing and talking with other women. Claira goes from feeling like she belongs to being assaulted by the conditions of the inmate bathroom. The bellowing voice of the officer redirects Claira's thoughts and actions: *"Hold it right there! What do you think you're doing? You know you don't use this bathroom!!"* The bathrooms represent two different categories of people with two different life possibilities.

Prison adaptation and desistance scholarship argue that the requirements of coping with and attempting to survive social death can deeply reshape a person's identity. In their study of formerly incarcerated people who served long sentences, Liem and Kunst found that people experienced lasting impact to their ability to connect, relate, and belong. Even after release from prison, people reported

> institutionalized personality traits (distrusting others, difficulty engaging in relationships, hampered decision-making), social-sensory disorientation (spatial disorientation, difficulty in social interactions) and social and temporal alienation (the idea of "not belonging" in social and temporal settings).[32]

Psychologist Kipling Williams studies the impact of ostracism and rejection and contends that a loss of social connectedness has the unique capacity to threaten one's sense of a meaningful life. According to Williams, ostracism, rejection, and exclusion threaten the four fundamental needs of humanity: belonging, control, self-esteem, and meaningful existence. Williams suggests that a life of meaning is difficult to discern without belonging, control, and esteem.[33]

People react to threats to fundamental human needs in three phases. In the immediate phase, the reaction is physical. The body experiences a range of emotions, including physical pain, hurt feelings, and mood disorders. These experiences can manifest as depression, anger, violence, and illness. *I struggled to believe I was really there. It was like I had died in a little courtroom. Yet, I was still breathing; a shell of myself.* These physical manifestations of pain are how the body responds to lessons in dying.

In the short-term phase, people attempt to regain the needs lost in social exclusion. They strengthen bonds with others, make self-affirmations, take control, and maintain cultural barriers. *I made some friends. I went to school. I got a better job.* This short-term phase is filled with optimism and hope that individual actions can resist further loss to fundamental needs.

However, Williams observes a different reaction among those who face long-term, persistent threats of exclusion. In the long-term phase, people begin to internalize the loss of fundamental needs. Some begin to self-isolate, choosing to be alone out of distrust and self-protection. There is a higher degree of learned helplessness whereby people become more dependent on institutions to exert control and relinquish the need for personal choice and agency. Self-esteem declines during this period, and there can be increased thoughts of suicide.

Students in Theology share similar testimonies to Claira, recounting feelings of despair, anger, and depression in the first several years of incarceration. They recall responding violently, staying in trouble, and getting into fights. They also remember turning inward and isolating themselves, failing to connect with others. Like Claira, after some time, students move from the physiological despair of incarceration into the short-term phase of seeking to reconstruct lost needs. Many begin to make friends, go to school, and get a job, each an effort to reconstruct belonging, self-esteem, and a meaningful existence. There is hopefulness in this stage, a sense that something can be done to re-create life in prison. This is the stage that most students are in when they first come to Theology.

Unfortunately, the impact of ostracism, exclusion, and rejection does not end after the initial moments of incarceration; they persist throughout the carceral experience. When a much-expected family visitation day is canceled, or a best friend is released, the need for belonging is fractured. When a student is abruptly and without warning moved from one dorm to another or from one prison to another, the need for control over one's environment is ruptured. When Claira enters the inmate bathroom, her self-esteem shatters. Social death practices promote fear of lost relationships and a permanent feeling of nonexistence, of never fitting in again outside of prison, and of fitting in too well inside. Fortunately, Williams' phases are not unidirectional or fully deterministic. Students whose self-esteem is diminished by the environment can find a sense of hope again. They can move from the long-term phase back into the behaviors of the short-term phase. Nevertheless, practices of social death education contribute to disconnection and disrupted senses of relationality.

Outcome 4: Dispossession of Dignity

Does my life matter? Living in a death-dealing institution provokes this question repeatedly. According to Claira, prison offers little help in developing positive, life-affirming responses. The one response it does seem to cultivate is the feeling of indignity. *The system pivots between being punitive and restorative and for the sake of rehabilitation inundates me with words like Character, Integrity, and Valor! . . . but never utters a thing about Dignity.* To feel indignity is to feel humiliation, shame, disgrace, embarrassment, and dishonor. Indignity is the lesson Claira receives, but she never hears anything about dignity. Claira does not explain in her homework assignment what dignity is, but we can get a sense of what dignity is not. Prison studies scholars contend that concepts like dignity and humanity "are difficult to operationalize" but insist that people incarcerated, like Claira, "know the difference between 'feeling humiliated' and 'retaining an identity.'"[34] For Claira, dignity is not communicated by any act or discourse of the prison, even when the prison claims to practice restoration and rehabilitation.

Dignity, as both a state of being and a process, is the antithesis of social death. Dignity recognizes full personhood, worthiness, and honor; it is constitutive of human beingness. In theological scholarship, dignity is conferred based on humanity being made in the image of God. It is an unearned feature of humanity that requires neither moral perfection nor conditional election. Humans are creatures with dignity by nature of our divine creation. To be human is to possess dignity. Social death systems attempt to stamp out the image of God. Carceral practices operate under the supposition that dignity is earned and can thereby be lost—that to be found a criminal is to forfeit one's claim to dignity, one's inclusion in imago Dei. The racist, sexist, and religious supremacist practices that undergird social death challenge the idea that all humans possess dignity by divine design. Instead, they operate on a belief that some people are less than human and thereby not made to possess dignity at all. In these cases, the image of God is not stamped out; it was never there to begin with.

Theological scholarship suggests that human beings enact, perform, and operationalize dignity. Vincent Lloyd describes dignity as both the result and performance of resistance. Lloyd investigates meanings of dignity that emerge from Black political thought, from people who intimately understand death-dealing systems of disenfranchisement and domination. According to Lloyd's analysis, dignity is the struggle against domination. It is action, performance, and practice. It is realized both in the work of resistance, and "when specific practices of domination end."[35]

Lloyd's description of dignity starkly contrasts the lessons in indignity offered in incarceration. Quoting from a woman named Tometi, Lloyd draws our attention to the relationship between dignity, agency, and self-actualization:

> Dignity is ascribed to those who struggle against domination. Those who dominate, or who participate in systems of

domination, do not have dignity. Those who are entirely dominated, to the point that all of their speech and actions are determined by the dynamics of domination, do not have dignity. But those who are subjected to domination and challenge that domination in whatever way, from passive resistance to active political organizing to aesthetic imagining, those individuals are properly described as having dignity.[36]

Quoting Marcus Garvey, Lloyd also writes, "This is dignity: realizing that systems of domination constrain our humanity, stamp out the image of God, and then creatively rebelling."[37] Practicing dignity in carceral contexts is to do as Claira does, becoming aware of how systems of punishment constrain quality of life and self-perception, and rebelling against those systems. Claira's rebellious decision to live and give meaning to her life is the performance of dignity.

Prison may offer lessons about character, integrity, and valor, but those lessons have nothing to do with the dignity of being made in God's image or the dignity of resisting domination. Prison's lessons do not cultivate, value, or encourage the type of dignity that Lloyd writes about, Tometi describes, or Claira personifies.

Outcome 5: Diminished Sense of Vocation

Who am I? Where do I belong? What kind of life will I have? Does my life matter? These are questions about constructing a meaningful life. To this practical theologian, they are also questions about vocation. Death-dealing education distorts and diminishes healthy discernment of vocation.

Christian theology and religious education have embraced various understandings of vocation: one's general call to Christian life, a call to formal priesthood or ministry, one's job or occupation, humanization, or self-actualization. But practical theologian Patrick Reyes' definition of vocation rings particularly relevant in prison contexts: "Vocation is a call out of oppression and into new life."[38] Humans can have many vocations and respond to many calls. But the first and essential vocational call is to live. Reyes defines vocation as the human work of hearing and responding to God's ever-present call to survive. God's call to live may be muted or distorted by systems, institutions, and trauma, but Reyes argues that those who have heard the call for themselves must communicate that call to others who cannot hear it.

Vocational discernment in death-dealing contexts begins with the recognition that you deserve to have life, that you deserve a life that matters. It requires an ability to believe against the death-dealing systems of disenfranchisement and believe another way is possible. Reyes' work helps us understand that surviving is the first vocation in a death-dealing reality. There is no shame in surviving. The first step in Claira's journey is realizing she is "actually alive." Not only is she alive, but her days had to matter, and she wanted to learn to live them.

Prisons are not places that support a vocation to live. According to Claira, prison wants her to accept another vocation: shame. The maintenance and production of punishment, guilt, and shame is the institutional vocation of prison. Shame becomes deeply embedded. *It has sunk down into the very core of my being. It hangs in my clothes. It sleeps in my body. I am wholly defined by guilt and shame*. If our first vocation is to survive, to hear and respond to God's call to live, then all forms of death-dealing education are a deliberate assault against God's hopes for humanity. Social death education is an affront to the divine calling to live, denying God's hope and possibility.

An education in social death is more than a pedagogical challenge to theological educators. It is a theological assault on the hope present in education. A social death-dealing process of formation attacks human dignity, both the innate dignity afforded to all human beings and the performance of dignity that involves human agency.

Claira's story illustrates the journey one woman takes from feeling like she has died to attempting to create a life that matters in prison—a hauntingly beautiful representation that even as people attempt to make a life for themselves in prison, they are constantly confronted with alternative messages to deter them. Like Claira, the students in Theology class desperately seek opportunities to learn, have substantive conversations, and critically explore questions important to their lives. But emergency counts and surprise inspections disrupt their efforts time and again. Nevertheless, like Claira's story, many students do not stay in a place of desolation. Students seeking to make a life for themselves in prison constantly resist lessons in dying and refuse to let a prison sentence be the final word for their lives. They, like Claira, decide to make their days in prison matter. They imagine the lives they want for themselves and learn to live them.

2
IMAGINING YOUR GOOD LIFE

> To image is to portray what is experienced in word pictures, stories and narrative, sound, movement, art. It is a nonexpository form of communication that mobilizes our imaginative faculties.[1]

Prisons are not designed to foster meaningful living. Social death as prison's educational disposition encourages purposelessness and renders the value of incarcerated people as human beings imperceptible. As Lisa Marie Cacho asserts, in a social death institution, those who are socially devalued are not expected to know or decide "what makes a life meaningful or the terms by which their lives are evaluated as meaningful or meaningless, as valuable or valueless."[2] Furthermore, Cacho argues that human value is ascribed and denied relationally in prison (and elsewhere) along racial, gendered, sexual, national, and spatial lines. But students in Theology refuse to allow a social death institution to have the final word over the possibilities for their lives. They define for themselves what makes their life good; what gives their life meaning. Students were asked to imagine that someone took a picture of a moment in their good life and to draw that image. Throughout the summer, these students name what makes their life meaningful and the terms by which they evaluate life as valuable.

After count clears and students return to their dorms for lunch, we make our way back into a classroom to prepare for our first group discussion. After arranging the tables into one large square, we wait. Five of the six people we invited return. Once we are all settled, I remind everyone of the purpose of the research and the confidentiality forms they signed earlier. When no one has any questions, I pass out name tags.

"For these discussions," I begin, "you can choose a new name. Please write that name on the name tag and let's introduce ourselves using the new name and one word that describes your experience in the Theology program."

The practice of introducing yourself with one word is something I have been doing to begin classes for years now. It is important for us to maintain continuity between class and research, to use practices and habits from our everyday Theology classroom. We want these groups to feel like any number of Theology classes—discussion based, embodied, inquisitive, curious, and fun. I maintain my regular role as educator and director of the program throughout the research—as one who asks questions, curates opportunities for storytelling and creativity, and facilitates collective analysis and imagining. The greatest difference between these groups and Theology class is the fact that there are two people feverishly taking notes. A stipulation of our research was that we could not bring in any recording devices. For this first group, I jot down key words and observations as I can, but the notetakers are capturing most of the details. Seated around the table but placed at the corners, they transcribe, interjecting every now and then as they would in any given class.

Meet Braley, Clarisse, Rylee, Briar, and Amari

We begin with introductions. With lots of laughter and good-natured teasing, we meet each other again. The first to introduce herself is Amari who describes Theology as interesting. Then is Clarisse whose one word to describe her experience in Theology is intrigued. Braley, who describes Theology as enlightening, introduces herself next. Next is Rylee who chooses the word "deepening" to describe her experience in Theology. The last to introduce herself is Briar. Briar is the only alumni of the program around this table. She has already graduated with her Certificate in Theological Studies and is pursuing her advanced certificate at the time. She uses the word "happy" to describe her experience of Theology. I have known Briar the longest.

Of the five students present, everyone but Amari is white. As I look around, I think to myself that the early years of the Theology program looked this way—majority white and Christian. It is no secret among students that whiteness and Christianity afford you certain privileges in prison, especially when accessing programs sponsored by chaplaincy. Over the past ten years, however, Theology has become more racially and religiously diverse with increasing numbers of students of color and non-Christian students. This has been an intentional goal of the program and a diversity we will see reflected more in later conversations. With new names chosen, we continue.

Drawing a Good Life

I give each person an 8.5" x 11" piece of paper with an image of an empty picture frame filling the page. Passing around colored pencils, I ask each student in the room to take a deep breath and imagine that someone has taken a picture of a moment in their good life. What do they see? I then ask that they take a few minutes to draw that snapshot on their paper.

Clarisse looks up from her blank page to me and asks, "Do you mean in *here*?" Her voice is thick with concern wondering if prison must be the location of her good life.

"It can be anywhere," I respond, and Clarisse's body relaxes as she takes up her pencils to draw. For several minutes, the room is relatively silent except for the occasional requests for different colored pencils accompanying the sounds of those scratching the surface of the papers, images of good life emerging. When it appears that most people are finishing, I add one final instruction: "Please give your image a title. OK, who wants to share first?"

Amari volunteers as she lifts her paper, moving it from side to side for all to see. "My picture is called *Going Places*." Amari shares a drawn image of herself and her son. Next to them, we see an image of a seed next to a flower. "This represents the journey with my son—growth. A good life is about family—family values and family goals. I want my son to have the life I never had."

Clarisse follows, showing us her picture titled *Getting Back to Basics*. It is a picture of a large house with room enough for her six kids. She laments the life she and her husband had when her children were young, saying that at least now her children have boundaries and her whole family goes to church every Sunday.

Braley presents her image next. At the top of the page, she has written the title "Happiness is . . ." She explains that happiness is this house she has drawn with herself and her four sons. "A perfect day is when everyone is home." Later, we come to learn that it was Braley who was seldom home, as she resents how much she worked while her children were young.

Keeping with the theme of home and children, Rylee goes next. Her picture is titled *Better Homes and Garden: the Rylee Edition*. Rylee did not hesitate when she received the instructions to draw a picture of her good life. She thinks about this question often, she informs us, especially when she peruses the pages of *Better Homes and Gardens* magazines. She loves looking at the illustrations of picturesque homes and family life but shares that it also makes her sad. "This is where I am *supposed* to be," she says as she points to her picture of a large home with a greenhouse out back. "Me, my baby, and my older daughter . . . and there might even be a husband floating around somewhere," she laughs.

The last to share her image is Briar. Briar lifts her piece of paper in the air with the word "Peaceful" written at the top. Briar has drawn an image of herself lying in a hammock tied to an apple tree "in the middle of nowhere." She confesses that her idea of a good life is one where she is alone with nature. By alone, she means no other humans, as her image includes a dog, cat, and two birds. One bird is blue and perched in a bush. The other bird is red "like Ms. Green's bird," she says. Everyone turns to me to elaborate. I tell the story about the red cardinal who has been coming to my house every morning and afternoon for months, pecking at the windows to announce their presence. This is the second season this bird has returned to my home, and the second season I have shared stories about them with students in Theology. Briar remembers my stories about this bird that returns and draws them into her image. "This is everything I need," she says. "Well, I guess I didn't draw myself any clothes," she laughs, "but the apple tree means I at least always have something to eat."

"Let's put all of the images in the center of the table," I suggest. "What do we see? What do they have in common? What is different?"[3]

Conversation quickly ensues about what these images have in common: houses, outdoors, no fences, no cars, no work, and bright days. The houses suggest that having a home and being home is an important feature of a good life. The house is where family resides. In stark contrast to the grayish concrete walls of the prison, bathed in artificial fluorescent light, images of sunlight, blue skies, and nature fill the pages. Finally, someone observes that these images convey simplicity.

Everyone returns to their seats as Braley lets out a sigh. "These are the things we just took for granted. I worked forty hours a week and did not care that I was barely home with my family. Now that I think back, a career is not that important to me." Clarisse agrees. "It's all about being together with those you love and who love you. In here, I miss so much, like the birth of my granddaughter and her birthday parties," she regrets.

Family is a central feature of a good life for most of these women. The one possible exception, someone notes, is Briar. "Briar's is the only picture with no family," she remarks. Briar does not respond. Briar is not the only person this summer whose image of a good life features solitude. Yet, even in the absence of other human beings, Briar's image like the others includes living beings where care can be given and received.

Briar has been an active member of the prison's Forever Friends K9 Rescue dog program. The mission of Forever Friends is to save dogs from being euthanized while providing people incarcerated with the training to teach basic dog obedience and learn animal care and grooming skills. According to the Department of Corrections, in addition to providing the dogs with love and care, women participating in the program earn their veterinary technician certification through the technical college system of Georgia, giving them valuable education and job skills that they can use upon their release. Students like Briar attest that caring for the dogs is one of the best things they have ever been part of. Briar often brings her animals in training with her to Theology. Her care and love for the dogs is evident to all who witness them together. I am not surprised to see animals as central to Briar's image of a good life.

Drawing our attention to the center of the table again, I ask, "What role do you play in making these images a reality?" I am torn about asking the question this way for fear of playing into the self-reliance, and hyper-individualistic notions of responsibility operating in carceral culture. The US punishment system is part of what Sered and Norton-Hawk call the "institutional circuit" of offices, systems, and services that govern the disenfranchised lives of the poor, sick, and criminalized. Based on five years of fieldwork in Boston, Sered and Norton-Hawk document the day-to-day lives of forty women caught in the institutional circuit and argue that the oppressive conditions faced by them are culturally believed to be the result of their "personal flaws and poor choices." Furthermore, these women believe "that their suffering is the result of the choices that they personally made: the wrong man, wrong education, wrong drugs, wrong beliefs, and wrong relationships" and not the result of larger structural obstacles.[4] Prisons feed on this radically individualized notion of responsibility using it to blame individuals for their suffering and extending it to make them wholly accountable for their rehabilitation and healing. Christian ethicist Elizabeth Bounds writes about the relationship between prisons and responsibility to "produce responsible persons, whose responsibility is demonstrated by obedience."

> In the US prison system, responsibility has been and continues to be a powerful moral term that is used to shape the meaning and purpose of imprisonment. While incarcerated, persons are supposed to be taking responsibility for their crime. A lack of responsibility, it is implied, has led individuals to prison and

their release depends upon their capacity to develop and practice responsibility. However, across these decades of prison history, the actual practice of forming responsibility has meant little apart from simple obedience to all possible regulations and commands.[5]

I am distrustful of the way prison culture uses individual responsibility to absolve itself of providing people with the resources, tools, and environment needed for healing and change to occur. But I do not want to assume that students lack agency to create some version of a good life for themselves, even in prison. In response to my question, the women around the table answer without delay: you must be a leader, do the hard work, focus on what is important in life, and not fall into temptation. I hear echoes of the Department of Corrections in these responses, but I also realize that another reality is simultaneously true. These women want to believe that they have some agency over actualizing the lives they desire. They are, by result, rejecting the determinism and fatalism that can easily creep into our structural critique of prisons. Their belief is not rooted in denial, however, but in hope paired with the reality that their good lives will not come without challenge.

"Are there obstacles to your role in creating these images?" I ask. Briar responds quickly. "Well, about temptation, you actually need to be out in the wilderness or else there will be temptations. If there are no people, there are no obstacles." We all better understand why Briar did not draw any people in her image of a good life. Briar is in prison for a crime that she participated in with four others. Through various interactions with Briar in class, I witnessed her try to make sense of what happened exploring topics such as sin, group think, and pack mentality. People and their temptations, unlike the animals in her image, represent possible obstacles to a good life and not its source.

"The biggest obstacle to a good life for us is our felon record!" The conversation shifts to discuss a topic about which everyone agrees. A felon record, accordingly, can be an insidious and long-lasting impediment to the good life these students desire. A felony conviction can follow someone for life, even after their prison sentence has ended. Unless a person can have their record restricted, a felony is a matter of public record. It can negatively impact everything from housing to employment, ultimately impacting how the mothers around the table are able to retain custody and care of their children.

Felon records, and the occupational collateral consequences that follow them, can drastically limit justice-involved people's ability to establish stable income, either through employment or government assistance. The women around this table understand occupational collateral consequences intimately. Formally, they are defined as "any law that restricts—either automatically or with discretion—a criminal justice involved individual's ability to obtain employment, by (1) limiting access to occupational licenses and certificates on the basis of criminal record; (2) restricting employment in a certain field; or (3) requiring criminal background checks for certain employment types."[6] A study on the gendered burden of criminal conviction and the impact on women's employment asserts that occupational restrictions can disqualify women more than men from gainful employment. For example, according to the US Department of Labor, two of the most common occupations for women are licensed nurses and teachers. Yet many states have historically had laws or customary practices that restrict people with felony records from obtaining the necessary licenses for these roles. In cases where licensing is not required, it is no secret that employers can be reluctant to hire people with criminal backgrounds, even in a Ban the Box state like Georgia. Georgia restricts background checks until after a job is offered and citizens have the right to expunge misdemeanors and nonviolent felonies four years after a sentence is complete. Nonetheless, students often want to know how they are supposed to talk about the fifteen-year gap in their work history. If employment challenges are not daunting enough, a felony conviction can also negatively impact eligibility for social benefit programs such as public housing, food stamps, and state and other forms of federal grants and financial assistance. The juxtaposition between the good life images on the table and the obstacles that come with a felony conviction is stark.

"We'll just need to do what we have to do" is the matter-of-fact response from the women in the room. I hear this as less of a concrete solution and more of a realization that a felon record is not going to make their attempts to live their good lives easy. Nevertheless, they begin talking about the people whose support will be important to living a good life, people like husbands, children, family, and groups like Narcotics and Alcoholics Anonymous. Clarisse summarizes by saying that what they ultimately need are positive people and not negative ones.

As I listen to the women around the table, I write a note to myself about the importance of community, specifically what some scholars have coined "community capacity." Community capacity refers to

> the ability of a given neighborhood to provide pro-social support to offenders trying to reintegrate into a community after incarceration. Without access to conventional institutions and their positive impact on improved life chances, women have narrowing options. In neighborhoods suffering from disinvestment, work is frequently reduced to employment in drug markets, crime, and both expressive and instrumental violence that often leads to subsequent imprisonment.[7]

As much as other people are important in their visions of a good life, Amari makes a statement that draws us back into focusing on individual roles. "My parents have supported me ever since I became incarcerated at nineteen years old. I need to show them that I am a woman now—I am not a little girl anymore." Amari's comment reflects a desire to be respected and viewed and treated as an adult. Prison is infantilizing and being incarcerated has eliminated many opportunities for Amari to show her parents that she has grown into a conscientious adult. She hopes that whatever good life is possible for her is one where she is no longer treated as a child. A good life is one where she can show that she has matured, one where she has grown like her picture of a seed transformed into a flower.

Rylee offers another source of support important to her, the church. Of all the people here, Rylee is the most open in talking about her faith and the importance of Christianity to her present and future life. Following Rylee's opening, I interject a question about God.

"We've talked about your role in these images and the roles of others," I recap. "What about God? What, if any, role does your idea of God have in these images?" The room quiets as each person looks back at their images as if they are looking for God to appear on the page. Breaking the silence, one person finally looks up and says, "Everywhere." "Yeah," Clarisse adds, "God gave me everything like my kids." "God gave me my very breath," another adds, "I'm grateful." Rylee looks around at the images and then back to me and offers the last remark about God: "He's like the frame, holding it all together."

Reading the room, I can see that there is little energy to continue along this line of questioning. I have noticed over the years that newer students are more reticent in their God-talk. Many are still trying to figure out what they think we, as instructors, want them to say. I once overheard a conversation between Briar and a new student that shed light on this. The new student was fretting over a homework assignment in Biblical Foundations. They complained out loud that they did not know if their responses were "correct." "I don't know if this is what they want me to say," I heard the person say to Briar. Briar responded with "Just write what you have to say, the teachers don't care what you say, just write something!"

I was compelled to interject. "We absolutely care what you say!"

Briar looks up and laughs at my defensiveness. "That's not what I meant, Ms. Green. I mean you want to know what we think, not like there is only one right or wrong answer. You don't care if we sound a certain way or not, as long as we are honest about what we think, that's what I meant." I laugh along with Briar as she returns to helping the new student understand that the ways of Theology are different from other forms of prison culture. To ask someone what they think, and remain open to their response, is not common in prison—especially when asking questions about God. Around this table, God is viewed as the giver of that which is good. It is not clear, however, how or if they believe God relates to the many obstacles that await to limit these good lives.

Watching the clock and knowing I have a few more questions, I move us along by asking one final question about the pictures: "What do you need for these pictures to come true?" The responses are immediate: a release date, parole, and freedom. "Well, my first thought was to say money," one person adds, "but even though an income is important, it's not the most important thing." Clarisse and Braley go back and forth here about what is most important and they conclude that being home is what they need the most and a release date, parole, and freedom are necessary for that to occur. "The worst thing about all of this is being absent. My kids really want me to be home." As the conversation continues, words like "strength" and "persistence" are added. But Rylee adds the last word: the thing she needs most to make her picture come true is "faith bigger than a mustard seed."

"If there is any one thing you could do to experience your hoped-for good life in the present, what would it be?" Going around the table, they each offer a response: "teaching by example, making wise choices, staying positive, having more compassion, and getting all the education possible."

Theology Helps Me Grow

There is widespread agreement that education is crucial to whatever good life is possible in prison. The ability to graduate from Theology with a certificate "gives you pride, and your family can see how you've changed. People can see that you've changed everything." Clarisse is referencing the value of proving to others that she is not who she once was. As she speaks, I remember Amari's hope that her parents can see that she has changed. Rylee adds that "knowledge is power," and being in Theology pushes her children to achieve since they can see she is fighting for education. This idea of graduating from Theology as connected to being a role model for children comes up several times throughout the summer.

The conversation turns to specific examples from Theology. One person proclaims that the first class new students are required to take, Biblical Foundations, "enables you to better see how so many churches and preachers are preaching at you." I have learned from my time working in prison that from the minute women are incarcerated, people start "preaching at them": family, chaplains, volunteer ministers from local churches, officers, judges, and sometimes other women inside. Whether this is unique to southern religious culture is unclear as every woman in this room was raised in the South. For many students in Theology, what they learn in the program helps them to reflect on how religion and religious language has been and continues to be presented to them.

"The knowledge you get in Theology helps you see why you and others believe the way you do." Rylee adds that "education gives advantages both in here and out there. It's good to be part of something, to be involved in something constructive." Rylee believes that other people in prison look up to her, asking for her help in reading the Bible, for example. "People assume you are super smart when you're in Theology." Everyone laughs.

For Braley, Theology is "humbling since you realize what you do NOT know.... I'm usually a confident person but have found myself humbled."

"I was more comfortable in Biblical Foundations than Theological Foundations," Briar adds. Theological Foundations is the second required course all new Theology students take. "But it is good to be told what you do not know," Braley interjects. Braley and Briar both like things to be more straightforward. Theological foundations, for many students, is a world more foreign than Biblical Foundations. At least with Biblical Foundations, there is familiarity with the Bible as a text even as people are challenged to think differently about it. Theological Foundations presents a new world of vocabulary and concepts that are unfamiliar to many students.

I ask about other educational opportunities in prison that are helpful, and a litany of classes and job training programs are shared. "But Theology is different," they say. "Theology allows us to have free expression where we don't have to be put in a box. Theology gives us evidence of what we have achieved (e.g., certificate). Theology gives direction, teaches openness to others, and how to deal with difference," Briar and Braley explain. "I'm now able to respond to Christians around me," Briar says. "Learning how to live with others is so important in open dorm areas—we have to coexist." Theology helps people navigate the diverse environment of prison life and how to deal with beliefs and people who are different from themselves. "I always hear those men [staff] arguing about Trump and politics every morning. I'm not interested in their arguing because I know it's not as important to be right. What is important is the ability to listen and respect difference and not to prove yourself as right and another as wrong. That is a survival tip for prison."

Clarisse interjects, "Theology helps me grow. I always have my roommates read my papers." "Every paper is important, you know?" Rylee adds. "I have a voice now." The women around the table start reminiscing about other papers and assignments that were meaningful to them. For Briar, it was her capstone project on sin as a form of bondage. For Braley, it was the "who am I?" assignment she completed in her Biblical Foundations course that she found most enlightening. "It was the first time I ever put my beliefs down on paper like that!" For Amari, it was the exegesis paper she wrote on Proverbs 31 where, for the first time, she truly considered the proverb as a conversation between a mother and her son, an example of how a mother might talk to a son whom she loves. As I listen to Amari, I look back at her image of a good life, the image of a mother with her son.

A Good Life Is Being Complete and Not Broken

At the heart of this research is a question about human flourishing in constraint. While we may talk about flourishing in the context of a theology classroom, flourishing is not a word I typically overhear in the hallways of the prison. Therefore, I ask what other words come to mind when students think of a good life. Words ring out in rapid fire: security, structure, consistency across officers, reliability, blooming where planted, growing, abundance, and wholeness. Clarifying what is meant by wholeness, they explain that wholeness is being complete and not broken. Then someone shouts out the word "freedom." "A good life is a life of freedom, specifically the freedom to make your own choices."

"Maybe," Briar interjects, "but the better choices you make in prison, the worse you are treated." For Briar, the freedom to make your own choices, even good choices, does not guarantee a good life, especially in prison.

In the cacophony of words and explanations that are in rapid succession in the room, someone offers the word "joy."

"What is joy? Is joy possible inside?" I ask. The overwhelming response is that joy is not possible all the time, anywhere. In fact, too much joy is "what got me here" was confessed with laughter. There is a difference here between happiness and joy, though what exactly the difference is became less clear as the conversation continued. What is clear, however, is the difference between being happy to be in prison and being happy in prison. These are two distinct realities. No one is happy to be in prison, but among these women, being happy in prison is not only possible but an essential need to survive. Amari reflects that it is important to stay happy inside and not let the reality of everything *in here* define her.

Taking a chance, I chime in with, "What about the word 'flourishing'?" With shrugs and slowly nodding heads, "Sure," someone says, "that works too, I guess." I laugh at their effort to affirm my choice of word and ask my last questions of the afternoon.

"Of all the words offered here or new ones that come to mind, if I ask you for one word that best encapsulates the idea of a good life, what would you say?" After a moment of silent reflection, the words "kaleidoscope," "security," "happiness," "flourishing," and "love" are spoken.

As the clock strikes 3:30 p.m., we hear an officer coming down the hall announcing the end of the track. We must leave. I ask Amari, Braley, Riley, Clarisse, and Briar to leave their drawings and thank them for their time. I hear laughter as someone asks if they can keep going by their new name. "We should do this again sometime," they laugh, "it was fun."

I am more than a little relieved at their joyfulness. As my colleagues and I take a collective breath of relief, we pause to take in what just occurred. We turn over the drawn images and write a few additional notes to help us recall these conversations: the importance of family and home, outdoors and nature, and the question of freedom. We walk out of the classroom energized and exhausted. As students return to their dorms, we make the journey back through no fewer than eight locked gates with the sounds of jangling keys and clanging iron serenading us out of prison to return next week.

It takes nearly six weeks before we gather students again to talk about a good life. After several failed attempts to have groups after classes on Friday afternoons, we pivot and decide to host groups on Tuesdays. I have never been to the prison on a Tuesday; I did not expect it to feel so different. The school hall on Fridays is usually empty when we arrive. Our programming and a popular theater-based class comprise much of the morning activity on Fridays, and Jum'ah prayer participants join the hall in the afternoon. On Tuesdays, however, the school hall is alive with GED and charter school activity, vocational-technical classes, and support groups. Officers appear to be at their assigned stations, and movement in and out of tracks goes more smoothly than I have seen for several Fridays.

In comparison, the prison feels more dynamic on Tuesdays, more structured, and less haphazard. Though the prison is short-staffed for correctional officers, fewer people call off on Tuesdays. It is also less likely that last-minute programming, random but necessary store scheduling, or one of the many "catch-up days" for spending state-mandated money on pizza or chicken dinners occur on Tuesdays. Tuesdays mean structure. Fridays feel like an afterthought.

We head toward the school hall when we arrive at the prison. But instead of turning right as we do to enter our usual hallway, we turn left and make our way to the chaplaincy department. Our group is scheduled to meet in the chaplain's conference room. The conference room is a narrow space with a long, rectangular table down the middle. If you sit with your back to the door, you face a wall of windows that looks out onto the courtyard. Trees with purple blooms sway with the wind, and birds perch on branches. It is the only external view I would describe as beautiful in this place. In some ways, it feels like a luxury to be in this space.

Though the prison runs smoother today, it still takes us nearly an hour to get settled and locate students, but all six people we invited show up—an accomplishment. We are mostly undisturbed as we situate ourselves around the table except for a counselor knocking to let us know that the Re-entry program will need the room for second track. I look to my colleagues, and one takes the cue, rises, and goes into the hallway to find another room for our following group discussion. There is also a woman not in Theology who is on work detail. She finishes cleaning on the far end of the room and closes the door behind her. Doors closed to the outside world, I welcome everyone and remind them briefly about the study, purposes, and confidentiality forms they have already completed. We then meet each other anew.

Meet Handsome, Cat, Cate, Nikki, Mena, and Spicey

The makeup of this group is more representative of the Theology program today: three Black students, three white students, four in the basic program, and two in the advanced. Their ages range from young to old, and they identify as Christian and non-Christian, religious and not.

Handsome introduces themselves first, greeted by laughter at the choice of name. They describe Theology using the word "freedom." Handsome is just over five-and-a-half feet and over two hundred and fifty pounds. Handsome could easily be intimidating if they chose to be, but I only experience them as reserved, thoughtful, and a quiet comedian. At twenty-nine years old and the youngest in the room, they have been incarcerated for eight years, and though their record states they have a maximum of ten years left to serve, they are confident they will be getting out soon. (Four years later, Handsome is in the transition center and will likely be out on parole by the time this publishes.)

Then we meet Cat and Cate. Five years into her life sentence, Cat is a sixty-two-year-old white woman who self-describes as an "old hippie" and describes Theology as enlightening. Cate is much younger, sprightlier, and with a much shorter prison sentence (maximum nine years served). She describes Theology with the word "empowering."

Next, we meet Nikki, Mena, and Spicey. Nikki is a few months older than Handsome, white, and one of the newer students in Theology. Mena, conversely, has been in Theology for years and is pursuing her advanced certificate. In her mid-forties, she is the only person in Theology who identifies as Jehovah's Witness. And finally, there is Spicey. Spicey, like Cat, is serving a life sentence and, like Mena, was raised in part as a Jehovah's Witness though she has not identified as such for years. She refers to herself as a Christian. They each describe Theology as eye-opening, unlimited, and stimulating.

Remembering a Good Life

Our introductions transition into five minutes of quiet coloring and sketching as I give instructions on drawing their visions of a good life. Mena draws a picture titled *True Happiness*, an image of a woman standing in green grass, basking in the sun's rays, under a blue sky, holding a Bible in her hands. "That book is my life core," she explains.

Cat's image is titled *Importance* and, because she confesses that she cannot draw, is a collage of words on the page: faith, family, and farming. Cat introduces her image by saying it represents everything important to her. She lived on a farm for a long time, so her image of a good life is on the farm. Spicey, a self-professed city girl, asks Cat to explain what is so special about living on a farm. Through Spicey's invitation, we learn that the farm, to Cat, represents closeness, working together, family, and seeing everything God has made. On the farm, her family shared everything they grew. She reminisces about an easter egg hunt saying the farm was an excellent place to raise kids and grandkids.

Handsome draws a picture of a house with two people standing outside, themself and their mother. Titled *Home Sweet Home*, we learn that their siblings and grandmother are also in the home (though they are not shown in the picture). Cate shares a drawn image of her parents watching her at a dance recital. "This is before they got divorced, supporting me doing what I love to do," she describes. For Cate, a picture of her good life is a picture of her parents "loving [her] unconditionally." Nikki shares an image of the sun setting over the ocean; its calmness is at the heart of her depiction of a good life. She titles it *Love, Serenity, and God*. Spicey shares last. With an image titled *Child-like-faith*, Spicey shares an image of a Black woman dancing, her body sketched to show movement and gracefulness. The woman is dancing for God, Spicey explains, and she calls it childlike faith because it represents a time from her childhood when she was "really small and still innocent, where God was like a daddy."

Unlike the last group, I did not have to ask about God's presence in these images. Unprovoked, Spicey describes God's presence in her image as "being in my heart," and Nikki locates God as the "creator of the beautiful world" she has drawn. For Mena, God is everywhere but "only as long as we allow Him in." Cate locates God in the love of her parents. "What my parents are doing in the picture shows love, and God is love."

These images of a good life are mostly memories for these students, recollections from a past life. But Spicey is the first to suggest that she can experience the feeling of her image even in prison. "When I praise dance," Spicey explains, "I can experience help now." More than a memory, Spicey's image is possible in the present. In fact, it happens when she dances and when she participates in worship. Cate agrees that through dance and the movement of her body, she experiences the feelings she hopes to convey in her pencil sketch.

For Mena, her good life feeling is possible "all day, every day" she expresses optimistically. Mena suggests that her good life is enacted in prison when she sees the good around her and reflects on it. "Growing each day" is what a good life feels like. Cat agrees that looking for the good things in this place she describes as "so crappy" helps her good-life feeling emerge. For Handsome, they can feel their hoped-for good life while daydreaming of their mother and siblings and thinking about going home. We learn that Handsome's siblings are also incarcerated, so Handsome spends much time daydreaming about what it will be like to "learn each other again."

A sense emerges in the group that a good life is something they each have some control over identifying or creating. Spicey explains it as a force that must be tapped into. "You have to tap into energy and feelings, position yourself to be thankful, and be healed. You have to surround yourself with good things. That's why I continue to try to embrace peace all the time. It is my responsibility. I can have a pity party, or I can rejoice."

Cate immediately agrees. "You have to see the good in things, even as things shift." She points back to her image of herself as a little girl dancing before her parents. "My parents are large in this picture, but they were actually not that big in my life as a couple after their divorce. There's nothing I can do about my parents' separation, but I can still recognize how they can give me unconditional love, each by themselves."

Though everyone around the table recognizes their role in creating their good life, they also acknowledge that a good life requires others. For Handsome, it is their grandma and mother. For Spicey, it depends on the season of her life, but anyone can "bring a little bit of goodness into her day." For Nikki, it requires her children, family, and God, and Mena agrees that God is central to realizing her good life: God, her children, and her spiritual family.

Mena on God and Her Spiritual Family

When Mena speaks of her spiritual family, she means the elders and members of her Jehovah's Witness congregation. Two days after this group, Mena explains in a private interview. "When I was in county, I kept praying to God. I had fallen hard and felt bad, so prayer comforted me. It was the only thing to lean on. The elders understood and they gave me biblical comfort. I got fellowship and knew I couldn't continue without showing repentance. I had strayed away from biblical principles and there were consequences. I had strayed away as a way to protect myself. But being inside the church has been a form of protection from straying. You can do your way for a little bit, but when there is harmony with God, He is protecting you. That protection reminds me of certain standards that are there for a reason. It's helped me see that all the things my great-grandmother was doing was for protection, not to restrict me."

"I know that I won't always fit in or agree with others. I don't agree with half the stuff other people do. Sometimes I don't feel like I belong, and it's natural to feel that way. I had to forgive myself and pour out my heart to God because God forgives. If you have guilt, that comes from within yourself, not from God." Mena attributes her ability to forgive herself and find the confidence to be herself to her spiritual family. She would talk to her spiritual family, those she describes as related to her in the faith. She would pray and do Bible studies with members of the congregation who would come to see her. Mena's spiritual family helped her understand God as forgiving, which allowed her to ultimately forgive herself. As I listen to Mena, I wonder if her spiritual family helped to communicate God's voice to Mena when she could not hear God for herself. "[God] is everything for me—not just Father Provider. God forgives everything, not just your 'above the surface' stuff. God is so merciful to me. I feel that I try to put in a lot of effort, but really, it's not that much. He has continually blessed my efforts. It may only be a little, but it is a lot I can give. He gives me peace, mental peace, so there's no worries, even in a place like this. I'm in prison, but it could be worse. I rely solely on Jehovah for a lot of things. Our deeds don't go unnoticed. He knows everything. I don't need approval from others because I have his approval. I'm happy to do the right thing. He's continuously protecting my family. There was something I prayed for some two years ago, and that prayer was answered this year. It wasn't on my time, but God knew when to answer it. I praise him even more."

Mena describes a spiritual family as essential to a good life. "Having a family with a spiritual foundation is the good life," she proclaims. "It's simplistic, ideally, a good life is a life with pleasant things like family. I really try to stress family values as the foundation for everything."

When asked if she tries to live into these values in prison, she says that she tries and immediately begins talking about

Theology. "Theology helped me to know that everyone doesn't share the same values as me. Some people do not have healthy values in their lives. It's a choice whether to do good. That's why I'm big on integrity. When you have integrity, you do good things. It's okay to be sad in prison. People say *I'm in prison, so what I do does not matter.* Yes, this is prison. But that doesn't mean you should make bad decisions because when you do, it comes back on all of us. Some staff are corrupt, but that doesn't justify you doing wrong. Doing wrong affects everyone else."

For Mena, integrity is a humanistic value. While integrity may be shaped by one's religious commitments, it transcends religion. Integrity operates both inside and outside of religious beliefs or allegiances. All humans can have integrity; all humans *should* have integrity, according to Mena.

Mena laments the decisions people make that jeopardize the lives of those trying to live with integrity. She shares a story about a group called Bead Amigas, who came to teach jewelry-making to people in prison. "The money goes back to women in Honduras who make the beads. The beads still smell like ash from lava." She continues, "Some people's values are warped in my opinion. That leads them to make unhealthy choices and that's how old patterns come back. Some people will say, 'I care about my family,' but they'll drink, smoke, and do drugs, which gets them in trouble in here. It's their choice whether they do drugs outside or in here. You cannot get mad at that, but when people take stuff from programs and stuff, that penalizes us. It can mess up whether volunteers are able to keep coming back in and can make the staff say that no one can come in. Certain crowds do wrong and that affects everyone else." We learn that a bag of beads brought in by the volunteers was stolen, and the group was halted immediately. "To steal from a volunteer organization shows you don't care. The same things have happened with yarn. Stuff like that removes any normalcy and connections to the outside. . . . We're robbed of that. It's not fair."

Mena is clear that she operates by a different moral compass from people who steal and live without integrity. "My way of living stems from biblical principles. Every day, you make adjustments to biblical standards, to his [God's] standards, not the world's.

You put him first and everything naturally flows from that. It helps you to have better conversations with people—I think before I speak, I consider how other people feel, I put their feelings above mine, I've learned to listen. Jesus Christ is the model for how to treat people. We have a choice whether we do it or not. There's only chaos without living with him. I can't do things my way and follow him—I did live separated from him but that led to chaos. Your life may not be perfect, but it's not as bad. I may face oppositions for being different, but most people respect it. I'm not an extremist—it's about balance. You can choose to lean on God or not. How I treat others has helped me mentally, physically, emotionally—in every sense. It helps me be a better mom and grandmother to my grandkids."

Mena never identifies anyone in Theology as belonging to her spiritual family, but she does value what Theology has helped her become while in prison. "The readings—they help me. I don't agree with some of them, but I still read them," she laughs. "Theology helped me understand other people and their views. Before, I would hear someone say, 'God doesn't exist' and I would think one way about them [negatively]. Hearing people's stories, though, made me better understand and not make assumptions based on one thing. I learned everyone's reasoning and why they feel certain ways. I know their triggers and what is sensitive when I interact with them, and I won't bring up certain things when I deal with people." Mena admitted that she has often gotten into confrontations with people because of religious differences, sometimes to the point of actual conflict. I could always count on Mena to challenge whatever interpretation of scripture or theology came up in class. However, she finds the approach to reading the Bible explored in Biblical Foundations, considering the world behind the text, of the text, and in front of the text, as a helpful framework for seeing differences. "When I engage a reading, I am not simply being oppositional."

Mena is not one to enjoy the creative or embodied arts in Theology. She calls herself "a deep analyst." She prefers reading- and writing-intensive classes. She also enjoys classes with practical application. "I loved the restorative justice class. It helped everyone with accountability, bridging gaps, paying attention to people you've hurt, calming down to get to the core of your feelings and apologize, and how to handle conflict. I also liked the Compassion[ate] Integrity Training," she adds. "I used to be bougie," she laughs, "but I grew out of that. I took inventory of myself and learned you can't be self-righteous. You have to work on yourself first before being of help to others mentally, physically, and emotionally. In Theology, I continued to learn and read the Bible. I learned honest communication. Even now if people ask, 'Why did you say that?' I'd rather speak the truth and have my conscience be free. I'd rather feel good that I told the truth. I'd rather bring praise to the God I serve, though the masses may disagree with something I did or said. If I did the right thing, I become happy by making my higher power happy. Integrity is doing right when no one is looking."

A Good Day in Prison

Here in the conference room, the sun dances light around the table, foreshadowing the laughter that would come with my next question, "What does a good day here look like?"

To my surprise, pizza was the first exclamation. We all laugh, and I quickly move on. I know this is partially a hint for us to bring in food like other programs do. The subsequent suggestions are more serious and consistent with what we heard several weeks before: A good day in prison is a day with no inspection, the least amount of chaos, and a day with consistency. A long conversation ensues about inspection, beginning with the fact that some officers will take their belongings. They complain that there is no consistent standard for inspection. A locker that may be fine to one officer is a real problem for another. The officers do not seem to abide by consistent rules or standards. Inconsistency breeds frustration.

Student descriptions of a good day are similar to others presented in prison studies:

> It is remarkable how the distinctions between a good and bad day in prison can be minute. Bad days do not generally occur because of the occurrence of physical or verbal threats, or any other major incident. Quite simply, "bad days" are days filled

with idleness and boredom. More importantly, the difference between a good and bad day in prison generally boils down to something as simple as a courteous greeting from a staff member in the morning. Prison officers are most instrumental in setting the tone for the day.[8]

To students in Theology, policies and practices seem more temperamental and erratic than procedural. "You can just look at an officer wrong and be in trouble." Cat shares a time when she got in trouble for having too many books in her locker. Cate interjects that she had to hide a water bottle in her pants just last night. She lifts up a bottle that looks like it was once a juice bottle, the kind you get from a vending machine. The juice and the label are long gone. Cate now uses the bottle as her water bottle. "Never in my life did I think I'd be hiding water in my pants." They explain that some of the officers do not like items that are not in their original containers.

Spicey keeps the conversation going. "A good day is when, instead of the dorm fighting after inspection, people let it go and help each other—when we just laugh a lot and let it go." Cate offers another story to illustrate. She tells us about the day her dorm was ransacked by officers after a "shakedown," and everyone's belongings were pulled out of their lockers and rooms, thrown on the floor, and left to be cleaned up. It is common for items to go missing after a shakedown, if not from the officers, then at the hand of an opportunistic member of your dorm. But this day was different. After the shakedown, someone turned on the radio, and everyone started cleaning and singing along to country music. "The dorm had been turned upside-down," Cate describes. "The officers could not believe it. Everyone just got down singing and cleaning." She laughs. "A good day here is when after an inspection, everyone picks up all of the stuff, and no one takes something that doesn't belong to them." Handsome agrees that a good day in prison is when everyone is together and having a good time.

Mena's optimistic outlook cuts the inspection conversation short. "Every day that I wake up. . . . When I have the privilege of waking up and am healthy, I choose to be grateful and see the good because many people don't get that opportunity. In spite of the environment, I am not going to allow it to disrupt me. . . . It's a choice. I choose not to let them matter." Mena tries not to let prison life's seemingly trivial but frequent nuances deter her. But when inspections, inconsistencies, and irreverence happen as frequently as students lament, I cannot help but wonder how they function as shaping principles in prison, shaping a disposition of distrust, unease, and uncertainty. In concluding our conversation about inspections, a voice emerges that describes inspection as "being in survival mode." People enter survival mode when they are trying to protect their life.

The conversation is lighthearted and humorous as students discuss a good day in prison, allowing me to see it as more than an idealized construct but as something that emerges in fragments in their time inside. Good moments can emerge in the worst of places. I remember a conversation from weeks prior about the difference between being happy in prison and being happy to be in prison, and I think to myself that good moments do not justify prison but rather point again to the resilience of people who can find and create good in the midst of it.

As we shift from discussing a good day to the possibility of living a good life in prison, Cat is the first to respond. Cat firmly states that living a good life in prison requires staying in your lane. Perhaps because she is the oldest person in the room, Cat looks like someone who minds their business. Cat was quiet as her colleagues' told stories about inspection, but I honestly cannot see Cat as someone who would take advantage of inspection chaos to steal. Neither can I see Cat singing along to country music afterward. Where I can see Cat, however, is in her room with one too many books or in the library. Cat is like any number of our older students who want more than anything to avoid drama and find a place to be at peace while they serve their time.

Spicey quickly answers the question about a good life in prison but with a different kind of response: "Jesus."

The conversation picks up pace as discussion ensues about the importance of stimulating your mind and continuing to grow, learn, and take classes if you want to live a good life in prison.

Relationships are essential, maintaining relationships with people outside of prison and building relationships with people inside. All of these actions require a person to be an active participant in living a good life. "You cannot just sit in your room all day and expect to live a good life."

Students admit that learning how to live in prison takes time. None of them were as thoughtful as they were now when they arrived in prison. Even Mena confesses that she had to "get a grip" with herself and go through the process of reflecting on what brought her here. "I realized that there are other people who were hurt in this process [of her crime]. But it starts with me. I had to focus on me first, then I could bridge all the gaps with my family and friends."

The point is made that if you want to live while in prison, you cannot "wallow in pity." You must recognize and accept that "this is prison. This is one step away from death, but it is not death. You can still live here." They mention how important it is to recognize that even in prison you can become a better you for yourself, friends, and family.

Handsome is energetic as ever at the turn of the conversation. "When I came here, I was a kid. I didn't know nothing. I didn't think about what I did until a couple of years ago [is now nearing the end of a ten-year sentence]. I can see how I have matured. And you're right," Handsome says as they look at the previous speaker, "prison is one step away from death, but I actually needed this experience—not that I should have been here this long. If I was out, I wouldn't have found me." Handsome explains that both the bad and the good parts of being in prison can be helpful. They stress that it is not just the good, reflective parts that can be instructive and formative. "What you see happening to [other] people, you learn from them, too. And the time is helpful. Time to sit back and reflect. *That* you wouldn't have done at home where you would just be going and going. In here, I've learned patience. I could get out today and be in a line of one hundred people, and I'd be like, you know, it's gonna be alright." Everyone laughs in agreement. As I listen to Handsome, I think back to how our last group was adamant that there was a difference between being happy in prison and being happy because of prison. I wonder if Handsome makes as clear of a distinction.

Cate's next comment makes me wonder even more. "I tell my family that everyone should do prison for a couple years." Cate is upbeat and smiling as she utters words that I try hard to suppress my shock over. For Cate, prison has afforded her opportunities she would not have had otherwise. She learned electronic engineering, which she never would have done because she already had a chosen career. Like Handsome, Cate sees prison as a time to reflect. "When you have a career and are busy, you just keep moving and don't often take time to think about life. You don't take the time to reflect on your life. In here, you can notice yourself."

Scholars describe the tendency to see a "silver lining" in prison as needing to create a purpose for imprisonment.[9] Cate's and Handsome's testimonies relay what several prison studies have recounted, that people in prison often identify positive outcomes of the carceral experience. Lila Kazemian writes,

> The most significant ways in which prison supported individuals in their process of transformation included the possibility of reflection time and introspection, a strengthening of bonds with the family, access to resources that were not available or used on the outside (education, training, etc.), and a forced interruption of criminal activity.[10]

No one else in this conversation or throughout the summer will go as far as Cate and declare that prison should be required attendance for others. But many throughout the summer agree that prison creates an environment for reflection, slowing down, and noticing yourself—who you were, who you are, and who you desire to become.[11]

Mena has learned not to take the simple things for granted anymore, like being outside or "walking on carpet." And Spicey has learned that she has some modicum of choice in what kind of life she will live. "When I first got here, I adapted to the climate of prison, fighting, going with the flow, just doing what others were doing. I got put in lockdown and realized *I can't do this.*

You only can bathe three times a week in lockdown and while I was in there, my cycle came on. The officer wouldn't let me take a shower. When they told me that they did not care about my cycle or my shower, it broke me. I had always had my way, but that day, I got a reality check that I can't have it my way in here. It made me see that lockdown is not the way I want to go. I realized that being rebellious wasn't doing anything and that's what made me start investigating other programs. I started to experience growth and I learned to be myself. It took a while." After Spicey changed her behavior and began participating in programming, she moved into the Faith and Character dorm.[12] Eventually, harassment by officers decreased, and she started to feel more respected. "Respect felt good. I got addicted to it."

Spicey, God, and a Good Life in Prison

When I asked about how to live a good life in prison, Spicey was the only person to utter the name Jesus during these conversations. In an individual interview with Spicey, we learn more about her religious life and what Jesus means for living a good life in prison.

Spicey does not say that her family was particularly religious, but growing up, she remembers her grandmother, a Jehovah's Witness, always telling her to pray for her mother, with whom Spicey had a contentious relationship. "I couldn't deal with them [church people] because of all the harassment. It just left me with a bad taste. They would come and give me all these books. They wanted me to sit with them and study. They were overbearing. You can't force someone to believe something. When I went to Kingdom Hall, the ladies would always comment on how I dressed."

Spicey recounts when she was ten or eleven years old and went to church with a relative. "I enjoyed the praise and worship, but one day when we were there, one of the deaconesses started praying for me, and she put her hands on me. I couldn't focus on what was happening because of all the spit on my face as she prayed. Then other people start coming around and they're telling me, 'Say "Jesus"! Say "Jesus"!' They're saying things like, 'Loose her!' 'I'm just not feeling it.' It's like, okay, now they think I have a demon possessing me!?! I was offended by what they were trying to do." This did not stop Spicey from attending church. Sometime later, she remembers going to the altar to give her life to Christ. "I tried. But no one ever explained what to do. No one explained how to walk with Christ or what that looks like. Everything that I knew to do, they're telling me I can't do—no hanging out at the gas station, listening to the radio and no rap music. My mom would put us on this bus to go to church. But it was just too much. The being saved thing just didn't work. One time, I was wearing bell bottoms at church, and this lady had something to say about what I had on. I was like, 'What does wearing pants have to do with what's in your heart?'" Spicey stopped going to church soon after.

As she remembers her childhood, Spicey laments that there was no foundation for her religious beliefs. "I mean, I see the sky, and I know he's there, but there's no foundation. The main thing I would pray about would be my mom, but she didn't change, so I couldn't keep praying when it wasn't working. I had no clues except negative ones about what to do. I knew Jesus was real; just maybe it wasn't my time. I found myself in this hopeless place, and that's how I ended up here, in prison."

For Spicey, God was insignificant for much of her life. "I didn't know who he was. I was just trying to follow other people's lead. . . . There wasn't anything significant, never a personal connection with God. There was nothing to hold on to or fall back on in hard times." Growing up, Spicey does not remember Bible reading as a common practice in her household, just an emphasis on prayer. And she quickly became disillusioned with prayer. "But that was a long time ago," Spicey confesses, "because I had no peace then like I have now."

When Spicey was first sentenced, she was in a fog like many newly sentenced people. "You know how it says in the Bible how Satan blinds the minds of unbelievers? I didn't realize the seriousness of what had happened or how to get out of it. I didn't understand that I was in here with murder charges." She did everything possible to find a way out, even concocting a way to escape. "But this is how I realized that God is real. I'm in my cell, and the door opens. The corporal came into my room and said, 'We know.' And I'm thinking she's just playing." But the officer tells Spicey that whatever she is planning is never going to work. From that point, Spicey is placed in a twenty-two-hour-a-day lockdown where she gets one hour out of her cell during the day and one at night. But for Spicey, the words from the older lady in the cell next to her change her life. "Listen," the older lady says, "you tried your way of doing things; now try God's way. God is trying to intervene in your life. You just need to listen. If you don't follow God, you'll end up going to hell." Her words impacted Spicey.

"I had Kenneth Copeland's 'Outpouring of the Holy Spirit' in my cell, and there was a salvation prayer in the back. I remember reading it and thinking it was so profound. When I read it, I got emotional and realized then that I needed to rely on something bigger than myself. I just started crying. I began to remember, right there in my cell, this lady at church from years ago. She just had this glow. I would see her and say, 'I want that glow. I want that peace that she has.'" Spicey believes she now has that peace.

Spicey believes that God thwarted her plans to escape. From that day, she began to wonder what could be so special about her that God would reveal her plan and save her life. After those days, Spicey decided to "turn her back on hate and to turn toward love. Everything I had loved, I now hated, and everything I had hated, I now loved. I removed all of my piercings. I broke off dealing with my ex. That day, I realized why I was in prison. I took somebody's life, and I couldn't let that go. I cried for two weeks. My grandma wrote me a letter that said that she and God had already forgiven all of us; we just needed to forgive ourselves. Reality finally hit me when I made this life turn. I would pray, 'God forgive me.' That's all I could say. When I got that letter from my grandma, I took a breath and said, 'I believe.' And that's when I realized that God had forgiven me."

After receiving forgiveness from God through the voice of her grandmother, Spicey wanted to know her purpose for living. "I wanted to make sure that no one followed in my shoes.

It became my ambition to make sure to tell these women, 'God set you aside for a moment to work on yourself. The road you're on can lead to other things you don't want. You can meet certain people and they'll lead you to prison. That environment is a gateway to other stuff.' I never did hard drugs because I would see even thick women fall apart, look like they were going to die. . . . That street life, selling your body, slinging dope, riding hard for your man . . . that wasn't the answer." Spicey knew what it was like to "go hard for your man," willing to lie to protect him, ready to go to prison while he remained free.[13] She did not want other women to suffer the same fate. It was not until she came to prison that she began to process the absurdity of it all. "Now, my purpose for life is about other people, to help women come to peace with their past. Now, you discover who you are and your self-worth and that you can't exist until you have a relationship with God and come to terms with your past. Before God, I didn't know myself."

Growing up, people always told Spicey she was intelligent, but several of her life choices obscured her intelligence from those who were not patient enough to see it, eventually including herself. In this prison, Spicey heard people talk about a program called Theology. "I used to hear people talk about having to write a five-page paper, or the people in the advanced program having to write a twelve-page paper and read all these books. I would tell them that I didn't want to do it, but they would ask me why not. I went into myself and decided to challenge myself to do it. Some people warned me that if you don't have a solid relationship with God, don't take Theology." Spicey heard rumors that some people stopped seeking after God after taking Theology, which made her even more determined to participate. "I'm going to show you what a woman of God is like," she chuckled as she remembered her stance when applying. "I decided to go and see what God had for me in the class. I've done it and I loved it. I conquered another fear."

After beginning Theology, Spicey applied to Life University, the only degree-granting college program in a women's prison in Georgia. "There were seventy-five interviewees and only fifteen slots. I just know it is my time," she offers optimistically.

Like most Life University students, participating in Theology has become a de facto feeder program, a preparation for further academic study. During her interview with Life, Spicey talked a lot about Theology. "I've gotten confidence with academics, and that's made me turn in a better direction. Creatively, I know what I possess. It just blows my mind the feedback I get from professors. The highest education I got [before prison] was the ninth grade, but now all of these college-trained professors are praising me," she squeals with excitement. Spicey attributes her participation in Theology to her improved sense of self-worth and value. "I used to fear certain things, but now, I love being challenged. I was stressing about this paper that was due today, and I don't know, I argued my point and when I started writing, it just started flowing. . . . I just thank Theology, because before, I would've just paid someone to write the paper for me. It's built me up and encouraged me to reach my full potential. As a mentor, I have to practice what I'm preaching. I can't be preaching what I'm not doing."

There Are Multiple Dimensions of a Good Life

Like the last group, these women express words to capture a "good life." They offer words like "love," "fulfillment," "hope," "stress-free," and "thrive." Then someone describes an image of a sphere. "Life is a cycle. It's like the earth, not just a circle but a sphere, because life has the possibility for multiple dimensions where you can still end up in the same place. A good life has multiple dimensions."

I offer some words into the room, inspired by my conversations six weeks prior. "What about joy, happiness, freedom, wholeness, or flourishing? Do any of these words strike you as describing a good life?" Freedom and flourishing get the most votes. "But freedom is not necessarily equal to not being incarcerated," Cate clarifies. Before I can ask Cate to expound, there is a knock on the door. The Re-entry class needs the room. Like many classes and conversations in prison, our discussion ends as haphazardly as the day began. Familiar with disruption, the students gather their things and prepare to go to their next locations. "See you on Friday," they say.

In the days and weeks to come, we will hear more about how freedom transcends physical location and why flourishing seems to resonate as a descriptor for a good life. But for now, we pack up our things and release the room to people preparing for re-entry.

Over the next two months, we host several groups and interviews as we listen to students describe their images of a good life. We see drawings such as *Home at Last*, depicting a student at home with her children, and *Our Family*, of a student with her husband, children, and grandchildren having a family dinner. We hear stories of vacations with images titled *Always Fun* of a lake in the South where a student went fishing with her family as a child, *Family, Sun, and Fun* showing a large family playing together while a grandmother cooked in the kitchen, and *Family Vacations* depicting a "black middle-class family on the outskirts of Maryland" who, in the student's words, "had it pretty good" growing up. These images are shared with laughter and fondness as students remember elements of their lives that they define as good.

Not all students find the idea of drawing an image of a good life easy or pleasurable. Some struggle to remember anything good while others draw a good life image that is more of a hoped-for future than a memory. I witnessed this struggle most in the last group of the summer.

Meet Harold, Ilillana, Arabella, and Claira

It is late in the morning on a warm September day when my colleagues and I crowd into a borrowed office to listen to four Theology students in what will be our final group conversation of the summer. For weeks, we have listened to stories about family and freedom, hopes and longing for home, opportunities and overcoming obstacles. We are finally sitting with our long-term lifers' group, people with sentences longer than twenty years who have served a minimum of ten already. I have been looking forward to these students' perspectives for the same reasons that Lora Bex Lempert studies life-serving women in prison, because "in a system of disadvantage those who occupy the margins have unique vantage points from which to assess and critique the center."[14] But personally, these are some of the students I have known the longest. Harold, Ilillana, Arabella, and Claira are the new names these lifers have chosen for today. As they introduce themselves, two of them laughingly ask if changing their name could mean changing their past. With their newly selected names, Ilillana and Arabella describe the Theology program using words like "empowering" and "fun," respectively, continuing the overwhelmingly positive trend of words used to describe Theology. That is until Claira speaks.

Claira's Critique

Claira and I are about the same age. But the year that I graduated college and moved to southern Ohio to begin my professional career, Claira left behind in Georgia her infant daughter for a life sentence in prison.

I first met Claira years ago, a quiet and pensive student in Theology. Claira is an insightful thinker and a gifted artist. At the time of this discussion, Claira has served eleven years of her life sentence and has been in the Theology program as long as I can remember. Of the students in the room, however, she has been in prison the shortest amount of time. While other students during these conversations have expressed an overall cheerfulness about their hopes and participation in Theology, Claira has a different take this morning:

> Five years ago, I would have said being in Theology was "rich." Now, that's a little depleted. At the beginning, the program felt exclusive, especially once it moved [here]. You had to apply to get in, like 75 women applied. Those in the program took it seriously, and assignments were graded more rigorously than they are now. Now, attendance is more lax and I know things are crazy in here, we hardly have classes any more. Everything feels like loosely held-together ideas. First-year students say things like, *this is boring, I don't know how to do this, how to write a five-paragraph essay, what's a thesis, I don't care, they don't even give us grades, anyway.* They don't seem to take it as seriously. They care more about "what I get from the program,"

rather than "what the program does for me and what I can do for it." And you'll hand assignments in which I've put my soul into and will not get them back or I will get them back weeks and weeks later without any comments.

When Theology began, it was an exclusive program. The first class of students were chosen by the chaplaincy department and as mentioned before, were predominantly white and Christian. Over the years, however, Theology has become more religiously and racially diverse. It has changed in other ways as well. For several years now, Theology administration has been more intentional about recruiting and welcoming a more expansive set of students. Countering the idea that Theology should only be a reward for the "best offender," we hoped it could also be an opportunity for those who wanted to make a different life for themselves. The program began to welcome younger people and even people with a history of gang affiliations. The hope was that Theology could be a welcoming space, but not all students agreed with the new direction.

Claira is not the only student to express disapproval at the "types of people" who were being accepted into the program. She describes these new admits as self-serving and lacking the respect she believes that previous classes had for Theology. When Claira speaks of the "first class" students, I think back to the many times lately I have heard vocal pronouncement against "young people" in prison. The newbies, as they are called, do not respect the ways of the prison and have no respect for themselves or the programs. According to students like Claira (and there are several), the newcomers do not care about anything but themselves. Admitting these students into Theology does not sit well with Claira.

Not only is Claira critical of the students in Theology, but she also voices criticism about how Theology operates lately. For several quarters, Theology classes have been inconsistently offered at best, a result of the prolonged staff and security shortage in prison. Staff shortage means the inability for classes to occur. Missed classes leads to fewer opportunities for instructors to receive and return homework. Plans for classes are so disrupted that at one point, we had to offer Theological Foundations twice because so many classes were missed the first time it was offered. As I listened to Claira, I began to wonder if we were doing enough to mitigate the disruptions. I began to wonder if even Theology, for Claira, was no longer a source of life but rather a simulacrum of the death-dealing ethos of the prison. I later find out that in addition to her frustration with Theology, Claira's application to enroll in the college program was recently denied.

Harold neither agrees nor disagrees with Claira. In fact, no one around the table chooses to challenge Claira's interpretation. Harold does, however, interject with a description of Theology as "learning something new." At the time of this conversation, Harold is nearly thirteen years into his life sentence. His five-foot six-inch, two-hundred-plus-pound frame affords him an intimidating stance in prison. When he wants to, or feels that he needs to, Harold can set firm his brown eyes and tower over others, his short cropped brown hair atop a head raised high. "Try me" is the message his body infers. The Harold I have come to know in Theology is not that. To know Harold here is to know someone contemplative, thoughtful, and wise.

Images of Freedom, Happiness, and Adventure

While each person around the table takes their paper and pencils to begin drawing their image of a good life, Harold sits slumped back in his chair. After a minute, Harold says aloud, "I'm stuck. I can't think of anything." Imagining a good life seems difficult for Harold, so I reassure everyone that they can use words or images or draw stick figures—anything that they want.

After a few more minutes, Harold is the first to share his image of a good life. We all move in a bit closer around the desk to look at Harold's drawing. On the left side of the page, the word "prison" is written in all caps, and several vertical lines like prison bars cover the half page. We see an image of what we come to learn is Harold, smiling with a green balloon in hand as he waits at the gate of the prison. The word "free" is written eighteen times in various colors over the bars.

On the right side of the page, however, there are no bars. We find Harold, still smiling but this time standing under a rainbow with two shining suns, one in each corner. In the white space between the rainbow and the suns are these words: freedom in mind, freedom in peace, freedom within self, freedom to love, God freedom. Harold explains, "The left is my life right now until I parole, while the right is still to come. But I'm also cultivating it currently; it's what I am trying to reach. It is happening now and hopefully more so to come."

Claira goes next. Her image of a good life is titled *Happiness Excess*. Claira describes her image as "a suburban, safe, clean, modern place with an excess of goodies." It is a drawing of a child's birthday party with "lots of presents, cake, and lots in the refrigerator." There are pets and a pool in the picture. It is the kind of neighborhood, Claira explains, "where you tell children they can grow up to be the president. This is a place where everyone thrives, everyone loves, and everyone laughs. This was my real childhood."

Her last words hang in the air like a cloud of contrition.

Arabella cuts the silence by presenting her picture titled *Happy*. I met Arabella in the first class I taught in prison. She has a joyfulness to her. Arabella describes her image: "Mine has two parts. On the right is me at the beach, floating on the sea in a raft. The second part is me in Paris. Here I am at the Café de Flore. I drew the Eiffel Tower even though I don't like it that much, [but] it shows you it's Paris." She points to her sketch of the Mona Lisa. "But yeah, I'd like to go there one day—to the Louvre." Arabella is currently seventeen years into her life sentence, yet she maintains high hopes for seeing the world. Of the students in the room, she has been in prison the longest.

Ilillana goes last. Ilillana is an artist. When there is an art-focused class in Theology, I can always expect hazel-eyed, brown-haired Ilillana to sign up. Ilillana is fourteen years into her life sentence when she introduces her image of a good life to us.

"The name of my image is *Let's Go*." Ilillana shares a pencil sketch image of a roller coaster. "I like roller coasters; I like the thrill. It's not stagnant. At first, I couldn't think of a specific time—it's hard to think of a perfect life. I can't really think of a lot of great times in my [life] experience because I spent a lot of time in YDC [youth detention center] as a kid. It's not that I haven't had happy times; I'm happy a lot, but a lot of it's been in bad places. So, the roller coaster is abstract—I like them."

"I feel like sometimes I was born [in] here," she continues, "like I've been here [in prison] my whole life. Here, what I do is that I have like twenty-seven details (jobs). I'm happy working—I generate my happiness in actions, not so much in thinking (can't have much of that, try to avoid it), or in interacting with people. This picture is an ideal. I drew this because to me a perfect life is always moving. When I was younger, I did a lot of BASE jumping off of buildings and cliffs. I love adrenaline rushes, to the point where it's almost a problem. They based the whole movie *Jackass* on me [laughing]. My idea of a good life is a life that doesn't have straight lines but lots of curves and ups and downs—it may go down, but it always goes up again. I didn't draw guardrails on the dangerous parts because that's how life is. I drew guardrails on the straight areas because you always need them when you think you don't. At the bottom [of the picture] I have a heart line [like an EKG line] because that's what's important to me—not having a house, a husband and family with 2.3 kids. *That* sounds like my private hell. . . . I drew this because to me a perfect life is always moving."

Harold, Claira, Arabella, and Ilillana's presentations are uniquely their own even as they began to crystallize themes and commonalities seen throughout the summer (figures 2.1–2.4). For example, student descriptions of a good life fluctuate between memories and dreams, between actual experiences and a hoped-for reality. Claira depicts an image from her actual life while the others present images that represent future hopes, even as they express elements of reality. Ilillana's life has been filled with thrill, but often, it was thrill that led to pain. Arabella draws a beach, which she has experienced, and images of Paris, which she has not. These images represent, in many ways, a hoped-for life. But the images also convey a sobering reality. Ilillana draws guardrails on her roller coaster to show "that's how life is," and Harold speaks of freedom while drawing prison bars. In the many ways that students depict and describe a good life, they do so with an awareness of the past and of a hoped-for future. They recognize what is ideal, what might be possible, and the gulf that often exists between the two.

Figure 2.1. Claira's Image of a Good Life

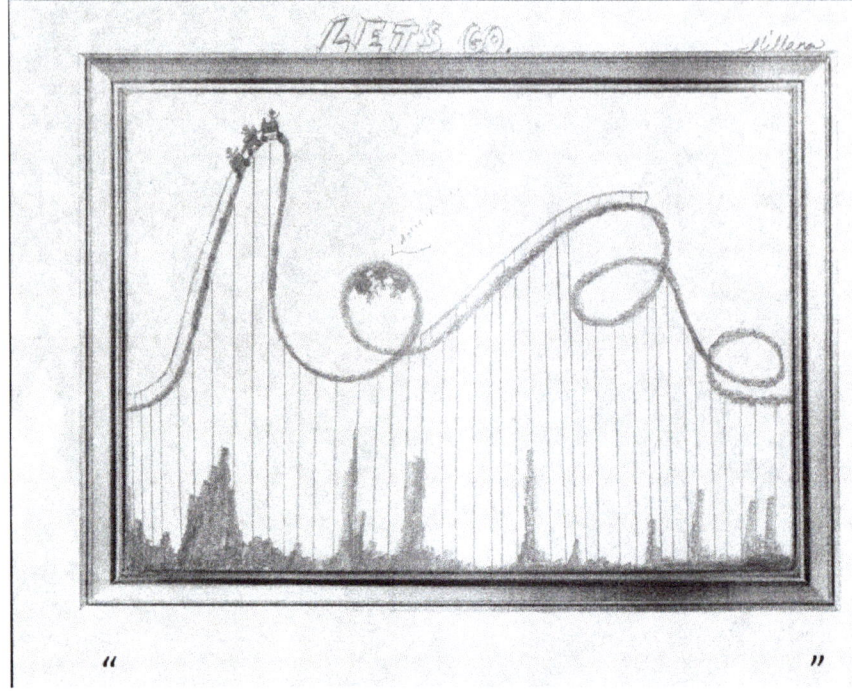

Figure 2.2. Ilillana's Image of a Good Life

Figure 2.3. Harold's Image of a Good Life

Figure 2.4. Arabella's Image of a Good Life

A Good Life in Common

Days after our conversation with Claira, Ilillana, Arabella, and Harold, I spread across a large table all images of students' good lives. Reviewing the images and the post-it notes that captured common phrases and hopes expressed by students throughout the groups, a bigger picture emerges. While there are differences and distinctions among students' visions of a good life, three themes surface. Commonly, a good life in this community involves meaningful relationships, opportunity for growth and change, and some experience of freedom.

Meaningful Relationships

For most students, a good life is a life that includes a variety of meaningful relationships—relationships that make them feel seen and safe, heard and happy, valued, loved, and missed. Claira's image of being surrounded by family and friends is one visual representation of the degree to which meaningful relationships are important. Another is from a student named

Morgen (figure 2.5). Calling the image *My Happy Place*, Morgen excitedly describes the scene, ending with a morsel of regret. "I'm eating dinner with my whole entire family; even my son is home (he is currently in basic training to go into the Navy). I took things like this for granted, I was always working."

Figure 2.5. Morgen's Image of a Good Life

The joy and regret with which Morgen recounted memories of family was shared several times over the course of the summer and was echoed in Claira's tone as well. Time and again students shared images with titles such as *Happiness*, *Importance*, *Unconditional Love*, and *Memories*—each image telling a deeper story of the important family and intergenerational relationships and places that constitute a good life. These pictures include parents, grandparents, siblings, and in a few instances, spouses. For many, these pictures included their children. One student shared an image that included twelve people: "It's me and my husband in the center surrounded by my son and his kids, my daughter and her kids—having family picnics." Another student described her image with a caveat: "I don't think there would be room for me to include everyone; there are a lot of people in the family picture. Grandma is in here, cooking, and there are people playing in the water." A good life is undoubtedly a life that includes a variety of relationships of deep importance. The images also show the meaningful places where these relationships are cultivated: kitchen tables, countries of origin, nature, and family homes. Being with people they love in places they love is the dominant hope conveyed in nearly every drawing.[15]

While most images depict family and significant others, there are a few images strewn across the table that do not include other human beings. Briar pictured herself in nature with several animals to accompany her, Spicey is dancing alone, another student drew herself driving a truck alone (figure 2.6), still another drew herself reading and "learning everything I can learn." As I reflect on the solo images, I recognize that another set of meaningful relationships is expressed—the relationship with oneself. Students frequently discussed the importance of knowing yourself and spending time in reflection. These solo images suggest that a good life also involves being in a meaningful and healthy relationship with oneself.

Figure 2.6. Honey Bee II's Image of a Good Life

I capture this desire for meaningful connection and relationships under the central idea of belonging. Belonging conveys the desire to matter to someone, some place, and oneself. It includes student hopes for a place to "be myself again." Recall from my earlier reflection on social death education that one of the learning outcomes of a social death institution is social disconnection. Social death by incarceration removes people from the people and places of significance and attempts to destroy a sense of meaningful belonging to others and to the self. In the depths of a social death institution, students draw images of belonging to others and to themselves as they imagine their good lives.

Dynamism

A second theme that emerges as I consider the variety of images and conversations is the idea of movement, possibility, and growth. A good life is a life with the possibility for change and adventure. For students in Theology, to live and to make a life involves possibilities for a future not dictated by the past or bound by the present—possibilities for growth, change, and transformation. Students express desire for the possibility to mature, develop, and evolve. It is a hope that life continues beyond the present condition, that there are possibilities beyond those prescribed by place that feels like dying.

Ilillana's and Arabella's descriptions of roller coasters, international travel, and BASE jumping represent these hopes for energy, vitality, and newness. Morgen's declaration that "I always want to be blooming; [in] a constitutional state of growing" also express this desire. Whether moving with unpredictable ups and downs as with the roller coaster, or blooming like a flower, students declare that a good life is active, energetic, moving, and full of possibility. A good life is dynamic; it holds within it the possibility for more than what has been—it is a life of ongoing creation.

I capture this feature of a good life under the term "dynamism." Dynamism conveys both energy (movement, vitality) and progress (growth, advancement). The image drawn by Amari of seeds transformed into a flower is a visual representation of this hope. She describes her image using the words "journey" and "growth," expressing both the desire for positive transformation and the realization that life is moving. Dynamism stands in stark contrast to the decay, stagnancy, and rot characteristic of the prison.

Freedom

A third theme that emerges is expressed in images of nature, vast oceans, and no fences and in discussions of parole, release dates, and the mind. Freedom is a third feature of a good life—freedom to be oneself, freedom to dream, freedom to live a good life. Harold's picture, *Free from Everything*, represents this third theme well (figure 2.3). Freedom for Harold is simultaneously already and not yet, something that is real on both sides of his page, in the present and in the future. The future image of freedom in Harold's picture suggests complete freedom, freedom from the confines and constraints of imprisonment. Student images of homes located in wide-open spaces and of nature scenes with vast depictions of ocean water or empty fields conveys this idea as well.

Harold's image suggests something more nuanced too. While physical freedom is a feature of a good life, Harold suggests that a person can live into other forms of freedom even in the absence of physical liberation. Harold is clear that freedom is something he desires and is working on, and freedom is something he has now. Freedom is both already and not yet.

To live—to have a life—is to be in relationship, to produce, to dream, to accomplish. Students' description of a good life as involving belonging, dynamism, and freedom stand in stark opposition to the prison environment. But are students' hoped-for good lives possible in prison? Are belonging, dynamism, and freedom achievable in a social death institution? Though not unanimous, most students insist that a good life is possible in prison. The next chapter explores how.

3
IS YOUR GOOD LIFE POSSIBLE HERE?

> Although some individuals succeed in achieving growth in prison, it is clear that the system makes it extremely difficult for prisoners to thrive during periods of incarceration. Prison causes harm . . . When positive growth is achieved, it is largely a result of individual volition rather than institutional support.[1]

It feels inappropriate to ask someone if they can live a good life in an environment of social death. So much so that I struggled every time I uttered the question, "What does a good life in prison look like?" The first time I asked it, without hesitation, Rylee twisted her face, looked squarely at me, and said, "I don't even know what that means. . . . Life in prison is jarring to think about. This *is* our life, I know, but I don't want to think about it like that. I *can't* think about it in the long term like that." Rylee's response is understandable. She does not want to think about a life spent in prison. Other students share her concern and would rather focus their thoughts on the possibility of a good life outside of prison. But most students, especially those with long sentences, have some understanding of how and why a good life in prison is necessary for them.

History is replete with stories of people who successfully struggle to preserve family, faith, community ties, and human dignity, despite domination and subjugation. I found comfort in their stories and in the scholarship of people like Patricia Hill Collins, one of many Black scholars who have written about "the creative tension between the desirable, the possible, the probable and the practical."[2] Her scholarship on Black women's visionary pragmatism reminded me that people can "operate in dual capacities, cultivating skills needed and making pragmatic decisions to survive while imagining a more hopeful future and working toward it."[3] To ask questions about the possibility of a good life in prison is to ask questions about the pragmatic responses and visionary hopes that animate people to envision lives of unrealized possibility in the midst of domination and disenfranchisement. I kept this tension in mind as I proceeded with my questions.

Throughout the summer of conversations, I learned that the desire to live a good life while in prison requires the audacity to believe in possibilities beyond present circumstances and the courage to conjecture about a world other than the one of profound constraint in which one lives. To define and enact a good life against all odds takes nerve. Stories about making a life that matters in prison reveal that students *do* cultivate meaningful connection in an alienating institution, experience dynamism amid stagnancy, and freedom in unfreedom. While not unanimous, most students in Theology believe that some semblance of their good life is *possible* in prison. Possible but not preferable. Possible but not desirable. This distinction was most evident in conversations with students serving long-term sentences.

The Journey Back Inside

It was the first day of the annual prison audit. I could tell three days before that something was up. When I arrived last Friday morning, there were more people than normal dressed in their brown Department of Corrections–mandated uniforms outside cutting grass, pulling weeds, and renewing mulch in the flower beds. Inside, the activity was equally increased. Several women went up and down the halls mopping the floors and washing down the cinder block walls with rags and disinfectant. Other women could be seen refreshing the painted bright red stenciling on the wall that read Suicide Prevention Hotline. Still others were inspecting the Prison Rape Elimination Act (PREA) posters on the doorways, replacing any that showed signs of wear or defacement. PREA was signed into federal law in 2003 designed to prohibit and eliminate sexual assaults and sexual misconduct in correctional institutions. The posters advertise, "It is not your fault if you were sexually assaulted. Sexual assault is not part of your sentence!" and list procedures for reporting sexual abuse and harassment, including displaying a phone number people can call. I do not know how effective the PREA procedures are at this prison, but in the calendar year of my research, there were over 1,671 PREA allegations reported in Georgia state prisons and facilities, half involving staff-to-inmate abuse and harassment, the other half inmate-to-inmate.[4] Of those 1,671 allegations, 936 (56%) were Unsubstantiated, 581 (35%) were Unfounded, and 82 (5%) were deemed Not PREA. Only 4% of the allegations were substantiated, the majority of which were inmate-to-inmate related (66%). Of the few cases of substantiated staff-related accusations of sexual activity or inappropriate touching (17), 100% are reported to have been "terminated or resigned from employment" and forwarded to the district attorney for review and, perhaps, prosecution.

I once heard a warden compare running a prison to operating a small city. Everything the prison needs to run operates on-site: sanitation, lawn maintenance, food preparation, health care, building repair, and sundry other "departments." If the prison is a small city, then the annual audit is the equivalent of a citywide spring cleaning on steroids.

Everyone is tenser than usual. The line to get inside the prison is slower today than on Friday; the officers at the front are meticulous with their procedures. I greet the security officer when I make my way through the front door. She smiles at me but does not say much, which is uncommon for her. She is an older woman from the area and, as she has said numerous times before, is close to retirement. She has grown more collegial with me over time, mainly because she associates me with "a good Christian program." More than once, I have heard her complain about other visitors, especially when "those Muslims come in here." Today, she is circumspect with her words. She knows that she is being watched, and so do I. As my bag goes through the X-ray machine and she picks it up to examine the contents, I think

I see her shoulders relax. My bag is much lighter than expected. Because we are only here to host a couple of conversations, I removed most of my Theology-related materials from the bag. There are only a few writing utensils, one folder, some mints, and my ChapStick. As she opens my bag, I think she knows she is far less likely to have to confiscate something today.

We make our way through security and are assigned a small metal tag that I attach to my volunteer badge. When we are ready to leave, this tag will allow us to retrieve our car keys and ID cards we must now leave behind. We make our way through the first set of gates into a hallway before the visitation area. We stand at the glass door, waiting to get the attention of another officer who controls the entrance in and out of the visitation area, which we must pass through to get to the school hall. It has been nearly a year since the time I was screamed at by an officer as I tried to enter this area alone. "What are you doing?" he yelled, which startled me. I turned and looked him in the eye, confused at the question. He looked at me and immediately saw my visitation badge dangling around my neck. Without apology, he said, "Never mind, go ahead," before opening the doors and allowing me to use the restroom. He thought I was an *offender*. I went back and told my colleagues about the incident, and they suggested it was merely an accident, probably because of what I was wearing that day, khaki pants, a white sweater, and a jean jacket. The state-mandated attire for people in prison is a brown or tan matching set of pants and button-up shirt. Many people wear a white T-shirt under their brown shirt. The uniform also comes with an oversized blue jacket which looks nothing like my jean jacket. I knew in that moment that if I traded clothes with my white female colleague, she never would have been stopped or spoken to the way that I was that day. By now I have been in and out of this prison so many times that most of the officers and staff think that I work here. But I think about that moment every time I come through this building.

Because of the audit, the count takes longer than usual, so we cannot host our first conversation. We wait for over an hour before the count clears and our second scheduled conversation can begin. We have trouble finding a space to gather as all the school hall classrooms are occupied, and so too is the conference room in chaplaincy. We stand in the hallway to intercept students while the college program director offers to let us use their relatively empty space, save for a couple of students using it for a study hall.

Meet Aminah, Karisma, Brouhaha, Zakkiyah, and Jordan

On this tense Tuesday, we guide five students into the room and gather around the table to talk. As we settle into our seats and the door closes, I am surprised how quickly we forget about the audit and everything going on outside this room. Aminah, Karisma, Brouhaha, Zakkiyah, and Jordan are the most diverse group we host this summer, religiously and otherwise. Aminah and Zakkiyah are longtime practicing Muslims and active both in Theology and Jum'ah on Fridays. Karisma would have called herself Christian at one point in her life, but today, she hesitates to place a label on her spirituality. Jordan identifies as "Christian, I guess," while with Brouhaha, it just depends on the day. Brouhaha has been in prison since she was a teenager. She has been piecing together her religious and spiritual life since I met her several years ago, trying on different practices and traditions, looking for something that fits her at the moment. "I'm really into African Religious Traditions now, Ms. Green, you know, like Yoruba." When Brouhaha introduces her latest religious quest, I wonder where and how this young white woman encountered the Yoruba religion in prison.

Brouhaha is a reader; she loves books and loves to learn. She stays open to possibilities and believes that everything has the potential to be helpful. Her bricolage approach to religion and spirituality is not uncommon in prison. Prison discourse can paint prison religion as feigned fundamentalism, but that is not the only manifestation of religious life in prison. There is much searching here as people look for systems and beliefs that might help order their thoughts or actions, become a source of comfort, or as they seek answers to questions that plague them.

Each person around the table is a lifer except Jordan. Jordan is in her early twenties and is four years into her max sentence of ten years. She is the youngest person around the table and the one who has been in prison for the shortest time. Zakkiyah, on the other hand, stands at the opposite end of the spectrum. In her mid-forties, Zakkiyah is the oldest to join this conversation today, and she has been in prison the longest of anyone here, for twenty-two years. Karisma is not far behind. In her mid-thirties now, she has been in prison for twenty years, more than half of her life. Brouhaha has a similar story. She came to prison nearly seventeen years ago and is currently in her late twenties. This leaves Aminah. Aminah and Karisma are about the same age, in their late thirties. However, Aminah was older than Karisma, in her late twenties, when she was convicted and sent to prison. Aminah is the only person in the room to have a life sentence without the possibility of parole (LWOP).

LWOP is rare but rising among women's prisons in the United States. One of every fifteen women in prison is serving life, and between 2008 and 2020, women serving LWOP increased by 43%, compared to a 29% increase among men. Statistics suggest that one in seven people (~14% or 200,000) incarcerated in US prisons serve life sentences, and 25% (50,000) of them are LWOP. In 2021, studies showed that the number of people serving LWOP—the most extreme type of life sentence—is higher than ever before, a 66% increase since the census in 2003. More than two-thirds of those serving life sentences are people of color.

At the time of this conversation, the state of Georgia had more than 7,700 people serving life sentences. Less than 5% were women. 55% were Black, 45% white, 3% Hispanic, and less than 1% Asian. Of the 373 women serving life sentences, 95% were mothers, and 93% had no prior incarcerations in Georgia before their sentencing. The year Aminah was sentenced, nine women had LWOP in Georgia. A decade later, that number is more than fifty. The last group of lifers I spoke with insisted that you needed hope in parole to survive prison. As we will soon see, Aminah has a different perspective.

Visions of a Good Life

We begin this conversation the same way we have several times before—with images of a good life. Zakkiyah presents first. She shifts in her seat, pushes her glasses up snugly on her nose, and scratches at the hair beneath her hijab. With pride, she displays an image she calls "Balancing." Her picture only covers one small corner of the page. She has drawn herself with her significant other, three dogs, mom and dad, her son, and her significant other's son. There is an image of a small building with the letters TAPS above it. "I want to have a chain of Train and Play Spas (TAPS) for dogs around the country. I'm going to school to finish my education, and then I will retire, but not before making great money while I'm working!" Zakkiyah's image is small but dense, with images representing the importance of education, housing, work, and family. Of all the images I see this summer, Zakkiyah is the only one to draw meaningful work as essential to her good life. I am not surprised by Zakkiyah's choice of business. She is an avid supporter of the dog program. There are several on-the-job training programs at this prison involving animal care: the Guide Dog Program, Veterinary Technician, Dog Grooming, and the Forever Friends Dog Rescue program. It is common for a Theology student in one of these programs to bring a dog to class. If a dog is present, Zakkiyah is almost always around providing care.

Brouhaha goes next. Her picture is called *Learning to Serve* and is an image of herself in cartoonish form. "This is me with a book and a huge brain where I am learning that the good life doesn't involve material things, just being with people." Brouhaha says that a good life for her is about "autonomy and possibility." A good life is one where she can give to others and do what she enjoys, pointing to the large brain and books as she explains herself.

Karisma's image of a good life is an abstract drawing she calls *To Be an Overcomer*. "A good life is about growth, unity, and the struggle," she says. "It's about finding the ability to overcome struggle to find peace." Going next, Jordan shares an image of a home with her future family, four boys to be precise. "*To Be Determined* is what I called my picture," she says. She pictures herself at home with a family and a good job and declares, "I will never stop furthering my education."

Aminah is last to lift her image displaying the word "freedom" written in all caps. Aminah has drawn a picture of children, herself, and her significant other, someone who was once in Theology but has recently been released. "This is me going home to my family," she describes. I notice she has drawn herself running toward her family and away from an illustrated image of a prison.

Unlike the other conversations this summer, no one has drawn an image of a past reality or memory. All these images are hopes and projections. For these hopes to be realized, students believe family, resilience, attitude, and perspective are necessary. "A lot of things can't change until you change something about yourself," Aminah adds. Karisma suggests that support systems are needed when you get discouraged, while Zakkiyah counters that even with support, "you have to have determination within yourself."

Maybe a Good Life Is Not Possible Here

Nearly everyone insists that a good life is possible in prison, but the optimism is not unanimous. Aminah is adamant that a good life is not possible in prison. "Look," Aminah begins, "I admit that you can have inner peace all day. You don't have to be miserable, but you are *not* going to have a good life in prison."

Quick to disagree, Karisma offers a rebuttal. "I think a good life is possible through our pursuits. We can fight for opportunities and the things we want like education and opportunities to grow. We can push back on the system and overcome the struggles we face to have the good life in here." After all, overcoming obstacles is central to Karisma's vision of a good life. "I've been locked up for more than twenty years, and I can still say I'm blessed. I can say that I have a good life; I feel like I have some of it here. I'm blessed in so many ways; I have much to be grateful for," she continues. "I live outside of here, and I pursue things that take me outside of these walls." I cannot tell if Karisma is trying to convince Aminah, herself, or some combination of both.

Unwilling to be deterred, which is typical for Aminah, she maintains her position. "Even if you do everything you said, it's not a *good* life. Because part of the good life is freedom. The good life requires freedom. You can *pursue possibilities* to the ends of the earth, but there is still going to be a limit. You *will* come to a stop sign."

"But there are people out there who aren't free," Karisma adds, challenging Aminah's insistence that a good life requires freedom. Karisma interprets Aminah's use of freedom in the literal and physical sense, but freedom goes beyond physicality. "There are people out there who are trapped in themselves."

In passionate disagreement, Aminah makes a personal declaration. "When I was free, everything was what I chose. Even if it was bad, I chose it. The ability to choose is freedom. The ability to choose is the good life." Freedom and agency are connected for Aminah, and both are necessary for a good life. Aminah is more than reluctant to associate a good life with incarceration; she is adamantly opposed to it. I do not consider Aminah any less optimistic than anyone around the table. Still, Aminah refuses to allow a conception of life apart from those she loves most to be considered good. I wonder if Aminah's disagreement would be as fierce if her significant other, who was recently released, was still here in prison.

"I was talking to a friend about this a couple months ago," Brouhaha interjects, easing the tension rising in the room, something I have witnessed her do many times before. "I wouldn't say this to a lot of people, but I feel quite privileged despite the circumstances. More than freedom, I have and try to build autonomy. I focus on making choices about decisions in here. It comes from perspective, appreciating both the good and the bad. I may not get to choose the clothes I wear, but I can choose how I spend my time." This is the second time that Brouhaha has mentioned the importance of autonomy. Debates about the autonomy of incarcerated people, especially women, have dominated approaches to criminal justice since the rise of gendered prisons. Brouhaha's assessment is in line with criminological research that suggests that women in prison constantly enact forms of autonomy even if that autonomy is constrained by the institution.[5]

Like Brouhaha, Zakkiyah wants to believe that a good life in prison is possible. "I don't think our circumstances create us, but they evolve us," she begins. "I have been here for more than twenty years too, and I have found understanding and have a sense of peace in myself, regardless of what anyone thinks." She adds, "We don't have control over what we can do; that is true. But we make the best of what we have." Zakkiyah believes that she has evolved, changed, and grown during her time in prison. "I think I see people here for who they are, and they see me for who I am." Before the optimism in her words has the chance to settle in the room, she quickly tempers her statement. "But it [being in prison] still suffocates me. It has suffocated a lot of us who don't have the will to do things for ourselves."

Jordan shifts the conversation back to the idea of freedom. "It's really hard for me because I was trapped at home as well as here." Jordan describes herself and her family as recovering addicts, where drug addiction is the source of their entrapment. "So, I was also trapped at home, physically free, but mentally trapped. Were it not for being in here, I would probably be dead. I owe my life to this place. I have to be thankful and find a way to do things." Jordan is not the only person incarcerated to attribute coming to prison with saving their life. For people like Jordan, prison creates a forced distance between the places or practices that could have killed them. They believe that prison saved them from imminent death. When I hear such testimonies, I always wonder what other people, programs, institutions, or interventions could have served the same purpose.

When Jordan was arrested and still in county (shorthand for county jail), her parents urged her to use her time in prison to *"become a better person, make good decisions, became aware of what life needs to be when you come out—come out different than you're going in."* Jordan believes she is living up to their expectations. "I've stayed out of trouble, never gotten a disciplinary report, and have taken college classes. I have found a kind of freedom here."

Freedom, Addiction, and a Good Life?

Jordan has found a freedom in prison that she has yet to know outside, a freedom she believes is diminished mainly by her addiction to drugs. Jordan was a teenager when she began using drugs; according to her, everyone in her family did drugs too. When drug use is not just an individual concern but a communal and intergenerational one, it can increase the anxiety about getting out of prison. "How will I know I won't use again?" is a question I have heard several times. People like Jordan who are trying to make a good life, a life apart from drug addiction, often seek out support and educational programming in hopes that AA (Alcoholics Anonymous), NA (Narcotics Anonymous), religion, or college might be the key to a different path when they get out.

Women are one of the fastest-growing segments of the US prison population, mainly because of draconian drug laws.[6] More than 61% of women doing time in federal prison are behind bars for nonviolent drug offenses. While drug use occurs at similar rates across racial and ethnic groups, racialized women are far more likely to be criminalized for drug law violations than white women like Jordan. Native American women are incarcerated at six times the rate of their white counterparts for drug-related crimes. Black women are almost twice as likely, and Latinas, like a student named Karma, are 20% more likely to be incarcerated than white women.

Karma is bright, joyful, and energetic, and I was so proud when she announced that she was going home. I have had the privilege of watching several people over the years be released from prison and, in an age of social media, become "social media friends" after release. One evening I am watching the local news, and I look up and see Karma's picture flash across the screen. She has been arrested again for a drug-related crime.

Drug treatment programs have grown in popularity with the rise in mass incarceration and public demand to offer a more just alternative.[7] Georgia has several residential substance abuse treatment programs where people reside at the prison but are not considered "incarcerated" in the same sense as others. The Residential Substance Abuse Treatment program

(RSAT) is a nine-month program based on the modified Therapeutic Community Model, which targets high-risk, high-needs offenders with a history of substance use as a crime-producing behavior leading to correctional supervision. There are also nine-month residential programs for probationers and those with mental health disorders. But Karma's conviction precludes her from participating in those programs.

Karma has been in and out of prison since her late teens, and it has all been drug related. "I've spent my birthday inside for so many years. I can't remember the last time I wasn't in here on my birthday." She has participated in drug programs, such as NA, both in and outside prison, several times. "I have a tendency to self-sabotage," she offers, I assume, as a sort of explanation. "When things seem too good, it's like I'm waiting for the other shoe to drop, to be abandoned. I've been working on my daddy issues since I've been here." Karma can only muster the following when asked about a good life: "I've never really thought about this. I still think about the picture-perfect family with a mommy and daddy—but I'm way past that. I don't know what a good life would be."

Jordan and Karma applied for Theology while in prison not because they believed Theology would provide answers to their drug addiction. But they hoped that Theology would give them something to do with their time, something else to focus on. "I would do anything to get out of the dorm," Karma states. For Jordan, Theology is one of the many programs she has done in prison, her way of fulfilling her family's request for her to "come out different" than she went in. "I know I am being good and doing good," she explains. Theology is one way Jordan attempts to do good while in prison in hopes she will do similarly upon release.

The way Jordan speaks about her participation in programs in prison reminds me of Todd Clear's research on religious involvement in men's prisons. He suggests that religion provides "a packaged alternative to previous ways of living," and the Bible is seen as a blueprint for how to live, a packaged guide for living a "good" life.[8] For students like Jordan, the emphasis is less on religion and scripture as prepackaged guides and more on the hope that religious and educational programming, like Theology, will serve as "documentation or proof of [their] ability to change, of remorse, rehabilitation, and redemption."[9] But as Karma demonstrates, participation in these programs does not guarantee success after prison.

Evolving Optimism in Prison

When Jordan arrived in prison, she knew that her sentence was relatively short, so she began, right away, to involve herself in educational and vocational programming to use her time well. But the other women in the room with life sentences did not have such a quick or positive adjustment to incarceration.

Zakkiyah racked up seventy-six fighting tickets in her first years inside. "It took my little boy visiting and asking, 'Why are you doing this?' to make me stop. He said, 'You're always telling me to do the right thing, but I can't visit you because of what you're doing.'" Zakkiyah believes that her participation in support groups and counseling programs helped, but her son's words ultimately made her want to change. "It took me understanding and loving me to get where I am today."

Karisma came to prison very young with a life sentence. "I thought to myself, why care about anything?" Although she does not confess to seventy-six fighting tickets like Zakkiyah, Karisma admits she gave officers trouble her first years inside. She remembers the moment when that changed for her. She met a woman who was also serving time. This woman told her that a life sentence does not mean she would never get out of prison—she could still have a life outside prison one day. Once Karisma realized that a life sentence was not wholly determinative, she attempted to change her behaviors. "It took me a while because I had to lose my reputation, but eventually, I proved myself." She explains that it is difficult to lose your reputation in prison once you have been marked by officers and staff as a troublemaker. "Even when I tried to do right, I was still getting targeted." But over time, Karisma's reputation softened.

Zakkiyah was less fortunate. "For some of *us*, we never lose our reputation," she counters. Zakkiyah does not elaborate here, but I know from previous conversations that Zakkiyah believes that Black women and Black Muslim women are treated more harshly in prison. "Here, they don't really see you or what you're trying to do, that you're trying to do better—they see it as a joke that you're in school. They don't take you seriously when you say you're trying to change. It's up to us to pursue change despite this negativity."

Brouhaha shares that she, too, stayed in trouble. "The police stayed on me, even when I wanted to change. I was on suicide watch, in segregation, because I wasn't seventeen yet. I thought I was going be in that room forever." When juveniles come to this prison, they are housed separately from the general population for their safety. Most are housed in isolation and must always have a guard with them. When they turn eighteen, they are transferred to the general population and live in the dorms. "Getting on the compound was a relief because I could socialize, but I was also targeted. There were people who wanted to take advantage of me [because of my age] and people who wanted to mother me. I guess that's a thing some people want." For older women in prison, especially those separated from their children or who never had children of their own, mothering or mentoring younger people is common. Juveniles transferring to the general population must be concerned with finding healthy relationships. "I was still very depressed and very exposed to a lot of negative stuff. I was not making good choices. It took people supporting me unconditionally for me to start to change. And then I had to fight for it."

Aminah smiles as she reminisces about her early days in prison, not so much because anything about that time was particularly humorous. Rather, it was utterly absurd in reflection. "I got in trouble a lot until the last couple of years. I was angry. When you're young, you think that life just is not fair. It's all about growing up—everyone must grow up and see things as adults. You can't do life through the eyes of a child. I wouldn't say I have a terrible life here, but it's not the life I should have been living." Aminah clearly sees a difference between the life she has been able to create in prison and the life she should be living had she not committed the crime that brought her here. For Aminah, there is a life you can manufacture out of scraps, but she does not confuse that life with the life she desires, with a good life.

Aminah is not the same person who stayed in trouble in the past. She looks at a member of the research team and begins, "Remember the first time you met me? I was beating up that woman in the Chapel!" The room laughs, and the researcher responds, recalling the story from her point of view: "I didn't realize that was actually the first time, but yes, obviously I remember." She remembers that Aminah was standing in the Chapel, ready to push a giant vase or pitcher through a glass wall. Aminah clarifies that it was actually the chaplain's communion cup. She went to lockdown for that event, but according to her, it was not for fighting but for denting the chaplain's communion cup. "She was livid about that cup!" The room fills with laughter at the image of Aminah and a dented communion cup.

Aminah believes that she has changed and names that change for herself. "It's not up to the State to say I've changed—I know I have. They'll see that eventually. But I finally got taken off the Top 100, and then Top 200 Most Violent Inmates list in Georgia." She smiles. This list includes men and women, and there are usually only a couple of women on it. There is a tinge of pride as Aminah describes both her previous placement on it and her removal. "I have reached some new goals," she continues, and one of those goals was graduating with a certificate in Theology.

You Can Flourish Here, but You Can Never Be Whole

As the time allotted for our conversation closes, I lay several words on the table: freedom, flourishing, wholeness, happiness, joy. While there are mixed opinions about the ability to experience freedom in prison, these women agree on the possibilities of flourishing and wholeness. They define flourishing as "living and growing right where you are" and unanimously agree that flourishing is possible even in prison. Life may be challenging and complex, and moments of goodness may be fleeting, but these women believe they can live and grow in prison. For Aminah, flourishing is possible in prison, but flourishing is not synonymous with a good life.

Wholeness is categorically different. Flourishing can withstand fragmentation and frustration, but wholeness cannot. Wholeness conveys completion. It is an all-encompassing idea that includes everything you desire in life, such as meaningful connections and opportunities for growth. "Think of it like a complete circle where everything important is included along the circle," someone begins. "Certain aspects [of a good life] may be there [in prison], sure, but you cannot connect it all together; there are just too many gaps in the circle," Zakkiyah utters. "Like being separated from your kids, how can you be whole without your children?" "Or for me," Karisma adds, as she voices something I imagine she realized years ago, "'How can you be whole like that when you really want kids of your own, but you know you will never even have the possibility of having them?'" Karisma was a teenager when she arrived in prison, and she figures she will be beyond child-bearing years when she gets out. Karisma's words fall heavy in the room. No one disagrees with her. For Aminah, Karisma, Brouhaha, Zakkiyah, and Jordan, wholeness is not possible in prison. There are just too many gaps in the circle.

A knock at the door jolts us back to wherever we each went in our thoughts, reminding us that we are sitting in a borrowed classroom, and it is time to leave. As we pack our belongings, I am left with the stark realization that if, as ethicist Emilie Townes suggests, it is in the relational matrix where wholeness can be found, the wholeness many of these students desire is something they are resigned never to know again.

An Imitation of Life

Most lifers insist that some version of their good life is possible in prison even if they disagree about what that good life entails. This same tension was felt when I spoke with Claira, Ilillana, Harold, and Arabella. When I asked them if the images they drew where possible in prison, Ilillana was the first to respond. "I get my adrenaline in my maintenance detail. My supervisor has a heart attack! I'll jump off things, slide down stair rails. Back in 2005, I broke my femur driving (equipment during yard detail) when I intentionally clipped the wheel on the gate so

Is Your Good Life Possible Here? | 111

I would spin around. I did it too hard and crashed, the motor block landed on my femur, breaking it. I vomited on the hot engine, and my only thought was, 'This smells' and 'Did anyone see that?' I was in a cast for twelve weeks—doing that in here [prison] was awful, the scratching nearly killed me. I have no sense of personal safety—but in the moment it's fabulous." Ilillana finishes her story of adrenaline and injury to the sounds of laughter and to the sight of scrunched-up faces in the room, mine included.

Claira interjects next. "I can re-create a version of [my image] here, in a way, and most people try to. You adopt friends and family and build relationships, celebrate, and mark time together in ways that seem normal. And with food and hygiene stuff you can improvise, can create nice meals—if you work at it, you can get comfortable, some things can be controlled. But there's something looming, it's generic, a false version of reality, it's that this is just an imitation of what real life is."

Ilillana energetically adds, "It's like a Family Dollar Store version of a Norman Rockwell."

Claira continues, "Sometimes [life in here] is fulfilling, and sometimes it's just a hollow, depressing outline of a longing that can never be fulfilled."

Claira and Ilillana express the sentiment that a good life in a social death institution is only, at best, intermittent. A life can be fulfilling one moment and hollow in the next. A good life is not static, nor is it an ultimate achievement. The good life that students seek and enact is the best possible option given their environment. Still, there are elements of their hoped-for good lives that simply are not possible in prison. Arabella passionately makes this point.

"No way, not happening, not even close! That sense of freedom of just floating out into the ocean [referring to her picture of beaches and trips to Paris], that can't happen here. The closest is by practicing astral projection. I study it a lot. The best time to do it is when my allergies are bad, and I take one of those yellow sinus tablets." We laugh at Arabella's confession.

"I knock out my busy analytic mind. I'm kind of like half-asleep, almost in a trance and relaxed. It's like getting outside of your body—when you're really good at it, you can even control where you go. That's only happened to me once—I went to Malta, and it was so cool. I talked to my friend about it."

Ilillana adds her perspective on astral projection. "It happens a lot when people see themselves about to die, at near-death experiences."

"I've been practicing a long time in prison," Arabella continues, "and I've only been able to get out one time. I'd love to travel, but Paris isn't happening—ever. Dreaming about it isn't the same." Here the sober reality of Arabella's sentence comes to the forefront, and simply dreaming of Paris, of a good life, to Arabella, is not sufficient or satisfactory.

Dreams Plagued by Prison

Claira carries forth Arabella's mentioning of dreams and adds with a heavy sigh, "Our dreams are plagued by prison." Using dreams as a metaphor, Claira expresses that whatever hopes people imagine for themselves, whatever good lives they imagine, can and often are corrupted by living in prison. Ilillana explains, "I have a dream where I'm a little kid in kindergarten, but I have to get back for count. Or I'm traveling and there's a time difference and I won't make it back in time for count." The other people in the room nod to affirm Ilillana's experience.

"It's like even *early* memories are plagued," Claira exasperates.

Ilillana continues, "I have to remember I wasn't born in prison. . . . It's hard to have a dream that's not prison related."

"It's hard because you wake up and realize that you weren't where you were dreaming," Arabella adds. "You're here. If you were dreaming of a stove, an oven, it's not there. . . . You realize you can't leave."

For Claira, her prison-tainted dreams started right away, but for Harold and Ilillana, the tainted dreams started after they had been in prison for a while.

"I was so batshit crazy my first years, and I had so much vitriolic anger that I cannot really remember my first years," Ilillana shares.

Claira continues, "After I got arrested, all my dreams were about my crime and the arrest, about the people around me. Eventually that transitioned to dreaming about incarceration."

"I never dreamed about my crime," says Ilillana, "only angry dreams, all of my dreams were about fighting. When I was able to get over it a bit, I started to have more real human dreams—but then you get woken up by things like a trash bag being opened or other prison noises."

"I was in shock for the first five years I was here," exclaims Arabella. "I was like, where's the golf course, why do I have to wear these boots, they're not name brand! I was used to wearing high heels!" We all laugh along with Arabella and ask her how she feels about the new state-mandated shoes that resemble Crocs. "Oh, when I saw them, I just threw them across the room, crying! When I was first in jail, I was on a PC, protective custody range because I was pregnant. I didn't believe I had committed a crime. I was up all night talking to the officer. I remembered this time when I was younger when my stepdad made a pretend newspaper for my mom for Valentine's Day, with stories all about them. So, when the officer brought me a newspaper with a story about my crime, I didn't believe it. I thought it was like my stepdad's newspaper back then. I kept thinking this is a joke, this isn't real. I kept expecting Ashton Kutcher [from the hidden camera–practical joke reality television series *Punk'd*] to show up. The only thing that kept me from starving myself was that I was pregnant. I would sing to myself so I wouldn't collapse."

Continuing, Arabella adds, "When I got here, I had never seen real crackheads before."

Claira interjects with laughter, "I was an actual real crackhead!"

Arabella smiles. "I had friends that used drugs recreationally, maybe a couple lines of coke, but that was it. That's one thing I feel like prison helped me with, if you can say that. I can understand how people do things like get involved with drugs, like I didn't before. I have learned from this experience. I have more compassion for different walks of life, for people who went down different paths that may cause trauma."

It's a Mind Thing

I turn to look at Harold who has been quiet during this exchange. "What do you think about all of this, Harold? Is your picture, *Free from Everything*, possible here?"

"I'm waiting on standing at the gate [upon release] with balloons. But I'm free *now*. I'm free within myself. There's nothing in prison that can make me feel not free anymore. I set my mind on freedom, take my mind on the other side. I picture myself riding around, going shopping. . . . Muscle relaxers help." Laughter and smiles fill the room.

"But that's not how it used to be," Harold continues. "Now, I have to focus on what is to come. If we look at reality, it's a mind thing. What you make your mind believe. In the beginning, I was really angry, I wanted to beat people up. It took me until forty years old to really accept I'm in prison. [He is forty-three now.] But God showed me something different. I came in early 2000s at age twenty-something, in my prime, wildin' out. I used to be mad because I was in prison; it made me think, maybe I should do some crazy shit. But not now. It is what it is. I think if I hadn't come, I'd be dead. I just didn't care. I'd shoot you, beat you. I was something serious, for real! My mom said she was glad I'm here, and I was like, 'What?' I could not understand this." Understanding laughter erupts around the table.

"But it was because she would have gotten that call, that I was dead or on a killing spree. But God got my attention. Too bad he had to do it that way. . . . Sad it took this long, but my eyes are wide open. Now there's so much I want to learn—but there's only so much you can do as a lifer."

Limitations for Lifers

"Why do you think that is?" I ask.

In a rapid back and forth between the four students, I hear the following, beginning with Ilillana. "They think we're gonna die in here anyway, so why waste anything on us."

"Their excuse is that the training we get would be obsolete by the time we get out," Claira explains. "That's their reasoning, but I think the values underneath are closer to what Ilillana said. They think it's a waste."

"Did you know that at the Angola prison in Louisiana, there is a program where lifers get to teach people with shorter sentences about different trades? Lifers are the teachers."[10]

"That's humane," Claira adds.

"It always makes you feel better when you can help someone," says Ilillana. "But here they don't care if there are ninety-six women in a dorm and only two have jobs."

In agreement, Arabella adds, "They don't really care if you go crazy in here, if you can't do anything, it's not their problem. But you know what? You don't understand my reality if you're not living my reality. If I have had good behavior, been DR [disciplinary report]-free for ten years, but someone else goes to lockdown every week, why are you giving that opportunity to her? Because she doesn't have a life sentence. They don't care about our quality of life at all. The public perception is that if you killed someone, [no one] wants you to come home."

Arabella adds a story about medical to emphasize her point. "A nurse fitting my brace said that to me, you didn't have compassion for the life you took," an explanation for why Arabella had not received the care she felt she needed.

Ilillana adds a similar experience. "There was a big deal up in medical because the doctor would flip to the end of your file to read your charges, in front of you, before administering care. She did this to me. I have a condition, so I have to be seen. And when I'm there, she goes into questioning, like, 'How long have you had this condition?' And I ask, 'My sentence or my illness?'"

The people around the table laugh while Harold remembers walking out of medical for similar reasons and Arabella describes the time she was prescribed "toxic" iron supplements and began arguing with the doctor about getting off them. Unfortunately, their stories about medical care are not uncommon; "the intersection of the identities of 'sick person' and 'criminal' undermines women's abilities to be treated as deserving of care."[11]

The lessons lifers receive are some of the worst. In many prisons in the United States, lifers have limited access to education and work programs. Over 90% of prisons have educational and chaplaincy programs, but on average only 2% of incarcerated people can access them. This leaves most people in prison with few means to improve their lives, especially lifers.

The Georgia Department of Corrections quotes the Correctional Education Association for the United States Department of Education in their response as to why they offer education in prison:

> "Offenders who participated in education programs while incarcerated showed lower rates of recidivism after three years"—a 29% reduction—and their "wages were higher." Ninety-five percent of offenders will one day return to society and this area is tasked with preparing offenders for their return to society as productive citizens. A recently published Rand Corporation study (2014), "How Effective Is Correctional Education, and Where do We Go From Here," reports that for every dollar in GED correctional education, there is future savings of $5.[12]

Education, jobs, and adequate care are for people who will go back into society and become "contributing citizens." To deny student lifers educational and vocational options suggests that education and work are goods that would be wasted on people who will die in prison, people who will not be able to use those goods in service to or to contribute to society. Students associate the ability to learn and work with quality of life and humane practice. As Arabella remarks, without opportunities to contribute meaningfully to one's growth or others, people can go crazy. It does not seem, to these student lifers, that the prison cares at all.

A Good Life by Your Own Bootstraps

Noticing the clock and knowing that at any minute an officer can cut our time short, I restate my question to the group, "Is a good life possible here? How can someone experience a good life in prison?"

"Well," Arabella begins, "you can pray over your food to start."

"Good can be misleading," Ilillana clarifies. "It's more of an inner process." Making a similar distinction to Aminah before, she continues, "A peaceful life is possible to best survive, to have comfort and humanity, with less waves." She defines waves as difficulties or obstacles. "I like adrenaline, but when *I* choose it. You can make dinner, iron clothes, do home things—small tastes of comfort, small tastes of home. This can add up to a decent existence—certainly not a life. So, you learn to pick your battles wisely. You can have certain choices, as long as you navigate them, understand them, and learn how to play the system. Circumnavigating. You occasionally play the system, that's what you have to do."

There is widespread agreement with Ilillana's assessment. "We're not as affected by their ideology, by the values of the system," says Claira. "They don't care about our humanity here, but we do. We can act as humans because we *are* human. Humanity is seen in our own interactions as well as with some staff. Our humanity is not policed so much on the ground. We lifers have worked around the edges to get ourselves into programs, to be productive, to get an education. It's cliché, but I'll say it: we've done it by our own bootstraps to get details (jobs). Most lifers get into the trade—we finagle. There is no help from the system—we learn to overcome obstacles through persistence and our own ability. We have a saying here about the squeaky wheel getting attention. Sometimes, you have to throw a tantrum and demand humanity. I think it wouldn't work as well if we were men."

Everyone chimes in to affirm. Arabella explains that she cries, and Harold explains that he threatens to "act like I used to... start doing stupid stuff, acting out to get attention."[13] Ilillana describes the process of finagling to demand humanity as learning to con: "In prison, you learn conning. But not to commit crime."[14]

"We're doing it to get an education," explains Claira.

"Or to get new pants or hot water," remarks Arabella.

"Or to get our toilet plunged!" finishes Ilillana.

Finagling for a Decent Life

According to Claira, finagling is required to live a decent life in prison. The word "finagle" became popular as an Americanism in the 1920s and connotes meanings such as obtaining, arranging, achieving something by indirect, sometimes deceitful methods, to use devious or dishonest measures to achieve one's ends. The word is often associated with the word "cheat." An early definition of "finagle" meant "to cheat at cards" and "to manage by trickery or sharp practice."[15] Despite its overwhelmingly negative connotations, students indicate that the skill of finagling is key to surviving in prison. It is how students exert control in seemingly uncontrollable situations. Finagling also refers to circumnavigating or conning the system. Students suggest that the only way to survive a death-dealing system is to manipulate the system to make it work on their behalf. Sometimes called playing the system, finagling is the cornerstone on which all other survival strategies rest.

As I understand Claira, to finagle is to manipulate present conditions to engineer new or alternative, better options. It is how students insist on their humanity and resist the colonizing threat of a constant lack of agency. Claira recounted, exasperated, that the prison does not care about the humanity and dignity of the incarcerated. Caring about human dignity is something students do for themselves as a way of resisting the dehumanization inherent in prison practice. To assert one's humanity is to use the system against itself. Finagling for one's freedom is a virtue.

Finagling has deep religious and cultural roots in the image of a trickster. In mythology and the study of folklore and religion, a trickster is a character in a story, a god, goddess, spirit, man, woman, or anthropomorphic animal that exhibits a great degree of intellect or secret knowledge and uses it to play tricks or otherwise disobey standard rules and conventional behavior. A trickster can change the course of events by taking definitive action using whatever power is available to him or her via trickery. Moreover, a trickster has a low or relatively lower social status, prohibiting gain or advancement through means available to others, so a trickster must employ wit and cunning to achieve their desired ends.[16] The trickster embodies a disposition of wisdom that requires the ability to evaluate the rules and procedures of institutions through a hermeneutic of suspicion for a better quality of life. If a trickster finagles the system by exhibiting a degree of intellect about the system, then the ability to analyze motivations, systems, and structures is crucial for the wisdom of a trickster. A trickster intellect requires the skills of social analysis and quick interpretation. By identifying finagling with a goddess attribute of a trickster, I hope to redefine it as a witty, intellectually skillful survival strategy.

Possible but Not Preferable

Whether or not a good life is possible in prison depends on how students image the good lives they desire. Lives of belonging, dynamism, and freedom may be possible in prison, but they are always at best incomplete. What is created in prison is a simulacrum of what it might be to live fully or to live in wholeness.[17] While Aminah, Claira, and Ililana might reject the notion that their good life is possible, their actions suggest that a life worth living might be. Aminah is one of the most respected persons in Theology and in the prison. She has been an encourager to teacher and student alike and has been a source of continuity, encouragement, and support for many of her peers. Aminah herself is a central factor in creating an environment for others to live a good life in prison.

The Possibility of Belonging, Dynamism, and Freedom

Cultivating Meaningful Connection in an Alienating Institution

Throughout our summer conversations, the ability to be with loved ones is *the* central component of a good life for most students in Theology. It makes living worthwhile, and for many, a supportive social network makes a meaningful future even imaginable. The desire to belong to people and places is a fundamental human need. Theologian John Swinton suggests that to belong, you need to be missed. This notion of being missed goes beyond mandated inclusion to something more profound; it means that others value your life and presence.

To experience meaningful connection and belonging in an alienating institution like prison requires the art of forming community out of fragmentation, where community is defined as "a group of individuals who share a mutual concern for one another's welfare." It requires the ability to create conditions to be missed, cultivate spaces to be known, and maintain spaces where a person can feel safe to trust.[18] Students' images and conversations depict these hopes for relationships grounded in mutual concern for one another's welfare. These hopes support a vision for life-affirming learning communities grounded in mutual concern for one another's welfare. Even scholarship critical of faith-based programs admit that faith-based ministries "can be a resource, a practice, a belief system, a sense of authority, and a space of belonging."[19]

Because prison disrupts meaningful relationships by separating parents from children, lovers from their beloved, and friends from friends, and because prison makes the restoration of old relationships and the construction of new ones complicated, people must create conditions to be missed by (re)establishing significant social connections by making friends and forming families *in prison*. In the absence of birth families, spouses, or significant others, students re-create family structures inside. Older students adopt younger students in a mother-daughter relationship. Students find "wives" and "husbands" and "sisters" and "brothers." They even find children. An older student declared that she never had children outside of prison, but inside, she had several. Many students who did not have children before coming to prison and whose prison sentence precludes them from ever having them find ways of "having children" as well. They befriend students with young children on the outside and become "aunts" and "uncles" from the inside. They share pictures and visitations so that outside family members become intermingled in the new creation of networks of belonging inside.

Cultivating Dynamism in a Stagnant Environment

Living a dynamic life suggests a desire to experience the ongoing nature of creation, an acknowledgment that creativity and possibility are essential to what it means to be alive and not dead. Dynamism suggests this desire to live fully, to experience the fullness of life—to live meaningfully, generatively—to feel fully alive.

Students and criminologists contend that one of the most effective ways to endure prison is to stay active. This desire to stay busy is a direct way of resisting the feared decay and deterioration of stagnancy and idleness. To experience dynamism in prison requires places and activities that allow students to experience growth, a sense of accomplishment, and newness.

Cultivating Freedom in Unfreedom

For students in Theology, to live and to make a life involves some claim to freedom. To experience freedom in the unfreedom of prison requires a particular capacity that practical theologian and educator Evelyn Parker defines as "the capacity of an individual to focus on what is hoped for, such as material freedom, while negotiating daunting circumstances of struggle and strife."[20] For Parker, freedom is both an ontological ideal, "a way of being in the world that defies oppression," and an "infinite aspiration," something hoped for in the material sense.[21] Parker's description of freedom as both a mindset and a practice resonates with students' debates about freedom. As a mindset, freedom "holds onto dignity and integrity when powers of domination seek to rob or destroy one of dignity and integrity. Freedom is a state of mind that governs the actions of the body even when abused, battered, and ultimately destroyed."[22] Freedom, as something practiced, is what a person or community does to move forward toward what is hoped for. The practice of freedom is the process of liberation. Student images and discussions of freedom suggest that a good life includes multiple expressions and experiences of freedom.

Harold's belief in the possibility of freedom in constraint is repeated several times throughout the summer though, as you recall, his belief is not unanimous. For Harold, freedom is a psychological state, a state of mind, predominantly because the mind is where he has the most control over his life. Harold may not control his physical freedom, but he can and does maintain a sense of agency over his psychological and emotional freedom. He may not be free physically, but he has freedom.

It is important to hold on to the tension between Harold's image of a good life and Aminah's insistence that it is not possible in prison. Harold's image propels us to continue to take little steps toward liberation even in a social death institution. Aminah's image compels us to take steps to dismantle the process of social death itself. For both students, the belief in a good life sustains and emboldens their survival practices. For Harold, it provides him with a vision to work toward, to actualize in the here and now. For Aminah, it provides her with a constant reminder of what is wrong with incarceration and gives her the requisite discomfort to refuse its colonization.

The created life in prison is not to be confused with delusional optimism. It is pragmatic, rooted in a realism that recognizes the limits of its practice. Students want to feel safe, be happy, have relationships of trust, and to believe that possibilities exist for their lives. While the prison constantly disrupts these efforts and tries to strip them of their significance, they are still good. Students press forward, recognizing the limits of their hopes but pursuing a good life in spite of them. They decide to make life matter in a place that treats them as if their living does not.

4
WHAT THEOLOGY MAKES POSSIBLE

> In this space where they offered alternative ways of thinking, a student could engage in the insurrection of subjugated knowledge. Hence it was possible to learn liberating ideas in a context that was established to socialize us to accept domination.[1]
>
> I'm not in prison when I'm in Theology.
>
> Briar

Though Clarisse was the most reluctant to imagine a good life in prison, when asked, she eventually responds by saying, "A good life in here is me staying busy. . . . and on Fridays, I come here [to Theology]." Over the course of the summer, there is widespread agreement that education is crucial to whatever meaningful living is possible in prison. As students discuss their hopes for a good life and what is possible while incarcerated, I began to piece together how they actualize some features of their good lives by participating in Theology. Students find people and a place to belong, opportunities to grow, change, and matter, and the freedom to be themselves. Some go so far as to say that Theology saved them. Listening to student reflections on Theology allows us to see how Theology becomes what bell hooks calls a place of possibility, where belonging, dynamism, and freedom—among other things—become possible in prison.

Meet Joan, CJ, Moon, and Honey Bee II

Joan has been in the Theology program longer than anyone I speak with this summer. When she learns that we are researching for the program, Joan, by her own accord, prints out a list of every class she has taken since 2009, when the program began. Fifty-seven classes and counting. Joan did not grow up in a religious family. She recalls going to "a handful of Catholic services" on Easter and other holidays, but that is about it. A self-described country girl, she grew up in the South with parents who were raised in the church, one Baptist and the other Catholic. To not create tension in the household, they decided not to stress religion with their children. When Joan was fifteen, her friends started playing volleyball with a local Methodist church's youth group. When those friends decided to get baptized, she figured she would as well. Joan did not attend religious services much until she married; her husband was a "hellfire and brimstone Independent Baptist." After their divorce, she "never really found another church."

Joan has been in prison for over a decade, serving a life sentence for a crime she contends she did not commit. When she was initially arrested and held in the county jail, she was treated well, felt the guards were kind to her, and hoped her charges would be dropped. But when Joan was sentenced to prison, her hope deflated. "I used to believe in the justice system, but now, no. I didn't know where else to turn, so I started to go to church on Sundays and Catholic Mass on Tuesdays. I lost faith in the justice system, and I needed to have faith in something." Looking for faith in something is how Joan ended up in Theology.

When Joan first heard about Theology, it was during its three-month trial run. A friend of hers was in the trial group and told her that she would love it. At that time, entrance into Theology relied less on applications and interviews and more on recommendations from a chaplain. Joan has been in Theology for more than nine years when she enters the classroom today. If you ask her why, she has a clear response: "I still learn something. You need something to ground you, a foundation you can build on."

Before Joan was arrested, she was three months shy of getting a degree in engineering. She is drawn to educational spaces, volunteering as a teacher's aide in prison. She recalls her favorite courses in Theology, like Preaching. Hebrew, and Greek. "A group of us in the dorm still work on Hebrew!"

Joan no longer attends church services in prison unless there is a special reason. She attends choir and praise band rehearsals instead. Like other stories I have heard, church services of late are less treated as religious rituals and more as social gatherings. "It's a lot of people trying to meet their girlfriend, and lately a lot of gang activity.... Last time I went, a guest chaplain had given the sermon. I tried to thank her for the service afterward, and she just turned to me and said, *Every time someone talks to me, they want something*. It hurt my feelings, so I rarely attend."

Nevertheless, Joan believes she has built a good foundation for herself in prison by being around like-minded people. "I want to be around people who are seeking the truth, even if their truth is different from mine. And to have enough people in my community that if I need to pray, I can find someone to pray with me. The Bible and Theology are still part of my foundation. I will continue to learn for all my life. I will never know everything in that book (Bible). Other practices bring me peace, too. Meditative practices like Buddhism and the Lo Jong practice that we did. Catholic contemplation and praying the rosary, too—I don't have to restrict myself to one denomination. I can be true to who I am and practice in any way I wish."

Religious and support groups have been essential for Joan over the years. Kairos is perhaps most important. "It stems around community. We meet once a month to talk about how we've seen God in our lives, what has brought us closer to God in the last thirty days, who we need to pray for, things like that. The people in Kairos are loving and nonjudgmental, making you feel like you are human." According to her account (which I am inclined to trust given her records about Theology classes), Joan has participated in more than twenty mental health groups for self-growth and advancement over the years. "The prison is not going to do it. They don't do anything to rehabilitate. It's part of why suicide rates have gone up." Joan's statement helps me make sense of the increased presence of suicide prevention hotline numbers plastered in red paint on the white cinder block walls around the prison. "There are lots of trade programs here, but not much for mental health—it's all volunteer run, like Narcotics Anonymous and Celebrate Recovery. They (the prison) don't do much to prepare you for society."

Joan believes that the Department of Corrections wants lifers to do twenty-five-plus years, even if they are under the seven-year rule. She is under the fourteen-year rule. Parole determination for lifers depends on when the person was sentenced. Parole-eligible lifers serving a life sentence for a serious violent felony committed before July 1, 2006, are initially considered for parole after serving fourteen years. Those who committed such crimes on or after July 1, 2006, will not be considered for parole until they have served thirty years. Most life-sentenced people convicted of serious violent felonies before 1995 were eligible for parole after seven years and have already received their initial parole consideration. Despite having no disciplinary infractions and doing "nothing but take classes," Joan received a five-year denial for parole a few months back. She is convinced that the system is "set up to knock you down" but believes that you must continuously try to make a life for yourself regardless.

For Joan, God is essential to her life, even if the church is not. "[God] is my creator, he's the one that gets me through. I've learned that when you don't look for God, you don't find God. But when you start to look, you find. So, I look everywhere. The first place you should look for God is everywhere." As she settles into a chair, waiting for our group to begin, I wonder where Joan has found God today.

Imagining a Good Life

Joan helps us push two tables together to form a square in the middle of the room. We find two additional students in the hallway who were, as I suspected, waiting for us in chaplaincy. A fourth is eventually seen coming in from outside, on her way back from her beekeeping job. It is time to get started.

We meet each other anew: Joan, previously introduced, Creative Justice (CJ), Moon, and Honey Bee II (HB). Compared to Joan, CJ is a newcomer to prison. She arrived not quite two years ago and expects to be paroled in five years. CJ is thoughtful and comes across as shy when you first meet her. She stands nearly six feet tall but carries herself lightly, delicately. CJ presents her image of a good life first. It is titled *Always Fun*, a picture of a lake with several people fishing. We learn that it is a memory from growing up in South Carolina, where she and her family would fish at a local lake. CJ smiles as she shares memories of home.

Joan shares an image of a house with herself and her three children. She titles it *Home at Last*. A good life, to Joan, is being home with her children. Moon shares next. Moon looks and sounds young, though she has been in prison for nearly ten years. She is serving a life sentence that began when she was still a teenager. Moon was born in Central America and her mother died when she was still a child, leaving her and her siblings to a life in and out of foster care. Studies show that women in prison are more likely to have been in foster care or another state facility as children.[2] Moon shares an image she titles *Heaven is Stable Family*. She has drawn a line down the center of her paper, splitting the image. One side represents the past, and the other is a hoped-for future. Representing the past, she has drawn a picture of her mother and siblings at home together. This past image of her family is less of a memory and more of a reflection of the life she wished she had. Representing the future, she has drawn herself with a husband and children of her own—a future she believes could still be possible. Moon must serve thirty years before becoming eligible for parole, but because she was so young when she arrived, she imagines her future image is still achievable. "Maybe I will live in Spain," she laughs.

The last image we see is from Honey Bee II. HB came from her beekeeping position, hence the choice of name. She lifts her paper to share a picture of herself driving a freight truck, something she describes as "the best times of my life, chugging along cross-country, spending time alone, just thinking my own thoughts." HB is the oldest person around the table. She is quiet and pensive and can spend entire classes without volunteering her perspectives. But this does not mean she does not have any. HB expresses herself well in writing and often listens more than she speaks. The image of HB happily driving solo in a truck is fitting for the person I have come to know.

As with the other groups, we reflect collectively on the images before us, and students name relationships, whether with family, a spouse, or just with oneself, as the most important common feature. Except for Moon using the word "Heaven" in her image title, there is no religious language used during the presentation of images. No mention of God. I ask about God's presence in these images, or if there is any. HB shares that driving in the truck alone brought her as close to God as she had ever been. For Joan, "God is present in everyday living." CJ sees God all over her image. "God created all this beautiful stuff. He wants us to fish. He created life to be fun and made sure I could experience it." Moon sees God in her image on both sides of her page. God is in the past picture of her mom and siblings as she describes what she thinks life would have looked like if her mother had not died. Moon also believes that God will make the future image of her husband and children a reality. According to these students, God desires that they experience a good life because it is God who makes a good life possible.

Parole, Family, Finances, and Personal Responsibility

As our conversation continues, four factors emerge, needed for these images to become a reality: parole, family, finances, and personal responsibility. Prioritizing parole does not suggest that good moments are not possible in prison. It does, however, emphasize that no one imagines their good life to be set within carceral contexts, mainly because the people involved in a good life (family, spouses, etc.) are not physically present within the prison. "Parole comes first," according to Joan, "and then you need to get back on your feet." This is where good family support and a good job becomes paramount. CJ affirms that getting back home is the first step in achieving her hoped-for good life. However, she acknowledges that returning home will be a different experience than she remembers. Nonetheless hopeful, she says, "It will be better. Sure, certain people will be gone, but it will still be a new life."

Moon insists that the first thing she will need for her image to be reality is a husband. "I have to find a husband," she begins. "Actually, I could just start with a boyfriend." Everyone laughs, and I wonder what others think of Moon's plan. She is not alone in thinking that a spouse will help her achieve a good life after incarceration. In fact, it is one of the most cited "next steps" that I hear students talk about when they imagine parole. Some students already have boyfriends waiting on them, boyfriends they have met via correspondence in prison.

Moon reflects that she has never had a job because she was so young when she was incarcerated. She feels she has never had the experience of "being able to do small things, be normal, be responsible." What worries her most, she shares, is that she has no idea how to be responsible because she has no experience in what responsibility is.

I do not know how much responsibility discourse Moon has heard over the past ten years. As stated before, prison is replete with responsibility discourse—the pull yourself up by your bootstraps, make good choices, try harder, individualistic kind. While talk of responsibility may seem to pair well with students' desire for agency over their own lives and decisions, prison discourse on responsibility seldom considers structural and deep-seated systemic concerns. Telling people to make better choices without surrounding them with the resources and community needed to make these choices actionable is insincere and harmful.

Everyone around the table believes that a good life is never yours to create alone. It takes other people, people who are mutually invested in your well-being, especially one's parents. Everyone, that is, except HB. HB, with the good life image of herself alone in a truck, insists that no one else is required for her to experience a good life.

Honey Bee II

HB describes her adolescence as a time of being lost. She left an abusive home as a teenager and moved in with a friend. After excelling in high school, HB received a scholarship to a Catholic university. She did not grow up religious and went to the university because of the scholarship. It allowed her to get away from her parents, who had since divorced. HB's mother is white, and her father is Native American.

HB started college amid the women's movement of the '60s and '70s. "Gloria Steinem, I remember. And Bella Abzug. I just wanted to study, study, study." HB was interested in the liberal arts and describes her early college years as going well until her third year when she got into a conflict with a Jesuit.

"He was demanding we write about an experience we'd had with God. I said, I haven't had one yet. And he said, oh, I'm sure you've had something. It was basically, do it my way, or I'll flunk you. We went to the dean, who tried to help us compromise. He started talking about euphoria and spirituality, and I realized he was talking about drugs. This was the early '70s," she reminds us. "He assumed I'd done them and was hinting I should write about that. He said to write about any kind of enlightenment experience. 'Do you have anything like that?' he asked me. I said, 'Nope.'" The assumption that she and her friends did drugs rubbed HB wrong. "I ended up dropping out of the class, and the whole university." HB transferred to another school and ended up majoring in accounting.

While in school for accounting, she met a woman who had "broken away from Catholicism" and was in Judaic Studies. "She opened my eyes to a lot of things as far as the Old Testament and the New Testament." This was when HB's interest in religion began. But it was short-lived. A family member soon died, putting HB into a spiral leading to numerous arrests and imprisonments over the next several decades.

HB has been in multiple prisons across state lines, so she knows how this prison compares to others. "This prison is very Christian based." HB attributes her characterization to the work of the chaplaincy department and the programs they support, like Kairos. When HB came to this prison, she decided to try Kairos and liked it. Like others we have heard, Kairos provides a sense of camaraderie. HB fondly recalls the unselfishness of the volunteers, and she felt like she understood what the speakers were talking about, even though she never considered herself much of a religious person.

She decided she wanted to do Theology because, as she put it, "let's see what they're thinking now." She thought that

Theology would introduce her to the newest ideas about Christianity and the Bible. "I love it. I would love to go to seminary when I get out." HB has enjoyed her time in Theology, especially the teachers, she confesses. She also speaks fondly of a Womanist & Black Feminist Intellectual Traditions class she took in Theology the summer prior. Given that HB has a college degree, seminary is a possibility, and she would not be the first person from Theology to enroll in seminary post-release.

HB expects to get out in a couple of years but the time between then and now feels enormous. She simply wants to complete her time in peace. One reason her sentence feels so tedious is because of the changes she has witnessed in prison. "It's like a dark veil is hanging over this place. It's partly the gangbangers. You'll be walking back to your dorm in the evening and look up and there are fifteen to twenty 'kids' [younger incarcerated people] stretched across the road, and you have to go through them. So, you never go anywhere alone."

"Take this past weekend, for instance. I was doing Theology homework and they [officers] said you have to pack up and move." HB was being sent to what used to be considered the elderly dorm. "It has been very nice, but they've started letting people in right out of lockdown. It was an elderly dorm, but they lowered the age from fifty-five, to fifty, to forty, and we're still getting kids. So, they changed it to the 'Cultivating Dorm,' but they didn't ask us about it at all." The Cultivating Dorm is the department's attempt to place older and younger people in the same dorm as a type of forced mentorship. "We don't want to mentor, and they don't want mentors." HB is clearly opposed to the change. "They get to the dorm and walk in and announce, 'This is my dorm now.' They take the TV controls, get people together at tables, everything. And I'm tired of it. So, I requested to be moved." HB was older when she arrived at this prison and looks at the people in their twenties with a tinge of sadness. "They come in their twenties and will be in their forties talking the same way—not having progressed. It's a shame for when they get out." In the meantime, HB wants to tend to her bees, come to Theology, and do the rest of her time in peace.[3]

You Have to Make Life Good

Despite the challenges, this group shows no hesitancy or reluctancy at the idea of living a good life in prison. "It's what you make of it," says Joan. "You have to make life good. If you just accept things with a positive attitude, just about any day can be okay. It's all in how you approach it." Joan believes that life in prison is endurable if she stays busy and occupies her mind with books. But for people who have done a lot of time without occupying their minds, Joan believes they will struggle when they go home.

Moon supposes you need to become settled in your thinking and accept the environment for what it is. "You don't have a choice [about being in prison], so you have to be realistic. You have to choose to do something with your life." Moon's pragmatic response recognizes the reality of what scholars call "constrained choice," yet insists that a person can still choose to do something good even with limited options. Moon insists that a job is among the many things required to live a good life in prison. But securing a job is not as easy as it sounds. There are far more people in prison than jobs to go around. Most people will not have a job, even if they want one. Like Rylee, Moon believes that staying busy is the most essential requirement for living well in prison: "If you're busy, the time passes, and you don't have time to think about it." Students and criminologists alike contend that one of the most effective ways to endure prison is to stay active. Staying busy is one way of resisting the decay, deterioration, and stagnancy of prison. But staying busy is not easily embraced by students with long or life sentences. Most longtimers are restricted from getting meaningful work and sometimes from participating in educational programming when space is limited.

"I don't want to work for the State," CJ continues. CJ is not rejecting the idea of work; instead, she is rejecting how work is compensated in prison. While some states have rules governing the payment of workers in prison, Georgia does not. At the time of CJ's declaration, people in Georgia prisons are not guaranteed compensation for their labor, so the minimum wage for

Georgians working behind bars is effectively zero. Nonetheless, CJ admits that keeping up a good work ethic is important, so she is prepared for life after release. "Those people Joan is describing who don't do anything with their time, how are they going to get back to work?" CJ sees staying busy through work and other programs as part of "investing in hope." But she warns people against using programs and details as a form of escape. "Instead of suppressing emotions, people need to understand their emotions," she adds. "If they don't understand them, when they go home, it all pours out."

CJ has not always been so measured in her assessment of things. She admits that when she first arrived in prison, she like many others was trying to stay busy as a form of escape. "When you have something to do, it gives you a reason to get up in the morning. The days go faster," one student remarked. CJ continues, "For me, I figured that hope can come later."

Hope, for Moon, did not come from staying busy, however; it came from someone who cared for her. In her words, "Hope comes from someone else's voice, someone who has been through it, who relates, and knows how I feel." HB, who has been relatively quiet these past few minutes, chimes in to agree that staying busy and participating in groups is vital to living well in prison. Like Moon, she also insists that you need a job. But HB declares, "I like the ones where I can work alone."

There are many forms of busyness in prison, and not all lead to a more meaningful life. Students like CJ suggest that living well in prison requires the ability to discern between constructive and destructive forms of busyness and the will to choose the dynamism that will improve quality of life and give life more significant meaning, or at least not deter one from it. Choosing constructive forms of staying busy is one way students exert agency over time. It is how they reframe time from being a reminder of punishment to being a source of potential development and a site of possibility. It is their counter-response to the stagnancy of prison.

Like other groups before, the women around this table believe education is essential to surviving prison. "Education means that you are doing something for yourself." Moon has a dream of going to college. She received her GED while in prison, which helped her believe she could accomplish something positive. "It gave me courage." Through a GED and Theology, Moon is making strides toward college in prison. Though she finds educational programs intimidating, her overall experience of education gives her a feeling of not being lost.

Joan affirms Moon's perspective. As someone who has worked as an educational aide for years, Joan attests that many people in the GED program believe they have never accomplished anything. Completing their GED in prison makes them feel capable, "disproving all of those [people] who didn't think you'd amount to much."

Theology Is Where You Get More Questions

As the conversation shifts to discussing Theology in particular, I find myself laughing along with Moon's reflections. "Theology is where you get more questions than you ever thought there were! But . . . I always want to know more!" "Yes," CJ adds, "the more I know, the more questions I ask!" These students paint a picture of Theology as a generative practice with an inexhaustible world of questions and exploration. Joan chimes in, saying that Theology has helped her read the world differently. "Because of Theology, I look for what the assumptions are and ask if I agree with them."

Not everyone speaks so glowingly of Theology, however. According to CJ, some people think Theology is "Bleep! Bleep! Bleep!" This is her effort at censoring the profanity used to describe the program by its naysayers. "Some people think Theology is devilish because people in it may change their mind about points of faith." But to Moon, Theology is where you learn to express yourself and your views, where you learn to ask questions. The questions and questioning are what CJ believes causes distrust of Theology. "Lots of people think you should not question the Bible because it is the word of God. And some people just think I am studying to be a pastor." She laughs louder than I have heard her laugh all day; the image of her being a pastor is incredibly humorous to her. I think to myself that CJ would actually be a wonderful pastor.

Someone Moon knows who calls herself a Christian told Moon not to ask any questions at all. She said the Theology program was just trying to confuse her. This seems to be another common concern among skeptics. Theology will either confuse you or try to convert you, but convert to what we are not quite sure.[4] Moon says she pushes back on those perspectives now that she is several months into the program. In response, she insists that Theology is about "studying and thinking—there is no believing required."

Theology differs from other religious programming in prison. "In Theology, a person can take two classes with two different teachers and get two different perspectives—which is one reason I keep taking courses!" offers Joan. Joan describes Bible studies in prison as "just studying one book (the Bible) and vocational-technical courses as having trade skills that don't change." But Theology, for Joan, is not only generative in the inexhaustible wandering and wondering it can engender but also dynamic in its ability to feel new.

HB experiences Theology as a place for the open sharing of different ways of thinking. Theology creates spaces where people who have lived around one another for years can learn things about one another they did not know before. "It gives you a different view of everyone."

Unlike the skeptics, the students around this table are not convinced that being a person who practices a faith tradition and being in Theology are mutually exclusive practices. "It is possible to be a person of faith and study Theology," Joan contends, but she does not think it would work well for anyone in a "strict religion." Like the groups before, these women clearly delineate between and among the different religious and educational programs in prison. Contrasting a course she is taking in Theology on Trauma and Healing to a support-group program on trauma, Moon complains that the prison support groups are "all about you." Prison groups focus on investigating the self, figuring out how to deal with your own trauma, and becoming responsible for your own recovery (maintaining a commitment to responsibility discourse). But in Theology, Moon states, "Here we study." Theology allows Moon to view trauma and healing beyond herself, beyond a personal, individualistic category. As I listen to Moon, I wonder if studying in Theology provides a respite from the constant analysis, self-reflection, and judgment that characterizes the support programs.

In the same way Moon distinguishes Theology from support groups, CJ does the same with Bible studies. "In Bible studies, you are not supposed to disagree, and you are not supposed to ask questions. But what kind of person doesn't have questions? In Theology, you can express yourself, you can listen to others, and no one is going to look at you crazy."

CJ on Theology

I am not surprised to hear CJ reflect so openly about Theology and how it differs from other religious programming in prison because CJ has been thinking about religion and education her whole life. CJ has fond memories of her childhood growing up in South Carolina, in a house where her father made her and her siblings read Malcolm X and Christian scriptures before they could go out to play. She attributes the emphasis on education to the fact that her father was a scientist. She always liked school growing up; math and English literature were her favorite subjects. She did well in the International Baccalaureate high school she attended and taught herself to play the trombone.

CJ does not describe her family as religious though they did go to church often. This could be because her father never went to church, even though he ensured the children learned the 23rd Psalm and the "Our Father." Her mother, however, was different. "With my mom, everything is God this, God that. Cousins too." She laughs when she confesses that she had difficulty understanding God from people who would "preach a sermon while smoking crack!" Growing up in South Carolina, CJ also witnessed many people around her practice voodoo. "My mom was very against it. I would be like, 'Auntie's gonna pray for me,' and she'd be like, 'No she's not. . . . No one is going to pray for you but me and God.'" CJ recalls many people in South Carolina who practiced Christianity and voodoo, including many in her extended family going back generations.

Though her dad did not go to church, she, her mother, and her siblings did—all the time. "We were in the choir and youth group," she explains. But church attendance was cut short at the Holiness church they attended when word got out that the pastor was having an affair. A few years later, she started going to a relative's church, where a woman was the pastor. "At that point, I did not think [a woman pastor] was right. I didn't believe a word of what she said because ladies aren't supposed to be pastors. Maybe they can minister to other women in the church, but . . ." She pauses and resumes, "I think I thought that because I was listening to my cousins."

In the early stages of her life, CJ saw God as something scary, something to be feared. "I was afraid, thought I was doomed and that He was there to destroy us. [God] was not loving." CJ held this belief for nearly ten years until she found herself in a terrible place in life. Then her mother told her she needed to return to God. CJ describes this period in her life as a time when she was "on a spiritual journey with no spiritual at all."

Fast-forward ten years, and CJ attends Theology faithfully in prison. In her mid-thirties, she believes she has finally gotten to a place where she understands God differently. "My mom says that God is always available to you in the same way. I say, yes, God is unchanging, but it is how we view him and deal with him that changes." CJ admits to being angry with God for years, so much so that whenever her mother would bring God up on one of their phone calls, CJ would hang up. "She'd tell me to talk to God and I'd say that I don't want to hear about God. And she would say if you don't want to hear about God, you're not talking to me." CJ felt her mother's redirection to God-talk was an avoidance strategy, keeping her mother from sharing what she truly felt and thought about things. "I wanted her to talk to me and all she would say is 'Talk to God.' That's the only direction she would give me. Like, you're telling me the God answer, but I want the mommy answer." Interestingly, CJ believes her mother's God-talk is a repudiation of responsibility, an inability or unwillingness to deal with challenging emotions, the very habits CJ feels people need to learn to do while in prison.

It is probably unclear to all besides CJ why someone trying to avoid talking about God would participate in a theology program. CJ realizes there is a relationship between rejecting God and desiring to connect with her mother. "I always come back to God—even when I've told everyone, including him, that I hate him. I'll turn around and say, God, how are you going to help me? That's what I know to do." CJ had plenty of love-hate conversations with God when she was sentenced to prison. A first-time offender, CJ was devastated when she was sentenced to twenty years. "We [God and I] were not friends after the sentence. I thought he wasn't a father but more like a husband who had messed up. I did not feel like I deserved the sentence I got. I could understand if I had done some bad things before, but I worked; I did not really do drugs [the *really* caveating the few times she smoked marijuana when she was younger]. I fell out with God. I thought that God would be mad for a moment, and I would be forgiven." At the time, CJ interpreted being forgiven as not being sentenced to prison.

Over the past two years, CJ feels that she has changed for the better. "I've learned to deal with conflict, take responsibility, be mature. Before, I was too afraid and lashed out, blaming things on others. Now, I allow people to tell me about myself. I accept constructive criticism and learn the value of it. I value understanding where others are coming from and seeing other opinions and viewpoints. I have matured mentally, and I make better decisions."

According to CJ, the best thing someone can do to change for the better in prison is surround themselves with good people. "You must be mindful of the people you associate with. Spend the least amount of time in the dorm as possible. Take classes, do lots of groups, and go to work. Start with yourself—come back to reality with yourself first and find inner discipline." While she believes that many people in prison have yet to find this community or discipline, she believes Theology has been helpful in her finding it for herself. Describing the people in Theology, she exclaims, "These are the kind of people it's good to be around. You may not know them, but I feel they're like me. I've found a new group of people I can associate with. They have great qualities; they help me be a better me. They help me through the bad times." I wonder if she is referring to the times when she pulled me aside to say she is depressed. "When you're going through things, you don't want a negative response. A lot of people in here will just beat someone up or sleep with another person's girlfriend." While I can attest that Theology is not immune from these behaviors, they are less common in Theology, and I can see why CJ finds respite here. "People in Theology and the conversations we have help you think about life. Class helps you—kind of like you graduate from one level [of awareness] to another. You start to see things different."

CJ speaks fondly of Theology but believes it comes at a price. "We definitely get pushback from correctional officers when we pursue an education in here. They'll say, 'If you wanted education, you should have never come to prison.' I think they're just mad because we're getting educated and they cannot just talk to us in any kind of way anymore. . . . They're mad because I know my own worth—if they even smell it [my worth], that's a problem for them. To them, I don't have worth because I'm a prisoner. Versus to me, I walk around with it, knowing my worth. I'm human."

For CJ, Theology allows her to surround herself with good people, which she relates to living a good life. In its ideal, a good life is a life where she is back with her family. In the interim, a good life is where she can surround herself with decent people, people she can confide in and trust. Ultimately, CJ says she is happy in prison (not happy to be in prison). "I'm happy I'm here [at this specific prison] because you can hear kids playing nearby." Of course, there are no children in line sight of the prison, but the prison is in a rural, residential area. There are homes all around. On a quiet day, it is not hard to imagine that CJ can hear the singsong rhythm of a metal swing swaying back and forth with children's laughter carried in the wind. "It's nice to hear them." The days in prison can be difficult, but CJ is assured that she is still happy. "I'm a witness. Think about it. Even lifers can be happy! It's the people with short sentences who are some of the most miserable people in here. The Devil is feeding you, but you have to find that sunshine."

Of all the people I sit down with this summer, CJ is the most comfortable talking about God and the most reflective about Theology. She describes Theology as "the study of the journey. The things we learn, the different pit stops, not one belief or another. Theology is like a shopping center, with rest stops," she adds. "I might believe one thing one day, and the next day something else. Theology is an ongoing learning experience."

God is still significant to CJ. She takes God more seriously now than before. "Someone in my dorm said they think they could give him another chance." Her voice takes a "can you believe it?" tone. "I don't think people really understand how big God is—you can never really leave him." To CJ, God is still mean, but she adds now that God is also "kind and loving, and that's primary." Thinking about her description of God, she adds, "You know, He's probably been to prison before." She laughs. "God has to be rigid, or we humans would run over him. That's just what humans do."

A Good Life Is a Life of Wholeness

Joan, CJ, HB, and Moon share their final alternative words for a good life: family, opportunity, and peace. As I did in previous groups, I offer words of my own: joy, happiness, freedom, flourishing, and wholeness. Despite focusing on happiness earlier in this group, there is little interest in discussing happiness now. Students are split on freedom and flourishing, suggesting that both are important and helpful words when imagining a good life. Freedom is related to parole for this group, while flourishing elicits more description than I have heard before. These women understand flourishing as an active concept "where a person keeps succeeding. Flourishing is opening up like a flower." Flourishing conveys the action of growth.

However, there is unanimous attraction to the word "wholeness" for the first time.

"Yes," they say as a chorus, "that's the word. Wholeness covers everything: heart, mind, and soul. It's about being emotionally, physically, mentally, and spiritually complete." A good life is a life of wholeness. I did not get to ask if a good life of wholeness was a real possibility in prison or anywhere.

Our time around the table has come to an end. HB, CJ, Moon, and Joan pack up their belongings and help us rearrange the room as we all prepare to leave the school hall, they to their dorms for lunch, and us to make the trip back to Atlanta. Before I can put my notebook in my bag, Joan stops me with one final comment. "Ms. Green, if you're looking for new course ideas, how about a class on the traditions and culture of the time of Jesus? It would really help us better understand the parables," she explains. She watches me write down her suggestion in my notebook, satisfied that she is not the only one to keep records of classes. As I place my notebook in my bag, I can rest assured that Joan will be the first to sign up whenever this class is offered in Theology, extending her list of Theology courses (figures 4.1 and 4.2) to yet another page.

Classes taken in my Certificate of Theological Sudies & Advanced Certificate of Theological Studies

	Name of Class	Start date (mm/yy)	End date (mm/yy)
1	Biblical Foundations	Jan-09	Mar-09
2	Theological Foundations	Apr-09	Jun-09
3	Reading the Bible from a Woman's Perspective (Womanistic and Feministic Theology)	Jul-09	Sep-09
4	Biblical Perspectives of Criminal Justice	Jul-09	Sep-09
5	Restorative Justice	Oct-09	Dec-09
	Certificate of Theological Studies	Jan-09	Mar-10
	Additional Electives taken:		
6	World Religions	Jan-09	Mar-10
7	Ten Commandments	Jul-10	Sep-10
8	Prophetic Preaching	Jul-10	Sep-10
9	Apocalyptic Literature	Oct-10	Dec-10
10	And Certain Women (Womanistic and Feministic Theology)	Oct-10	Dec-10
11	Spiritual Development	Oct-10	Dec-10
12	Introduction to Koine Greek	Jan-11	Mar-11
13	Theology in Film	Jan-11	Mar-11
14	Seeing the Sacred: Intro into Liturgical Art	Jul-11	Sep-11
15	Salvific Encounters	Jul-11	Sep-11
16	Crying, Cursing, and Other Poetry from the Darkness: The Lament and Cursing Psalms	Oct-11	Dec-11
17	Contemporary Ethics & Women: Love, Relationships & Intimacy	Oct-11	Dec-11
18	Ethics in Film	Jan-12	Mar-12
19	Theological Foundation Aide	Apr-12	Jun-12
20	Public Theology	Jul-12	Sep-12
21	When Faith Meets Facts: Exploring the Relationship between Religion and Science	Jul-12	Sep-12
22	Her Story (18th, 19th, & 20th Century Women Theologians)	Oct-12	Dec-12
23	Theology and Story	Oct-12	Dec-12
24	Ending the Cycle of Violence	Jan-13	Mar-13
25	Women's Styles of Preaching	Jan-13	Mar-13
26	Spiritual Practices in Prison	Apr-13	Jun-13
27	The Revelation of John	Apr-13	Jun-13
	Advanced Certificate of Theology started:		
28	Footsoldiers for Justice: Profiles of Faith Inspired Activism	Jul-13	Sep-13

29	Ethics of Paul	Jul-13	Sep-13
30	Pastoral Care: Mosaic Conversations	Oct-13	Dec-13
31	Theologies of Non-violence	Oct-13	Dec-13
32	Discovering Self: Identity and Personal Theology	Jan-14	Mar-14
33	Research and Writing Seminar	Jan-14	Mar-14
	Advanced Cetificate of Theological Studies	Jul-13	Apr-14
	Additional Electives taken:		
34	Psalms and Hip Hop	Apr-14	Jun-14
35	Faith and Female Mysticism	Jul-14	Sep-14
36	Sustaining a Life in Ministry	Oct-14	Dec-14
37	Reading and Writing Spiritual Memoirs	Oct-14	Dec-14
38	Theological Approaches to Suffering and the Role of Ritual	Jan-15	Mar-15
39	Introduction to Judaism and Islam	Apr-15	Jun-15
40	Biblical Hebrew	Jul-15	Sep-15
41	Religion and Mythology Discussion Group	Jul-15	Sep-15
42	Tabetan Buddhism: The Lojong Way	Oct-15	Dec-15
43	A Theology of Creation	Jan-16	Mar-16
44	Cultivating Community	Jan-16	Mar-16
45	Spirituality in the Arts	Apr-16	Jun-16
46	Encountering What Matters (creative writing & drawing)	Jul-16	Sep-16
47	Book Club-Novel Discussion -no credit class	Oct-16	Dec-16
48	Biblical Greek	Jan-17	Mar-17
49	Biblical Greek II	Apr-17	Jun-17
50	Biblical Greek Study Hall	July~~Oct~~ 17	Sept 17
51	Christology in the Gospel of John	Oct-17	Dec-17
52	Ancient Arithmetic: The Birth of Mathematics	Jan-18	Mar-18
53	Scandalous Women: Crime and Sin in Postcolonial Women's Writing	Jan-18	Mar-18
54	The Fall & The Redemption-"The Apple Doesn't Fall Far From the Tree": Another Perspective on the Fall and the Redemption of Humanity	Apr-18	Jun-18
55	Christian Spiritual Formation	Apr-18	Jun-18
56.	Theology & Film: Practicing Cultural Exegesis	Jul-18	Sept 18
57.	Hebrew Introduction to Biblical Hebrew	Sept 18 -	present

Figures 4.1 and 4.2. Joan's List of Theology Courses

Educational, Self-Help, and Spiritual Programs

Theology is not the only meaningful program available to students, but it does hold a unique place in what is offered. Students describe Theology as "an educational outlet on something spiritual." Theology, for these women, sits at the intersection between education and spirituality, the mind and the heart. "It teaches you how to grow," they add, "shows how religion effects everything." It is not necessarily Christian, they clarify, but it is spiritual.

Students offer an example of a recent class on Ancient Math taught by a PhD student in Mathematics. This class was not explicitly Christian but covered the spirituality of mathematics. Described as a research-based course, students studied and explored number systems, arithmetic, and geometric patterns of ancient civilizations, as well as the cultures and religious traditions that used them. They kept a journal of drawings, symbols, patterns, and notes on traditions that interested them, concluding with a research project presented in class. More than a few times, students asked me if I knew about the Fibonacci sequence because they planned to find examples of it the next time they went outdoors. The idea that there could be a relationship between religion, spirituality, and math was intriguing and bolstered a perception among students that Theology was different from other religious programming offered in prison.

In addition to Ancient Math, students mentioned their participation in CIT and AVP, two courses offered through the Theology program. CIT, or Compassionate Integrity Training, is a program developed by the Center for Compassion, Integrity and Secular Ethics at Life University. The first time they offered their program in this prison was through a partnership with the Theology program. CIT is

> a multi-part training program that cultivates basic human values as skills for the purpose of increasing individual, social and environmental flourishing. By covering a range of skills from self-regulation and self-compassion to compassion for others and engagement with complex systems, CIT focuses on and builds towards compassionate integrity: the ability to live one's life in accordance with one's values with a recognition of common humanity, our basic orientation to kindness, and reciprocity.[5]

CIT is a program founded on "a secular approach to universal ethics based on common sense, common experience and science, rather than a particular culture or religion." The program advocates that secular ethics "can be useful to people of any or no religious background, while not being in any way in conflict with any particular religious values. The word 'secular' in no way implies a stance that is against religion; on the contrary, it implies inclusivity and a respect for all." Its presence in the Theology program creates among students a perception that Theology is inclusive and reinforces the idea that religious belief is not a prerequisite for participation.

Another program mentioned in the discussion was the Alternatives to Violence Program, or AVP. Like CIT, AVP is a program designed and developed by external volunteers but offered to Theology students. AVP describes itself as "an experiential workshop that draws on the shared experience of participants with interactive exercises, games, and role-plays to examine how people respond to situations where injustice, prejudice, frustration, and anger can lead to aggressive behavior and violence. Participants learn conflict management skills that can enable them to build successful interpersonal interactions, gain insights into themselves, and find new and positive approaches to their lives."[6] AVP began in 1975, when a group of incarcerated people at Green Haven Prison in Dutchess County, New York sought to work with youth gangs and teenagers at risk but were having difficulty communicating their message about the consequences of violence. They got help from the Quaker Project on Community Conflict which sent an interracial team to conduct a workshop for them. It was so successful that requests were soon received for more. The AVP organization was born and grew quickly.

AVP programs are currently in federal, state, and county prisons in most US states. It soon became evident that the program designed for prison could be useful to everyone. As a result, AVP training and workshops are now offered to the general public. In its origins, organizational structure, and philosophy, AVP has ties to the Religious Society of Friends (Quakers), but today, AVP is a nonsectarian, nonpolitical, and nonprofit volunteer organization dedicated to reducing interpersonal violence in society. According to its description, its board members and volunteer leaders are Quakers and non-Quakers from a diversity of backgrounds.

Through the presence of classes and programs like Biblical and Theological Foundations, Ancient Math, CIT, and AVP, students have an expansive imagination of what is possible within Theology. When asked what other classes they would like to see in the program, they exclaim, Gender Theology, World Theology, Occult, Mythology, and Life after Death.

To get a clearer sense of programs they find meaningful, I ask if they can place these programs in categories. First, they group educational programs such as GED, Charter School, Vocational-Technical school, and Life University (associate degree program). These programs are located within the education department and offer credit-bearing courses culminating in a degree. Students explain that these programs "are about the mind," where there are clear right and wrong answers with predetermined, set ways of learning. A second category they name is support groups. Alcoholics Anonymous, Narcotics Anonymous, Trauma, Grief, and Loss, Parenting, and Confronting the Self are mentioned in addition to Department of Corrections–sponsored cognitive-based programs such as Thinking for Change and Moral Reconation Therapy. They describe these programs as having "some spirituality and some education but are focused mainly on improving the self."

Finally, they name spiritual programs. These include the many religious services that occur each week, including but extending beyond chapel, such as the Episcopal group, Catholic Mass, Baptist services, Jum'ah prayers, and several volunteer-run Bible studies. Unlike the educational programs housed within the education department, these programs are sponsored by the chaplaincy department and primarily concern themselves with spiritual growth and development. The women around the table describe these programs as "being about the heart." One prominent program within this category is Kairos.

Previously discussed, Kairos is one of the most well-known programs in prison. It is offered by Kairos Prison Ministry International, an interdenominational Christian ministry that aims to address the spiritual needs of incarcerated men, women, youth, and their families. When Kairos comes to this prison, their gatherings often occur over the course of three days. Rylee describes Kairos fondly as a "place where the Holy Spirit roams freely." For her, Kairos "feels like a retreat where you will encounter every kind of person on the compound and come together as a unit, feeling as one." Many students in Theology have participated in Kairos at least once, and many serve as volunteers. It is generally a welcomed event by students. For some, it is because of the Holy Spirit; for others, it is because of the promise of a hot meal and fresh-baked cookies, or simply because it breaks into the mundane reality of the prison. Briar offers a less glowing recollection of Kairos saying that she was forced to attend even though she "didn't believe any of it."

As students see it, prison offers three types of programs: religious or spiritual programs for the heart, educational programs for the mind, and support groups for self-help. Theology transgresses these divides. Unlike some of the spiritual and support programs that reinforce the idea that students must fix themselves, Theology feels judgment-free. Unlike the educational programs with inflexible ways of learning, Theology feels more flexible. Though not credit-bearing, Theology provides a sense of achievement with the receipt of a certificate at a public graduation. It provides creative ways of expression and learning while teaching skills students describe as essential for living in prison: how to deal with difference, learning how to coexist and respect others who are different from you, especially when you live so close together. Theology, for these women, is about the head *and* the heart.

Getting oneself into a program like Theology is not an easy feat. When people arrive in prison, they are told that the administration or staff are the primary sources of information. But that is not true for the students in Theology. "If someone wants to learn about programs in prison, the best way to find out is from other people trying to live in prison. Sure, some counselors will introduce people to programs, but it varies and is more the exception than the norm." Years ago, people used to put flyers on dorm bulletin boards announcing programs for all to see. But like so many other things, that does not seem to happen anymore. "You have to want better for yourself in order to get connected to programs," Cate explains. "You have to want it. You have to make it happen."

Programs like Theology give people a sense of accomplishment, a way of recognizing their ability. Especially for those "with time" (long sentences), programs like Theology provide ways of cultivating and enhancing self-esteem and creating a sense of normalcy. "Having some normalcy is good for me. Before Theology, I soared up and down, big swings in mood and outlook," a student named Mena explains. "Now I spend my time working, teaching, and attending school. Before Theology, I had a closed mind. Now, I have an open mind to understand others' views. It's also helpful to still be in the know and to be able to have intellectual conversations with coworkers."

A student named Nikki discusses other vocational programs she participates in, programs she believes will be helpful for her once she gets out of prison. "I'm getting lots of certifications that will be helpful outside like learning to operate the forklift." This southern prison has several certification or on-the-job training programs including small engine repair, auto mechanics, auto paint, woodworking, cosmetology, electrical wiring, welding, food service, educational and library aides, culinary arts, dog grooming, and more. Theoretically designed to increase the likelihood of an incarcerated person's ability to make a living wage post-release, these certifications are difficult to obtain for most people. Nikki can participate in these programs because she will be paroled. But for lifers, these programs are hard to come by. Though she praises her certifications for their possibility to assist her economically upon release, Nikki praises her time in Theology for different reasons: "It has been helpful for making me more open to other people's religions and different backgrounds, and for forming new relationships. Theology sort of opens up new doors where you are relating to people you wouldn't normally relate to." Mena describes Theology as "a place of productivity in a place that is truly designed to break a person down, to make them inhuman. I can say I'm still human, I still have a voice."

Theology is different from many of the other religious programs offered in prison. Described as "more worship based, and more fully Christian, most religious programs in prison share a Christian message." Though Theology is offered by Christian seminaries and primarily reads Christian perspectives, Theology is viewed differently. "In Theology, we're studying." I find student attempts to distinguish Theology from other religious programming intriguing. Take Nikki, for instance. When she comes to

Theology, she says she can "kind of set my beliefs to the side and academically learn."

In many ways, I am not surprised at the distinction students make between Theology and other religious programming. From the time most students step foot inside the local jail once they are sentenced, they "have a Bible thrown at them, and someone preaching to them." Religious discourse is given to them, spoken over them, and even used to judge. Seldom, if ever, is it a topic for critical debate and discovery.

Theology is many things to these students. Theology is for expanding your mind, getting out of ignorance, and learning for yourself versus relying on what someone told you. Theology is opportunity. It is a chance to stop being so superficial and get a deeper understanding of yourself, to find yourself. Theology is deciding not to allow your mind to go to mush, a decision to stay away from "nonimportant" conversations and turn instead toward conversations that matter. And to Mena, Theology in prison is how you "be not conformed," echoing the words of Romans 12:1.

To Mena, every prison should have a Theology program because "an idle mind is a sad waste of time. I have always loved God with my heart, but through Theology I have learned to love God through my intellect. Personally, the program has assisted in normalcy behind these walls. In an educational setting, I have a normal mindset like I have at home."

Students believe that Theology broadens ways of thinking, allowing people to live better with one another. Karisma had this to say about Theology:

> The program has challenged my way of single-mindedly looking at who God is and what God expects. That means a lot to me because it has allowed me to appreciate the realization that I don't have everything figured out and probably never will. I have learned that not knowing is okay and also that everyone's point of view counts. What stands out for me is having an opportunity to just come and discuss the realm of possibilities on God. The Theology program is for anyone who wants to study and learn, grow and expand on the knowledge of God.

> The prison is a place where it is easy to become stagnant, so having a program that explores different avenues of knowledge, that challenges us to question any and everything, can create confidence within individuals that they can do and rise above many more challenges in life.

Theology provides a place where students can come together with, in CJ's words, like-minded people. It is a place of progress amid stagnancy. Overwhelmingly, Theology is about growth.

Meet Scott, Hope, Sister, Morgen, and Spirit

Friday the 13th, during one of the hottest Julys on record, would be the smoothest running day this summer. The morning Theology classes came and went without disruption, and now I make my way to a classroom across the hall to host another conversation with students. Scott, Hope, Morgen, Spirit, and Sister are already seated around the table when I arrive, in what sounds to be an intense conversation about military recruitment and service. Four of the five women in the room have a child or sibling in the military. I enter the middle of a debate about whether the military is beneficial or burdensome. Someone is arguing that military service can offer important benefits, especially financial ones, to people who otherwise would not have them. No one disagrees, but someone points out that money is often "dangled" in front of people without much discussion of the responsibility required or the reality that lies ahead. As I take my seat around the table, the conversation ceases as they look to me to begin.

Each woman has been in prison for less than ten years, but all are lifers under the thirty-year rule. Scott, Hope, and Sister are in their fifties and sixties, while Morgen and Spirit are both in their thirties. Scott grew up on the East Coast in "a Black middle-class family that had it pretty good." Hope is a salt-and-pepper, wiry-haired woman raised in the "Southern Baptist South." Sister has lived all over North America but was born and raised in the Caribbean. Under the thirty-year rule, none of these women will be released from prison before their late eighties or early nineties. Morgen and Spirit are younger in comparison: both in their early thirties. Under the thirty-year law, Spirit could possibly be released before her sixty-fifth birthday, the youngest in the room. Though Morgen is also in her thirties, like Spirit, she is serving consecutive life sentences of thirty plus thirty. If she believes the paperwork, she will serve a minimum of sixty years in prison.

The reality of life imprisonment is sobering to hear, but none of these women who are relatively early in their sentencing seem to despair of the facts. Their images of a good life are filled with family, memories of the past, and hopes for their future. Scott shares an image of herself with her parents, siblings, and uncles on vacation. Sister draws a picture called *My Island Home* and depicts herself lounging on the beach with a piña colada. "This picture shows what I want to do when I get out," she laughs as she explains her hopes of rediscovering the island she has long left. Morgen draws an image of her family seated around a dinner table, twelve people in all, including her son, who is currently finishing basic training for the Navy. She calls it *My Happy Place*. Similarly, Hope draws a picture of herself and her husband on a family picnic surrounded by their children and grandchildren. Spirit declares that there is no way a single piece of paper could fit everyone in her family as she shares an image called *Family, Sun, and Fun* of her grandmother cooking and people playing in the nearby water.

These women are convinced that their memories turned hoped-for futures are possible. Sister and Scott believe it will take persistence and perseverance on their part; Morgen believes it will take dedication and discipline. "For me, it will take self-will to resist my old rodeo life. I enjoyed the family dinners [referencing her picture] but liked fast money more." Morgen describes an earlier time when she made "big money" working in the rodeo earning between $50 and $90,000 for a win. "It was my addiction; it's something I battle with a lot." Morgen acknowledges that the rodeo lifestyle remains a temptation for her but contends that she will do everything to avoid it. As Morgen talks, it becomes clear that she believes she will be released as early as this summer. "I'm fixing to go to court this summer."

Spirit's hope to be surrounded by family again will "take faith in the unknown, in what hasn't happened yet." She believes that the problem that led to her incarceration was a bad choice of people. "Now, I want to have faith in myself, to leave more mature, and pass on wisdom to my kid, to build a better life," she explains. She knows on paper that she has a life sentence but quickly says, "I don't believe in my heart that I will do this time. As of now, it is on paper, but it is not in my mind." Spirit has decided that she is not accepting her life sentence as an actual truth about her life. A life sentence does not mean what it conveys. "I don't claim it," Spirit says. Instead, she proclaims that she will keep her dreams open, hold on to memories of family, and hope in the process.

The women around the table affirm Spirit's optimism with a depth of certainty that differs from lifers who have been in prison longer. "I know in my heart I'm going to get out," Sister says. "I have it as my visualization, and I use that to get through the day, every day. I'm in my sixties, but the Bible says we get seven-score and seven." Sister was in her twenties when she left the Caribbean. She says that after having children, she gave her all to them. Now that they are grown, Sister wants a life for herself. "It's time to focus on me and give myself the treatment I deserve. Being in here doesn't matter," Sister states confidently. She can still have a life of her own, even with a life sentence.

Perhaps to justify the optimism that so thickly surrounds us, Morgen interjects that some people in prison get life without the possibility of parole at all. "At least none of us are in that category. God is the God of miracles," she adds. I wonder if she would have uttered those words if people with life without parole were seated around the table. I find myself thinking again of Aminah.

"You have to keep hope. There *is* nothing if you don't have hope." I smile at the fact that it is Hope speaking these words. "If I give up the hope of getting back to my family, what point is there?" Hope refers to getting out of prison, hope in the reality of parole. "The Theology program helped me keep my sanity. Otherwise, I would just be going over and over everything." Theology gives Hope something to think about other than worrying about when she will get out. On paper, Hope is not scheduled for the Transitional Center until she is 114 years old, and I realize that Hope, like Morgen, is also serving a consecutive life sentence. Nonetheless, Hope expects that she will return to court and get out. "Then I can have the picnic with my grandkids."

Scott sums up the sentiment of the room nicely: "You have to frame your life with the words coming out of your mind," she tells us. "Some of my family say that I need to accept the fact that I have a life sentence. But no, I cannot live without hope."

Finding Hope and Comfort in Theology

For Hope, Theology helps her to resist the despair of having a life sentence. It gives her something to focus on, something to orient her thinking. As the conversation continues, I learn more from these women about other ways that Theology helps them.

Spirit shares a story I have never heard her discuss before. It is about losing her daughter. "I was lost in my grief of losing my daughter, asking why, why, why, why, God? What did I do that was so bad to deserve this? Am I being punished? I didn't find [answers to] all of the whys in Theology, but I did find a lot of comfort." Spirit says she found some answers, namely that God did not do or will her daughter's death. "I'm at a better place; I'm not so strangled by grief anymore," she says. "I didn't find a lot of answers, but I found a lot of healing. I found myself and now I want to be helpful to others in their grief." Spirit shares that over time she found a calmness of spirit and has replaced anger and resentment with love and joy. Now she wants to advocate against domestic violence, which I assume is related to why her daughter died. Spirit wants to honor her daughter's life through advocacy. "This will make my life meaningful."

Sister remembers being excited when she was accepted into Theology. A practicing Muslim, she wanted to learn about different religions and was quickly intrigued by the other things she learned, such as restorative justice. "I wrote a letter based on my restorative justice class and gave it to the governor, the commissioner, and three parole board members," she says. The governor of Georgia visited the prison to attend the GED graduation ceremony. It is common for government officials and administrators from the Department of Corrections to show up on such occasions and have their pictures taken for local newspapers, evidence of the "good things" taking place in prisons. "I thought it would get me in lockdown, so I told my roommate to pack my bags in case anything happens. I hid the letter in my pants, so it couldn't be seen. The governor helicoptered in and had his own secret service security with him. After the event, I walked right up to him, which stopped him, the secret service, and CERT in their tracks. [CERT refers to the Correctional Emergency Response Team. They differ from other officers; imagine people who look like they belong in SWAT.] But the governor said, no, let her come. And he took the letter and handed it to his wife." Sister is beaming as she tells us the story of her bravery. It seems of little importance if the governor or his wife read the letter, and there is no way of knowing if they did. For Sister, it is the act itself that she is proud of. "What I live for now is to see my fellow inmates get out. I will continue to use the power of the pen to do this." Sister's letter explained the importance of restorative justice and lamented the harsh realities of prison life. She hoped her letter would make a difference. "If [being in prison] is what the Most High has willed for me, I will do this until He decides otherwise. But I wouldn't have known I could do this without the Theology program." By this, Sister means her ability to use writing to make a difference in someone's life.

Sister: From Jesus to Malcolm X, Jum'ah to Theology

Sister does not describe her upbringing as particularly religious. Her father, a government worker in the Caribbean, never went to church. Her mother taught her to "go to church and love God." As she neared her preteen years, she began attending a Pentecostal church with her mother, which she did until she left the Caribbean. Later in life, she encountered the *Autobiography of Malcolm X* and was drawn to an image she saw of him dressed in all white. Malcolm X reminded Sister of Jesus. "I connected what I was taught about Jesus, with how he looked wearing white, with how we are supposed to pray." Sister is speaking of images of Malcolm X after *he* transitioned to El Hajj Malik El Shabazz and embraced Sunni Islam. "One day I saw a group of brothers dressed in white—like in the book! One approached me and started talking. They were teaching." The one who spoke to Sister would eventually become her husband and the father of her children. "They were from the Islamic Hebrew Mission and were teaching doctrine. I converted to Islam and took the Shahada. I was in full khimar for thirteen years; no one knew what I looked like." After several years, Sister's marriage dissolved faster than her practice of Islam, which would also eventually cease. She said she stopped practicing slowly. It began when she was instructed by the masjid to stop wearing the khimar for fear of being targeted (this was after the 1993 World Trade Center bombing). She went from full khimar to no head covering at all. She tried to keep the practices of Islam going at home by teaching her children to pray, but without her husband, she did not believe she understood enough about the faith to teach her children well. "I blame my husband for not teaching me more. At that time, it was women in the back, men in front—he could have taught me more, and then I could have taught the kids more. I tell everyone, I didn't really understand the concepts fully until I came to prison. That was when I started reading the surahs and learning more."

Sister did not practice Islam again until she came to prison, but not immediately. "When I came to prison, there was a sister here from Pakistan. It jerked my memory back. She'd ask me when I was going to come to Jum'ah." It took Sister nearly two years before she would find her way to Jum'ah, long after the sister from Pakistan was released. It was in Jum'ah where she met K, a student in Theology. On any given Friday, one-third of the students attending Theology classes are Muslim. Mornings are spent in Theology, and the afternoons are spent, more or less, in Jum'ah.

The Qur'an invokes the importance of Friday as a sacred day of worship in a chapter called "Al-Jumu'ah," meaning the day of congregation, which is also the word for Friday in Arabic. Jum'ah refers to Friday prayer or congregational prayer. Until recent months, the Muslim chaplain dressed in colorful khimar would join us in the school hall in the afternoons. While we hosted afternoon classes, she gathered Muslims (or those interested) for prayer. The prison revoked her volunteer privileges, leading the students to believe that the prison (and chaplaincy) is biased against Muslims. Even so, by law, students must be permitted to pray and eat halal, so students continue to gather on Fridays to pray.

Sister was in her fifties when she came to this prison, and when she arrived, she decided that after all that time raising children, this was her time to think about herself. She applied for the Faith and Character dorm and was there for fourteen months, where she facilitated groups and reentry activities. Public-facing reports about the program suggest it equips participants to "choose alternatives to criminal thinking and behavior through emphasis on spiritual, moral, character development, and life skills training."[7]

While Sister was in Faith and Character, she pursued academic educational certification starting with Adult Basic Education (ABE). The Department of Corrections lists several academic education programs available in Georgia (including literacy programs, GED preparation and testing, charter high school, and even braille) though access varies by location. Sister completed her GED and one trade: small engine repair. "It took me a year, and only two of us finished. But I like to finish what I started." After completing these programs and meeting K in Jum'ah, Sister applied for Theology. "I didn't want my brain to stop. In Theology, I found out I could write, which I had never known! In Theology, I started to realize I could do something. After that, I got into the gospel choir."

Sister believes that Theology opened a door for her to explore other religions and help her figure out where she belongs. "It did a lot for me. I tell people sign up, and it will take them places. I wish there was an Advanced Advanced! It makes you think outside the box. And it does a lot—especially for lifers." Over the summer, Sister mentions several times how she never would have found out she could be a writer if she had not come to Theology. It started in a class on spiritual writing where an instructor left one single comment on her paper: "You are a good writer." For Sister, this is never something she considered for herself. "I didn't know I had that. If I get training, I could be a *really* good writer." Sister imagines writing persuasive pieces like the letter she gave to the governor. "And creative stories," she adds, "like the one I wrote for Scandalous Women." The Theology class Scandalous Women (a title that received more than a few raised eyebrows from the administration) considered how crime and sin are conceived and expressed in a variety of women's writings from Charlotte Brontë (1847) to Zadie Smith (2012). Sister used postcolonial and feminist analysis to examine how crime and sin are used as frameworks to define, subjugate, and at times liberate women in varying historical, social, and geographic contexts. "I wouldn't change this time for anything—I've learned so much. And learning to be with women—so talkative! I need to put in earplugs sometimes," she laughs. For Sister, time in prison is spent on herself, developing and nurturing her own hopes. She has decided not to take this time for granted. After all, as she says, "If I'm able to get out, I have grandkids I have to go and raise up!"

Lessons from Theology

The idea that being in Theology is connected to investing in oneself is an important and recurring theme. Theology helps Sister see herself beyond the role of a mother, as a writer and an advocate. Other people around the table share additional lessons they learned in Theology, beginning with Morgen.

Morgen admits that she had no interest in doing Theology when it first began in 2009. "I was very angry and just wanted to fight. I would bust you in the side of the head back then." She laughs now, the image hard to imagine. "But the chaplain *read my spirit*, called me in, told me that I needed to apply, and handed me the application. On the interview day, I was pissed off because I didn't want to be there, but I ended up getting in. I was early on in my sentence then, and initially I did the program just to pass the time. I figured to myself, *I might as well do it; I'm here for life anyway.* And besides, I had a list of unanswered questions."

Over time Morgen's outlook on the program changed. "I found out there was a closeness between women in the program. We missed seeing each other every week." Morgen believed a true dedication formed between people in the program, and she started to bond with people, which caused her confusion. "That's personal dealings, and you're not supposed to do that; it'll get you in trouble," she thought. Personal dealings are usually associated with inappropriate relationships between outsiders and people in prison, typically involving contraband such as drugs, cigarettes, or cell phones. Morgen interpreted the feelings of connection between herself and the instructors as wrong. "But I felt love and compassion from the program, and I just started having compassion for other people! But then I had Theology on the anniversary of my daughter's death and stayed in the school hall over lunch. I could talk to the Theology volunteers about it, which was a turning point for me, when I could talk without being judged."

Morgen found Theology classes to be self-reflective and engaging, mentioning Hip Hop and the Psalms, the Revelation of John, and a course on Discovering Self: Identity and Personal Theology as some of her favorites. Before Theology, Morgen saw herself as a closed-off person, but her opinion changed when she wrote a poem about *taking the mask off*. "People encouraged me to do what I wrote about. I'm still kind of an introvert, but I'm opening up more. I can act a fool, and people laugh, but I know they're laughing with me and not at me. I learned that my ideas *do* matter. My ideas aren't stupid but interesting. I'm learning to ask why people are doing things if they're acting out. I am not so narrow-minded about other people, not so judging. I have become more open." For Morgen, Theology is more than something to do on Fridays now. "This changes people's lives; it helped me shift out from my anger and gave me something to look forward to."

Spirit finds herself nodding in affirmation. "You can't do prison by yourself. You need a group of people to help you get through it." Spirit tells others that they can find these people in Theology. "Everyone wants real connection, not just the kind of relationships built on exchange where I'll do this for you if you do this for me." Transactional relationships are common in prison. "Theology is a place where you can be safe to be yourself." Sister agrees, adding that people want a place where they can show their potential, find their voice, be heard without being overlooked, and sometimes even learn things that may help them with their cases.

Spirit discusses the culture of people who have been in the Theology program for a while. "[They] welcome new Theology people into the program. You can feel it when everyone is getting ready on Friday mornings. We want our appearance to be good." People take special time with their hair and makeup on Fridays. "People want to be welcomed into that type of fold, into a space that is open." "Our behavior here is different," Hope adds, "not like what happens on the compound. We want to protect Theology."

Scott describes Theology as providing "the strength to go through this journey . . . or just the week." Scott was an ordained minister before coming to prison and had trouble figuring out how to adjust. "I wanted to be with my peers. It was hard to deal with things in here, and I needed assistance—like when doctors need someone to care for or do surgery on *them*. It was easy to minister to others but difficult when things were happening to me." Scott applied for Theology, hoping to find some assistance. "I do this not so much for the religious part but for being able to interact, let anger and sadness out, and interact with people who have *somewhat* like minds."

Scott is not the only minister to participate in Theology. There have been others, like a woman named Mickey. Mickey was ordained in the Sanctified Church in the 1980s. "Everyone was doing it. It didn't really hit me until my early twenties. People would meet me and say, 'You look like a pastor!' or 'You look like you could be an evangelist!' Once I saw that Bible, I said, 'I'll do my calling.'" Mickey feels that Theology has helped her in her ministry. "The Sanctified Church doesn't know about the

Septuagint—they'd say, 'Septua—what?!' Theology has helped me be more formalized." Mickey believes she needs formalized training because "even if you're called, you're dealing with people who want structure and training, and training shows in your message and in your delivery." Since being in prison, Mickey has been able to experience other churches through the traveling choir. "One time, Chap took us to a Pentecostal church—it was full of Caucasians. Where I'm from, Pentecostal meant Black! The Sanctified Church was the place with all the Black folks shouting, where you could get fish fries and chicken dinners. So, when we go to this Pentecostal church, I'm like, 'Where are all the Black folks?!'" Mickey laughs at the memory before being critical of the preaching she witnessed there. "Something is wrong if your level of preaching is still at 'Jesus loves you, now shout to the Lord!' Preaching needs more substance." This is one reason Mickey takes Theology classes inside. "I need training. It has its place. I can't be on Facebook looking like a fool because people will laugh at you. Now, I look at the exegesis of the text. It helps me structure my sermons better. It's one thing to have enthusiasm; it's another thing to do so where people can relate and connect. On Facebook, you don't want your message to be part of folly. You have your training and that leads to a more effective gospel message." Mickey sees Theology as preparing her for more effective ministry when she gets out, a ministry she believes she will pursue, at least in part, on Facebook. While Theology helps Mickey with her practice of ministry, it is, at least at this time, more of a respite for Scott, who still struggles with being in prison.

Hope also struggled when she first came to prison. "When I got in, they told me they didn't have any programs for me." Hope had a high school degree and a bachelor's degree in business. "There were no college-level classes available, so Theology was an intellectual exercise I actually qualified for." Hope continues to take Theology year after year. "I do this for the ability to talk about something other than how bad the food is or how mean an officer is! That all gets redundant fast." Like Morgen, Hope was angry when she arrived, but her anger was not violent, she clarifies, at least not toward others. "It was inside me—and it was just so much anger. It took me a long time to realize I had to forgive what was done to me in order to be forgiven for what I had done. Now I see these kids coming in who need love and compassion and I try to get them interested in Theology."

These women not only have meaningful memories of Theology as a community, but they also have meaningful memories from specific classes. "I will always think about the Ancient Math teacher—he's just wow, so enthusiastic. When he left, we were sad; it felt like something had been taken away. One thing he taught us I will never forget is the Fibonacci series and about how it's everywhere, in lots of things in nature. Now I look at fruit differently! I'm always looking around, trying to find it."

For Spirit, it was AVP, the Alternatives to Violence Project. "It was healing for me. I'm a social preacher; I like to be around people." AVP is an interactive program that uses embodied pedagogies as central to their operation. "Class always involved movement and hands-on activities, which were healing. I got addicted to it and did it lots of times. AVP helps break down barriers between people and helps us address our emotional needs. It taught me communication and conflict resolution skills that I take back to my dorm. We have AVP days now in our dorm, where we play the games we learned in AVP after we do cleanup. Everyone participates—it's festive. It's fun." Spirit is one of many people in Theology who takes what happens in class back to the dorms to share with people who otherwise do not have access.

For Morgen, it was a class she took on the book of John. "It had already been a favorite book of mine; I still have all my notes. We had quizzes and a final test! The teacher wanted to make sure we really understood. I got excited about my paper for that class and ended up writing a really long one. I eventually sent it to my friend. I said, 'Here, look at this paper I wrote.'"

"I think we discover hidden talents here," Hope interjects, picking up on a recurring theme. "The program helps build self-esteem and confidence. I remember one time when, years ago, we had a study hall to learn Hebrew. We were writing it on the board, and the director came in, and she was like, 'Oh, I didn't know Hope knew Hebrew!' And it was just this moment of 'Ahh, yes, see what I can do!'" Hope is glowing as she recalls the moment. "I always share what I'm learning with my son—he writes Hebrew in his letters to me. He wants to learn Klingon! And now there's a computer language he wants me to learn." Hope's son is also incarcerated.

Hope on Faith and Justice

According to Hope, Theology gave her a whole new perspective on life. "I learned that everything I learned as a child was wrong. I had to apologize to my sons because I taught them that way too, because that's how I had been taught. I went to church and had a Christian home but never explored theology in depth as I have now. And I never thought I should contribute to other people's lives. I had no sense of injustice or sympathy for those inside because of what I had been taught. But it is nothing like that. There are so many beautiful, amazing women who don't deserve to be here."

Hope grew up in a religious family that constantly changed churches. "It was always Protestant, though. We were living in the North. We went to a Baptist church when I was very young, then a Pentecostal church, then a Nazarene church. We never went to a Lutheran church. It was a small town—the kind with one stoplight and five churches." Hope went to whatever church her mother picked for the moment. "She went to all but the Catholic one. Mom was anti-Catholic. Really, she was anti-anything she didn't understand. She believed the rumors. Churches then often taught against other churches. It's worse down here [in the South]. Catholicism is more mainstream up there," she explains. Going to church was mandatory growing up for everyone except Hope's father, who only went on special occasions like holidays.

Hope describes her mother as strict. "Mother was against alcohol because there was alcoholism in her family. Father worked a lot, and people often gave him alcohol as gifts. He would only drink maybe one glass per year. Mom didn't allow us to be around it. We didn't play cards unless it was Old Maid. It was easy to get your mouth washed out with soap. There was no cussing. Mother was against a lot of things."

When Hope had her own children, she also made sure they attended church. "I tended toward Baptist churches. I just picked a church near our home that didn't follow my mom's teaching. It was more modern. They didn't see any harm in a deck of cards, but a Ouija board still wasn't welcome!" Hope prides herself in teaching her children the importance of education. "I encouraged them to study. During the summer, I told them to pick a subject, and they would get books from the library and read. They would ask questions, and I wouldn't always know the answer, but I'd know where they could look for it!" When I learned this about Hope, I began to understand more deeply why she is passionate about Theology.

"Being in prison has changed my views of the world. I found that much of what I was taught, especially by my mother, wasn't necessarily true from the world's perspective. It's helped me mature my own thoughts. You know, we take our embedded theology and add to it."

Hope thinks much of what she believed about the justice system came from her mother. "In prison, I learned that ignorance of the law is no excuse. I didn't know things about the law, that I could have been arrested. I learned that innocent until proven guilty is a lie. My mom used to say that only bad people go to jail or that people in prison are a danger to themselves and others. That's not true. My perspective has shifted."

This is not the first or last time that Hope will mention losing faith in the justice system this summer. No person of color utters anything similar. I suspect that it is not because they think the justice system is fair, but because they never expected it to be. Hope's expectations of justice are rooted in her identity as an upper-middle-class White woman. "As upper-middle-class people, you can delude yourself to thinking that you can't do anything to get arrested. People don't know how close they are. Don't tell me it's by the grace of God you're not here or that people in prison did something you could never do. I thought that. I was wrong." Hope is unsure if her mother's religious background contributed to her misinformation about the justice system. She thinks it could be possible. "My mom's church experiences all taught [false lessons about justice]. They were good Baptists, steady people. In her experience, no one in their family got in trouble with the law. I was a good, law-abiding, tax-paying citizen—what happened? It was a rude awakening. My thoughts on the justice or injustice system have changed. I had a sense of entitlement toward Calvinistic thinking. It's how I was brought up. My mom came from Puritan stock, frontiersmen."

The theology Hope learned as a child was "strict and limited," but her time in prison has expanded her beliefs. "I have broader experiences and thoughts. I understand more diversity in religions and enjoy having a diversity of religions in the classroom—it makes a better class because different people bring different ideas. I have learned that people don't all believe the same things about Jesus; not everyone believes what I was taught. Other beliefs are interesting and have broadened my outlook in numerous ways."

Hope is passionate when she talks about her life, but her disillusionment with the justice system fires her up the most. "I was never taught that the system is so wrong. Listen to these lies I was told: the police are your friends, authority is to be trusted, you are innocent until proven guilty, there are only bad people in prison. When I was in the county jail, the first thing I said to my mom after I saw her was, 'You lied!' She did not understand. And I said, you lied about how this works. And now I understand I need to help make a change—my son sees this too; it's in the letters he's written, when we get out, things are going to be different as we cannot ignore what happens inside."

Hope believes that the average person thinks people in prison are just hardened or desperate, exaggerating what life is like inside. "But we're not. That's one of the first things volunteers learn; they look around and see someone lied to them. Sure, some dangerous people are here, but many have mental health issues. They need to be in a care facility. No one should be here for drugs. They should be able to go to rehab as often as it takes—my sister did AA three times before getting it right. And if you're in here for money crimes? It only costs the government more money for you to be here. The whole system is messed up and we can do something about it, I am sure we can, but it's going to take a lot of people on the outside." Hope does not want people outside to help out of pity. "Do not feel sorry for the women in here; help because it's <u>wrong</u>." Hope has channeled her anger at the justice system into a desire to advocate for people in prison once she gets out.

Freedom and Flourishing

I look around the table at these women. Everyone is confident that there will be life after their life sentence, a life they sketched just over an hour ago. For these women, a good life is a life of freedom, but freedom is more than the absence of physical restraints. "There's a kind of freedom we have inside," Morgen says, "whereas the officers, a lot of them are trapped in themselves." There is an interesting disagreement between Spirit and Morgen on the relationship between freedom and flourishing. For Spirit, you must be free to flourish. But for Morgen, freedom comes as you flourish. "If you're flourishing, you are blooming, you are in a constitutional state of growing!" Whether freedom is required for flourishing or not is less of a matter for the other women around the table. But everyone is emphatically sure that freedom and flourishing, happiness, joy, and wholeness—all are possible in prison. How? "Well, it starts with yourself, by working on your inner self." The final word is this: "You have to learn, learn everything, and then keep learning."

Theology Saved Me

For many students in Theology, participating in educational and religious programming has a redemptive tone, serving as motivation for and proof of growth, change, and improvement. This theme was particularly relevant among lifers. Back in the room with Aminah and her colleagues, the conversation reveals several programs these students have found helpful over the years. Several I have mentioned before, like the Faith and Character dorm, the dog program, and the new college-in-prison program. Aminah mentions the Inside-Out program, which brings undergraduate students from one of the Atlanta universities to study with students who are incarcerated. For

Karisma, the computer technology classes have been particularly enlightening. "You can take the computer classes as part of the other trade programs, and I'm grateful because I haven't been exposed to technology because I've been in here so long. It helps me not feel so lost when it comes to technology." Karisma and Brouhaha begin a back-and-forth conversation about the benefits of participating in programs. They describe the programs as providing motivation, rehabilitation, knowledge, purpose, confidence, and autonomy. For these women, programming in prison provides spaces where they are "free to do our *own* work and critically use our *own* mind."

Zakkiyah chimes in, "I think of myself like a piece of clay. Every class and group I've participated in has been molding me, starting from the bottom and piecing my way up." I wonder if Zakkiyah has a vision of what she is being molded into or if she is open to becoming whatever emerges.

"So, what about Theology? What has this program been for you?" I ask.

Aminah immediately responds, almost before I can complete the question. "The Theology program saved me," she stated, and not metaphorically. "It was strictly enforced so you couldn't do it and go to lockdown. I got kicked out five times," she says, smiling. "But I eventually got mad and became determined to show Chap a different me. I went from 'going to jail' every other week, to about once a year, to not at all now." Like many programs sponsored by the chaplaincy department, participants cannot have disciplinary reports and remain in the program. It is a stipulation of participation, a code of conduct agreement of sorts. Aminah's previous behaviors were incompatible with the requirements of the program. When she received a disciplinary report or was sentenced to lockdown (isolation for punishment), she would be suspended from the program and need to reapply the following year. While Aminah never admits such, someone in chaplaincy or Theology must have had a soft spot for her to keep allowing her to reapply.

"I felt like I knew what I believed when I started, and now I'm questioning more," Karisma explains her participation in Theology, and her tone suggests that what she is describing is good. "The program challenges me to think about what I want to believe in. I've gotten to where I wouldn't call myself an atheist, but the sky is the limit—I can challenge myself to understand new ideas rather than just passively reading the Bible. I like that the program has diverse classes also. It's good to challenge yourself."

Brouhaha agrees. "A lot of people struggle with the hard questions about God and religion, especially here. People sign up for the program to get answers, but it doesn't give you that. What it does give, though, is the ability to think. You learn to embrace your own reality and not take things at face value." Brouhaha has summarized several prevalent themes heard throughout the summer. The first is people often come to Theology seeking answers to unanswerable questions. *Why did this happen to me? Am I a bad person? Can I be forgiven? Why didn't God save my child? Where is God when bad things are happening? Why didn't God make my life different?* People come to Theology seeking answers often to find more questions. According to these students, Theology does not promise answers to life's enduring questions. But it does develop the capacity to live *with* the mystery of life, in ambiguity and uncertainty. Unlike other educational or vocational programming, Theology facilitates a way of thinking where answers are not the only or most essential outcome of learning. In Theology, students situate their questions alongside other enduring questions throughout time, wrestling with how other people have attempted to make sense of their lives, even as they attempt to make sense of their own. Sometimes the conclusion is what Morgen expressed: "I didn't find answers, but I found a lot of healing."

Brouhaha credits the Theology program with nurturing the ability to think. A recurring fear among students is the fear of losing their minds and being unable to think for themselves. In many ways, the regimentation and discipline of prison dulls the senses and constricts agency. Prison, as a death-dealing institution, cultivates a mistrust in one's ability to decide. Prison teaches a person not to trust themselves. Theology, however, is one place where students feel equipped to think for themselves. If, as

Aminah suggests, freedom involves the ability to choose and, as liberationists proclaim, the ability to self-define, then Theology provides space for this expression of freedom to emerge.

Brouhaha continues, "Theology is something constructive to do and keeps people out of trouble. And, for me, it made me more comfortable with not having a religious label," though Brouhaha currently describes herself as agnostic. "Sometimes in here, you kind of feel like you've been thrown away. But seeing volunteers who have care and concern makes me feel confident again, like we're still part of the world." Brouhaha has named a third theme—being in Theology helps students feel connected to the outside world. Beyond the administrative staff, Theology volunteers change each quarter ushering in new teachers and new experiences. The consistency of some volunteers and the fresh faces offered by new ones make students like Brouhaha feel connected to a world outside prison.

"Okay," I transition, "Theology applications are coming out again soon. What would you say if someone asks you why they should apply?"

In rapid succession, their answers come unhindered: "It will change your life! It will take your life down a different path. . . . It will change your mindset. . . . It helps you focus and find purpose. . . . It gives freedom of mind, in more ways than one. . . . It challenges what you believe. . . . It enhances who you are becoming. . . . It's the least judgmental place you'll find in prison."

Anticipating hesitancy about the perceived workload, their pitch takes a preemptive turn. "People don't want to do the work, but I will tell them that it's not unbearable. You can write the papers; you don't have to be a number one scholar." This idea that Theology does not require academic perfection or exceptionalism, I have heard before. Karisma explains that people are often intimidated because they feel they cannot do the work and are scared to try. She is committed to helping anyone who wants to enroll.

"My mentee wants a safe haven," Zakkiyah continues, "and has been asking me where to find it. I tell her Theology, and now she's always on me about it. Theology is a safe haven of the mind." For Zakkiyah, Theology is "where you are allowed to have a voice" and where you can put your voice and emotions onto paper. Jordan agrees. "I'd tell them that Theology is a place you go on Friday and actually feel like yourself again."

"I would tell people that you can be as creative as you want in Theology," Brouhaha offers. "I did a final project on Jesus being a magician!" I laugh along with Brouhaha, remembering her class presentation where she tried to perform a levitation of another student to suggest that Jesus' miracles can be read as a form of magic or illusion.

"I tell people that you'll go in with one thing and come out with another!" Karisma resounds, stating what she believes to be an asset, while another student suggests that many people could have a problem with that very idea.

Aminah imagines speaking to her Muslim peers. "I'd tell them that it's not all Christian. I'd tell them about the electives and different classes." Over the years, because of people like Aminah sharing their experiences of Theology with their peers in Jum'ah, each Theology admittance season sees a growing number of Muslim applicants. Aminah continues, "Christianity tells you to believe one thing—the Jesus story. Islam says to believe all the books—which means you must have knowledge of them. Even if they are not all *true*. After all, in every lie, there's some truth. . . . You have to learn how to eat the whole fish and spit out the bones." For Aminah, studying theology in a Christian program is not incompatible with her beliefs. In fact, she believes that Islam encourages learning about multiple religious traditions, including those that differ from its tenets and practices. "Theology is a good stepping stone for me. After all, I've always wanted to get a master of divinity," Aminah adds something that surprises all of us. "It's about knowledge for me."

Zakkiyah offers her perspective to accompany Aminah's. "A word I would use for Theology is *opening*. Theology is an opening of the mind, mentally and emotionally, and I've learned how to speak about things. Theology gave me a voice I didn't have before." Agreeing with Aminah, Zakkiyah adds that converting to Islam taught her to respect all forms of learning. "I appreciate that there was no judgment about my religion in the program." Pausing for a moment, Zakkiyah looks off in the distance before she continues with an example. "Theology is like our dance at graduation; you can combine aspects from all different religions!"

Dancing Is Theology

A few months before this conversation, we hosted a graduation celebration for graduates of the basic and advanced certificates. While the graduation programs have always included opportunities for graduating students to speak, this was the first time we added a segment on the program titled Theology Thru Dance. Zakkiyah (Muslim) and Cate (Christian) worked together to choreograph an original dance to embody and enact what Theology means to them. They recruited several students from the program of various ages, races, and religious commitments to perform with them during graduation. The music, like the dances, varied in style and sound to signal differences in cultures and beliefs. From liturgical dance set to contemporary Christian worship music, African-inspired movements to syncopated drumming, to a dance using bright ribbons set to Indian-inspired beats, students allowed the music and their bodies to move in and out of different traditions, with no one tradition dominating the performance. This is how Zakkiyah views Theology: inclusive, embodied, and intercultural.

For graduating students, Theology graduation is a time to demonstrate their accomplishments, show family they have grown and changed, and be proud of who they are becoming. But the ways that Theology students choose to express themselves do not always sit well with the prison administration. Graduations in prison are opportunities for administration from the Department of Corrections and sometimes state government officials to come to the prison. News articles will be written, and photographs will be taken to communicate "the good rehabilitative work of the department." However, the type of performance Cate and Zakkiyah constructed did not receive accolades from the prison. Prison administration desires two things at graduation: praise of Jesus and praise of the Department of Corrections.

If we are light on either, I can rest assured word will be delivered to chaplaincy questioning the "Christianity" of our program.

But for Zakkiyah, it is precisely the welcoming of different beliefs and perspectives that makes Theology a place she returns to and a place she continues to recommend to her peers, Muslim and otherwise.

Not everyone insists with Aminah that Theology saved them, but most would agree that Theology changes their lives. When asked about the importance of Theology, Ilillana from a previous group had this to say:

> The information you have access to, the classes and resources, are priceless [here]. Prison, by nature of the beast, is restrictive not only in body but also in mind. The ONLY place to exercise the muscle of your mind is to become a functioning, dedicated member of the Theology program. Words cannot describe what the Theology program means to me. It means an end to the stagnant mind I'd had for fourteen years. Theology means perpetual motion within myself for mental, spiritual, emotional evolution. From artistic/creative endeavors, to self-awareness, to questioning who am I, who are we, I've learned to look at the picture outside myself. To be conscious of self without being absorbed in self. I have learned how to reach people and how to change lives through both scholastic and literal creativity. This prison must have a theology program. For those who have a GED and cannot get into college, it is the only avenue for continued mental enrichment. A mind is a terrible thing to waste, regardless of society's restrictions on the body.

Claira admits that she enrolled in Theology just to get a picture with her friend. "They said they took pictures at the Theology graduation. I got that picture and I still have it, and now that friend is gone. But Theology changed my life. Nothing had asked me to be DR-free before, to be accountable. I held myself to a standard and I haven't had a DR since I started the program."

For Arabella, it was her love of learning, especially religious studies. "It was how I grew up; my family all had different religious backgrounds."

Uncharacteristically full of energy, Harold in that same conversation added spiritedly, "I let people see ratchet, ghetto, fabulous, but what I never show people is that I'm smart. One day someone said to me, 'Why don't you use it [your smarts]?' I like to challenge myself. I don't do DRs, I don't get in trouble. I want to do charter school to flip my GED to a diploma. When I see the class list for Theology come out, if there's something I want, I gotta have it. I learn more. I want to know more."

Ilillana continues, "When I get out, I don't want to speak to someone and they know I was in prison, like if I'm talking to them on the phone. I'm afraid that I have a sign on my forehead stamped 'felon.' I think those of us in Theology feel more assured that this won't happen. Theology is the only thing offered for us [lifers]."

"I feel like it's [felon sign] a shirt you always wear, though," Claira says, challenging Ilillana.

"Yeah," Ilillana rebuts, "but I can put another shirt on over it."

Harold replies that he now has influence and is seen as a leader. "I talk to the young people, they'll be ready for me to do something real crazy, and I'll be like, oh, got to go get this book, let's go to the library. They're shocked! If I said, let's go fight, they would be ready for that, but books?!?" Harold laughs. "But if I fight, what can I accomplish? I want to know everything there is to know, everything. I want to know about computers. I now know freedom is possible through learning."

Arabella sighs. "People assume we all come from a life of crime. But I had a great life before, but prison gave me a deeper meaning."

Despite living in a social death institution, students in Theology have hopes for a good, meaningful life. Though not preferable, many believe that some version of their good life is possible in prison. Students define their good lives in many ways; commonly, it involves the qualities of belonging, dynamism, and freedom, which students actualize through creative, pragmatic, and mundane actions. The Theology program is one place in prison where students attempt to create some version of a life worth living; one place where students try to create a life that matters.

We never quite get used to the weight of the stories that we carry throughout this research. As we leave the prison, we begin to reflect on what we heard, making connections to other groups and ultimately, each of us, wondering what to do with it all. I leave considering what these stories imply for the practice of theological education both in prison and beyond.

5
FOSTERING LIFE-AFFIRMING PRAXIS IN THEOLOGY

> The very process of education depends upon what Débora Junker describes as embodied redemption. The process does not simply point to redemptive ends, but is itself a redemptive movement.[1]

> Redemptive communities are spaces pregnant with the possibility of sharing experiences, of weaving new narratives, a space for a communion, for dialogue, for cooperative work, for inclusion, and for learning as a process of change—the visible anticipation of God's peaceable kin-dom.[2]

As I sift through a summer of stories, images, and artifacts, I reflect on what I learned about students in Theology and what they taught me as an educator of religion and theology. When students are in Theology, "it feels different." A Theology classroom becomes an "elsewhere" that transcends the concrete reality of prison. With knowledge that students participate in Theology, in part, to create lives of meaningful connection, dynamism, and freedom, against the threat of a social death institution, I went back to the Theology classroom to begin to name the practices that affirm students' hopes for their lives and asked how, with greater intentionality, Theology might become *more* life-affirming. The task in this chapter is to name the life-affirming practices in Theology. Life-affirming practices are those that free people from the constraints of oppressive systems of social death, alienation, and degradation. They are practices that normalize living as embodied and relational and that indict social death as a form of sin. In the death-dealing context of the prison, the life-affirming practices experienced in Theology make people feel human again. The working conception of a good life that emerged throughout the summer, as belonging, dynamism, and freedom, became a frame through which the life-affirming practices of a classroom can appear. In this chapter, I invite you to return with me to the beginning, to the Theology classroom where I ask: What are the classroom practices that affirm life, thus redeeming (rescuing and freeing) life from social death? What are the classroom practices that might nurture belonging, dynamism, and freedom?

A Theology of Life-Affirming Practice

Theologically speaking, life-affirming practices are how human beings mediate God's redemptive reality, where redemption is understood in a liberative theological sense as the divine work *and* human social practice of freeing life from oppressive control. With God and humans as agents and copartners in redemptive work, redemption is something people receive from God and extend on God's behalf for the experience of others. This understanding of redemption is not primarily an otherworldly concept but a concept rooted in the here and now.

A life-giving understanding of redemption can be found in the original meaning of redemption used in Hebrew scripture, where redemption refers neither to life after death nor to a millennial hope but rather to a concrete act of freeing enslaved people from bondage. In her work on feminist theological perspectives on redemption, Rosemary Radford Ruether argues that ancient understandings operative in the Hebrew scriptures define redemption socially as liberation from bondage. Redemption is thus a this-worldly social definition, mainly egalitarian, overcoming gender and class hierarchy.[3] This structural understanding of redemption as liberation from present conditions of bondage is prominent in liberation theologies. In Black theologies, redemption is always connected to earthly liberation from oppressive, dehumanizing forces. Any promise of future redemption without the subsequent struggle against forces of oppression in the present is fatalistic hope and death-dealing.[4] In womanist theologies, redemption is never only individualistic but always concerns social reality and communities.[5] Liberation theology contributes to an understanding of redemption that is more life-giving in prison, where redemption may be defined as the restoration of human dignity and relationality through diminishing harm and oppression. This is God's redemptive desire for the world.

Life-affirming practices participate in God's act of redeeming the world by bringing about glimpses of a good life as best as we can discern and interpret it. They perform an in-breaking of grace into a death-dealing world in the here and now, even if incompletely. Life-affirming practices in the classroom encourage participants to experience a way of life that unshackles from the burden of shame, frees from the degradation of dehumanization, and creates space to live into a vision of life beyond the confines and constraints of social death. When practiced over time, life-affirming practices build resistance to oppression and cultivate skills needed to survive and defy the systems that confine and constrict human life. They embolden participants to live into a vision of life informed by God's desire for goodness and justice. When education participates in God's liberating mission, it becomes a redemptive movement, an embodied redemptive experience.[6]

Characteristics of Life-Affirming Practice in Theology

With common elements of students' hopes for meaningful connection, experiences of growth and transformation, and freedom as our frame, life-affirming practices in Theology can be identified as those practices that encourage relationality, possibility, and liberation. In theological and pedagogical terms, these practices are characterized as relational, futuring, and liberating.

In the anthology *Being Black, Teaching Black*, Lynne Westfield writes about the importance (and difficulty of) relational pedagogies—incarnational approaches to teaching that seek justice—in countering the dehumanizing ethos of many classroom environments.[7] Relational pedagogies are those that "teach toward humanness," where participants of the learning community strive to "hear and understand each other and the subject at hand for the healing, redemption, and liberation of all." They stand in stark contrast to pedagogies of domination "where students are silenced and merely recipients of information for memorization in [*supposed*] politically neutral encounters." Life-affirming practices in Theology are those that nurture growth-fostering relationships with self, others, and for some, with God—practices that reconnect people to themselves, their communities, their histories, others, and the Divine. As I considered the Theology classroom, I looked for practices that encourage listening, understanding, and sharing of stories.

Life-affirming practices are also *futuring*. Educational scholar Maxine Greene calls theological education a process of futuring rather than the insemination of ideas. By futuring, Greene means going beyond the now and pointing toward future possibilities. Greene asserts that "transformations are conceivable, that learning is stimulated by a sense of future possibility and by a sense of what might be."[8] Life-affirming practices create a sense of possibility and generate an imagined future toward which to live. Futuring is more than an obsession with life to come, it is a preoccupation with making the future possible now, even if only partially and momentarily. In the Theology classroom, I looked for practices that generate a sense of possibility and newness; practices that promote growth, creativity, and imagination.

Finally, life-affirming practices are *liberating* because they free participants from the totalizing effects of oppression, even if momentarily. Pedagogically, liberating practices stand in contrast to practices of indoctrination or subordination. In emancipatory learning, liberating practices focus on enabling persons to recognize lacks or deficiencies so they may learn to repair and transcend them. Emancipatory education seeks to equip students to understand the history of the knowledge structures they encounter, the paradigms structuring thought, and their relation to human interests.[9] Liberating practices participate in the praxiological process of identifying, naming, and transforming conditions that distort, diminish, or delimit human possibility and potential.

The liberating nature of life-affirming practice has both spiritual and social dimensions. Emilie Townes asserts that liberation aims "to restore a sense of self to the oppressed" by cultivating a strong sense of pride and self-worth.[10] Accordingly, the spiritual dimension of liberating practice "concentrates on the acquisition and possession of power that enables the individual to be her or himself fully."[11] *To be fully human* is the spiritual telos of liberating, life-affirming practice. Theology student Cate defines redemption in a way that recognizes this liberating character. To Cate, "redemption is becoming the self you were meant to be." In the Theology classroom, I sought to identify practices that might promote students to "feel normal" and "feel like a human being again."

If the goal of punishment through social death is to create nonbeings, strip agency, and stagnate growth, then the goals of life-affirming practices must resist and transform these acts into practices that humanize, increase opportunities for agency, and contribute to growth and human flourishing. Life-affirming practices create and operate within alternative spaces in prison, transforming classrooms into hush harbors and sanctuaries.[12] Life-affirming practices are informed by a discerned vision of God's goodness and justice, supporting a life we believe God desires for God's people. When learning communities enact life-giving practices in death-dealing spaces, they participate in God's redemptive project, liberating human suffering with experiences of grace. Life-affirming practices promote the fullness of human life, even in contexts of social death. A classroom can become a respite for redemption.

Six Life-Affirming Practices

Identifying life-affirming practices in the Theology classroom requires an interpretive theological logic that assumes that altered social conditions—feeling like dying to feeling like myself again—is an indirect sign of God's redemptive presence.[13] I suggest that the scenes from the Theology classroom that opened this book point us toward some of the practices that embody a socially liberative notion of redemption and that affirm life as theo-pedagogical practice. These practices are not exhaustive, but they are paradigmatic of what I have observed over the years, practices common to Theology that make Theology feel like an elsewhere in prison. These practices include coming together, choosing names, considering one another, critical questioning, creating theology, and celebrating growth.[14]

Coming Together

The obstacles to attending Theology classes in prison can be numerous, and attempts to capture the difficulty in writing cannot do justice to the magnitude and depth of harm experienced by the pervasive and systematic attempts to thwart human gatherings for education. In Theology, the practice of coming together is the intentional act of showing up to be with others. In prison, coming together is a defiant stance against the alienating and isolating mechanisms of social death. Coming together nurtures intentional presence and conveys that each person (their body, history, stories, and experiences) matters in the classroom. In the opening scene, teachers reinforce the importance of each person's presence by calling each person's name, even those who are not there. The physical act of gathering takes effort and cultivates an implicit pedagogical lesson that presence matters.

Community formation is essential to the humanization project. It happens mysteriously and is so complex that it eludes formula. It does, however, happen over time through "the power in small but important elements of being together."[15] The practice of coming together is the practice of intentional community cultivation. Community formation practitioner Peter Block suggests that community precedes "from an expanding shared sense of belonging."[16] Block also suggests that communities are built from the assets and gifts of its citizens in places where people choose to come together to produce a desired future.[17] Theology is a gathering of people of diverse backgrounds and perspectives coming together over a shared belief in the possibility of healing and growth in prison. The future desired by Theology students is a future with meaning and purpose. In this sense, they are a community of practice—a group of people who share a concern or a passion for something they do and who learn how to do it better as they interact regularly.[18] The "something" students are learning to do, in this context, is to resist the threat of dehumanization and fulfill a desire for growth and development.

The values that structure coming together are accountability, trust, and respect. Coming together in a prison classroom is one of the few places where students actively *choose* to cross boundaries of difference to be with and learn from one another. In most other places (dorm, work, etc.), students are forced together with little consultation. Though students complain about forced togetherness, they actively choose to be together with the diverse and disparate group of people who come to Theology.

Coming together in prison is an act of resistance and fortitude. It takes perseverance to combat the desire to stay inside, avoid guards, and be targeted for getting an education. It is a risk to gather. But bell hooks reminds us that building community "requires vigilant awareness of the work we must continually do to undermine harmful socialization that leads us to behave in ways that perpetuate domination."[19] Within these actions, certain values emerge: the respect of bodies, trusting relationships, safety, accountability, and being seen. These values are the internal results of the practice of coming together. They are good in and of themselves.

Central to the idea of coming together is the pursuit of belonging. Theologian John Swinton defines belonging as the need to be missed. In it, I find helpful guidance for theological educators wanting to "come together" to cultivate belonging against a death-dealing system:

> To belong you need to be missed. People need to be concerned when you are not there; your communities need to feel empty when you are not there. The world needs to be perceived as radically different when you are not there. Only when your absence stimulates feelings of emptiness will you know that you truly belong. Only when your gifts are longed for can

> community truly be community. When we belong, people long for our presence in the same way as the prodigal son's father longed for the presence of his wayward son (Luke 15:11–32) and in the same way that God longs for us to be present with God. It is in precisely these ways that we are called to long for one another in the midst of all of our differences. Such longing is not discovered through politics or argument, but only through the gesticulations of God's love towards human beings as they are embodied within the lives of those who have come to know and love God and who long for the love of God to become the pivot point for the redemption of the world. To be included you often have to conform or have your context conformed to some kind of relational, social or legal norm. To belong you simply have to be noticed as yourself. To be included you just need to be present. To belong you need to be missed.[20]

Swinton suggests that belonging is not "a matter of choice, freedom, individuality, justice or equality. Such things are consequences of belonging, not movements towards it. We need to belong before we can understand the true meaning of such things as autonomy, freedom, and self-representation."[21] Following Swinton here, cultivating a sense of belonging is thereby the first step in resisting and transforming social death's attack on identity and freedom. Cultivating a sense of belonging, in this vein, requires cultivating opportunities for students to be missed, to know one another, and to feel safe. It requires asking about Tonia and Monica even when they are not in the room.

As a participant with students in the classroom, I have witnessed and felt the transformative and transcendent nature of being together in the classroom. It *feels* different. Once the door closes and class begins, our bodies change. We relax. No longer concerned with the gaze of an officer, we are simply together. Students express this sensation as "feeling normal." The Theology classroom becomes a site of normalized humanity, and it is good.

Choosing Names

Recall again the scene from the Biblical Foundations class where I called the names of each student: Fly, Storm, and Fierce. These are not the formally recognized names of anyone residing in this prison. However, on the first day of class, we ask students two questions: what they want to be called and what pronouns we should use. These acts are common today in many university classrooms, but they are a particularly radical act in prison. The official modus operandi of the Department of Corrections states that all inmates must be referred to by their government-identifiable names. While this is fine for many students, there are those who have an aversion to their given name and prefer another. To honor this decision, we transgress the official rule and call students by the names they choose for themselves.

The practice of choosing names, or self-naming, is a radical act. Endorsed widely across liberation theologies and critical pedagogies, self-naming is a liberative, emancipatory practice that acknowledges that freedom comes with the ability to name oneself. Freedom is the ability to choose. The intrinsic value in naming is the affirmation of personal agency. Students engage in agential identity construction that allows them to name themselves apart from an inmate identity. They engage in a retrieval of individual uniqueness and an ownership of themselves.

One student, whom I will call Darla, once declared aloud, "You know who I am out there, but in here, you can just call me Darla." In class, Darla was able to be a version of herself that was distinct from the person she was outside of the classroom. In class, she is not the guarded self that must always perform for survival and protection. She can live into a version of herself that she desires, emerging, embodying, and enacting a hoped-for self. The name "Darla" represents the self she can be when she is free from the threat of death-dealing practice.

Educator Paulo Freire contends that there is power in naming one's context, and educator Maxine Greene argues that a naming praxis contributes to one's becoming or humanization.[22]

The practice of choosing names signals not only that a person can have the agency to choose the name they desire for themselves, but they can also express agency in naming the world as they experience it.

Considering One Another

Considering one another is a practice of care and refers to the acts of listening and sharing stories and perspectives with one another. "Theology is one of the only places to have a decent conversation all week!" A Theology student offered these words once when I asked her why she keeps attending classes though she graduated many years ago. This student suggests that the ability to have a conversation about something important is humanizing and constitutive of feeling normal. Another student suggested that Theology opens a depth of conversation that does not naturally occur in everyday life. "I've been living with these people for a long time but never knew this much about them." Considering one another goes beyond gossip and chatter and involves significant conversations about matters of life and death. It is more than listening to other opinions; it involves taking a view from a different standpoint and learning to appreciate other perspectives. These are skills that are lifesaving in contexts of social death.

The essential elements of considering one another are conversation and dialogue. Ethicist and educator, Rev. Dr. Katie Cannon observed that classrooms which function with a communal logos necessarily promote dialectic-dialogic conversation.[23] bell hooks adds that conversation is the "central location of pedagogy" and can promote humanization when it values and affirms the knowledge and wisdom present in the common vernacular of the students.[24] Dialogue supports a relational pedagogy as it emphasizes relations between participants in the class (between students and between students and teachers). Dialogue is fundamentally relational, refusing to let students "wither away in isolation."[25] It saves students from the fear of loneliness and abandonment and promotes a relation of empathy nourished by "love, humility, hope, faith and trust."[26] These virtues of love, humility, hope, faith, and trust are values intrinsic to dialogue.

Through conversation and dialogue, students practice hearing one another, understanding different viewpoints, and speaking back in a way that acknowledges the other without suppressing the self. Mary Pellauer contends, "If there's anything worth calling theology, it is listening to people's stories—listening to them, honoring and cherishing them, and asking them to become even more brightly beautiful than they already are."[27] In this regard, the practice of considering one another is a necessary theological practice. Womanist and feminist theologians argue that "theology is shaped in dialogue between and among ourselves—who we are, what we are doing, together or separately, in concert or at odds with one another. The study of theology takes place in this dialogue, between and among ourselves, as well as between ourselves and the authors of the texts as we engage them in our disparate life situations in our common educational praxis."[28]

In considering one another, students learn to respect multiple types of knowledge and to see their knowledge and the knowledge of the community as valid and valuable both as sources of truth and as valid sources of critique. Students practice offering their reading of the world and they recognize that there are other ways of reading the world different from their own.[29] They, in turn, not only learn to recognize and deal with differences in the classroom, but they are also able to do so in their broader lives.

For example, in Biblical Foundations, we engage a historical critical reading and study of scripture. The first activity students do is to name what the Bible is to them and where these beliefs come from. Over the course of the quarter, we explore multiple ways of reading the text: the world behind, of, and in front of the text. One student, Briar, had this to offer:

> My grandfather always throws the Bible at me as if that is the only thing he can talk about. I think he does it because he wants to make sure I'm saved, whatever that means. I used to ignore him, but the last time I was able to have a conversation about Genesis. I told him there were two creation stories. He about lost it.

What was told as a humorous story is evidence of a deeper transformation in how Briar has used her study of the Bible both to consider her grandfather's standpoint and to challenge it. She was able both to consider his care for her as the impetus for his behavior but also to assert her own agency and knowledge into the conversation such that biblical speech was no longer one sided. Considering one another in dialogue, through conversation, and by working together creates a critical attitude.[30]

Critical Questioning

"What kind of person doesn't have questions," Creative Justice declared, more as a statement than a question. CJ expresses a significant truth captured by liberative pedagogues about the centrality and importance of questions to the project of humanization. Freire admonished educators that we cannot "as imaginative, curious beings, . . . cease to learn and to seek, to investigate the 'why' of things. We cannot exist without wondering about tomorrow, about what is 'going on,' and going on in favor of what, against what, against whom."[31] For Freire and for CJ, critical questions are fundamental to living.

Critical questioning refers to the deconstructive work of meaning-making and is fundamental to moral life. It gives rise to a critical consciousness that resists temptation toward the indifference, stagnancy, and decay that petrifies the human mind. The term "critical" refers to the human capacity for self-reflection and the task of engendering multiple ways of reading the world to expose systems and structures of power and relation. Critical also refers to consciousness-raising, awakening, or "perspectival grasping," a mode of moving outward, coming in touch with the world. Critical questioning includes acts of "imagining, intuiting, remembering, believing, judging, conceiving, and (focally) perceiving."[32]

The consciousness shaped by critical questioning leads to what Greene and other philosophers have termed "wide-awakeness." To be wide-awake is to perform the conscious endeavor to elevate one's life by becoming aware and intentional in action.[33] The goal of wide-awakeness, Greene insists, is to encourage students to pose "searching and significant questions with respect to what conditions them . . . to learn how to recognize mystification."³⁴ Wide-awakeness therefore has a "concreteness"; it is related to being in the world:

> By the term "wide-awakeness" we want to denote a plane of consciousness of highest tension originating in an attitude of full attention to life and its requirements. Only the performing and especially the working self is fully interested in life and, hence, wide-awake. It lives within its acts and its attention is exclusively directed to carrying its project into effect, to executing its plan. This attention is an active, not a passive one. Passive attention is the opposite to full awareness.³⁵

Critical questioning is an active process of discernment and curiosity. In Theology, the dominant source of critical questioning is lived experience; students' lives and the contemporary world are the most poignant and frequently engaged site of critical questioning. In addition to reading the human web of life, students engage in critical questioning of written texts and art. Students engage what is considered "traditional" academic theological texts, but also and often with more rigor and curiosity, they practice theological reflection using other literary forms such as fiction novels, nonfiction autobiographical writing, and film. These materials act as other "bodies" in the room, giving the class additional perspectives and experiences from which to reflect. Various modes of art have also been useful in this process. Music and dance are other sources of reflective content. All these modes act as sites from which students can begin the process of critical questioning and reflection.

Most students do not come to Theology with "academic theologians" to dismantle. They come with theologies of culture, church, community, and the US justice system that must be critically analyzed and assessed. Even while class activities will, at times, deconstruct traditional academic resources, the primary focus is to develop the tools and transferable skills needed to deconstruct and reconstruct one's own theologies.

Critical questioning as deconstructive work seeks to contribute to wide-awakeness by fostering the skills needed to see, name, analyze, and transform contexts. Greene argues that reflection requires that we be awake to the world and conscious of our own consciousness; that we embrace ambiguity and that we engage the process of thinking about our thinking. Though the prison is, in the words of bell hooks, "a context that was established to socialize [persons] to accept domination," students suggest that the critical questioning in Theology offers them space to practice alternative ways of thinking and living.[36]

Critical theological questions elude clear, quick answers, making them essential for understanding, surviving, and transforming contexts of social death and oppression. Peter Block asserts, "Questions that have the power to make a difference are ones that engage people in an intimate way, confront them with their freedom, and invite them to co-create a future possibility."[37] Furthermore, Lynne Westfield proclaims, "Interesting questions are those which invite the Holy Spirit to show herself in new ways, act in new ways, bless us in new ways. Interesting questions are open and honest—they demonstrate curiosity, empathy, and hope."[38] Theological questions are never exhaustive and always contextually driven. They provide persons resisting social death with a constant source of active, generative content. Questions create space for something new to emerge. Questioning is a futuring and liberating practice. "The future is brought into the present when citizens engage each other through questions of possibility, commitment, dissent, and gifts," writes Block.[39] In communal dialogue, questions require each person's participation to bring about meaning. As a source of spiritual intrapersonal development, critical questions inspire wrestling with personal belief and action, and they unsettle us. Finally, critical questioning leads to a critical awareness that is fundamental to the project of emancipatory education.[40]

Creating Theology

Theology is about imagination. To James Cone, theology "is symbolic language, language about the imagination, which seeks to comprehend what is beyond comprehension. Theology is not antirational but it is nonrational, transcending the world of rational discourse and pointing to a realm of reality that can only be grasped by means of the imagination."⁴¹ He goes on to write that "theology is thinking about God who escapes our comprehension. . . . Theology is paradoxical language with no easy answers to ultimate questions, and that we need imagination to think about transcendent reality. What we call 'God-talk' is imaginative language, like poetry, not rational language."⁴² A social death institution cultivates disimagination, limiting a person's ability to imagine a life of dignity, a life with and for others, a life with God. Creating theology nurtures the imagination needed to resist and counteract disimagination.

Creating theology stands in contrast to a practice of receiving theological information.⁴³ Instead, creating theology is a constructive and generative practice that students engage with their bodies and their own language.⁴⁴ The theologians of the Mud Flower Collective suggest that "to consume passively theologies produced by others is not to do theology. . . . We have been discovering theology as a creative act that incorporates our present experience and is resourced by our roots—the traditions from which we have come. . . . The most important features of the creativity are that it is foundationally oriented toward justice and that it is relational in character."⁴⁵ The production of the Genesis creation stories described earlier is an example of how students use their bodies and creativity to do theology in the theological classroom. Students also create in various art forms such as poetry, dance, spoken word, drawings, and even radio podcast. Theology here is something that is constructed more than something that is read or memorized.

The central feature in the practice of creating theology is creativity. Practical theologian Courtney Goto defines creativity as "the capacity to make what exists into something new or enlivening to oneself. Where there is peace and freedom, creativity flourishes. However, creativity also assists in survival and resistance because it summons possibilities, grants agency, and fosters hope."⁴⁶ Even though forms of oppression place limits on creativity, Goto suggests that *critical creativity* is the "brightest hope for transformation."⁴⁷ What Goto points to is the dialectical tension between creativity and freedom. On the one hand, creativity thrives in freedom. However, it also assists and persists in times of oppression, disenfranchisement, and confinement. Angie Titchen and Brendan McCormack define critical creativity as a pedagogical strategy in which the assumptions of the critical paradigm are blended and balanced with the creative for the purpose of human flourishing. They suggest that human flourishing, in critical creativity, focuses on maximizing individuals' achievement of their potential for growth and development as they change the circumstances and relations of their lives.[48] The critical in critical creativity links the deconstructive work of critical questioning to the constructive work of creating theology. After the cognitive or embodied critique of deconstructing a context, situation, crisis, contradiction, or dilemma, students then reconstruct it for the purposes of transforming practice. This kind of reflective reconstruction is a creative process that uses imagination and expression to access embodied, tacit knowing.[49] Together, critical questioning and creativity form an embodied cognitive critique of practices of degradation, a way of deconstructing them and then reconstructing possibilities. When used to do theology, it helps students deconstruct and reconstruct belief systems about God, self, and others in ways that incorporate the traditions from which they come but that also point toward a future hope that begins to manifest as they create.

As a practice, creating theology is a relational task and often requires students to work together in its production or to bear witness to what is produced. For example, each year new students present capstone projects to members of the Theology community. Dance, spoken word, and critical essays are applauded by the community. After each presentation, we hold space for anyone present to share what they appreciated about the work and how it inspired them. Creative expression from members of the community yields a fruitful and thought-provoking discourse that brings theology to life. The practice of creating theology in prison not only contributes to meaning-making, but it also contributes to community-making and a sense of belonging.

Critical theological understanding assists students in making a distinction between punishment and the sin of social death, between needing to be accountable for their crime and being unjustly assailed by oppressive, inhumane prison practices that systematically degrade and dehumanize. Theological study enhances students' ability to discern, analyze, and construct religious speech for themselves. In criminal justice contexts, where religious concepts and punishment practices are intertwined, critical theological engagement that affirms human life and mediates God's redemptive reality over and against the prison's is a redemptive practice.

Celebrating Life

An education in social death is an education in despondency, joylessness, and overall apathy about life, so celebration is an essential component in redeeming life from the grips of social death. Celebrating life describes the practice of observing, commemorating, and affirming instances of growth, development, accomplishment, and positive change. In Theology, the ultimate moment of celebration occurs during the annual graduation where students, with cap, gown, pomp, and circumstance, graduate in front of family, friends, and visitors. The community comes together to celebrate student accomplishments. For some students, Theology graduation is the first and only graduation they ever attend. But moments for celebration also occur in smaller and ordinary ways, through the applause given after a classroom performance, through words of affirmation written on a homework assignment, through hallway conversations praising a fresh idea. In death-dealing contexts that refuse to honor the life force of individuals, recognizing and celebrating a person's creativity, resilience, persistence, and intelligence is an act of defiance.

Celebration is also how a learning community in a social death environment practices joy. Willie Jennings speaks of joy as "an act of resistance against despair and death . . . a work, that can become a state, that can become a way of life."[50] Jennings defines joy from the lives of Black church folk who understand what it is to be dominated and subjugated. Joy work that emerges within domination begins with renouncing despair;

it is a decision to "do something with the given reality instead of simply giving in to oppression, suffering, pain, and fear." In the words of a Theology student, it is the recognition that "this is prison. This is one step away from death, but it is not death. You can still live here." While students throughout the summer insist that joy is possible in prison, they were reluctant to define joy explicitly. Instead, joy is the feeling of a good day, of caring, safe relationships, of an interesting conversation, of seeing your loved one. The joy that emerges in prison is an "oppositional joy [that] humanizes dehumanizing conditions."[51]

Be(com)ing a Life-Affirming, Redemptive Learning Community

The redemptive practices of coming together, considering one another, choosing names, critical questioning, creating theology, and celebrating growth are just some of the many practices that seek to redeem life in prison. These practices form the substance of redemptive pedagogy that can in turn shape a redemptive community. Evelyn Parker, in her work with incarcerated girls, identifies four elements of a redemptive pedagogy that adequately summarizes the pedagogical goal of redemptive practices. These practices facilitate embodiment of God's tangible grace, include activities that engage the whole body, engage in practices of critical questioning (emancipatory learning), and, in contexts of death and degradation, cultivate the experience of fun.[52]

The practices engaged in the Theology classroom are corporately produced practices that students and teachers do together and that shape a way of life that extends beyond the classroom. This way of life has the capacity to address the fundamental human needs of the persons engaging in the practices—needs for belonging, growth, and freedom. In this light, these practices mediate God's goodness and grace, becoming places where the power of God can be experienced.

If theological education in prison seeks to be *more* life-affirming, it should intentionally cultivate healthy opportunities for students to belong to themselves and their histories, to others, and to God. In an institution that cultivates alienation and distrust, pursuing education is one place where students create networks of belonging. Remember Morgen's story about how the loss of being with her own family made it difficult for her to make connections when she arrived in prison. She self-isolated, barely speaking for several years. For Morgen, Theology became a place to establish trusting connections, a place to be missed. It became an elsewhere in prison to practice knowing and being known differently.

A pair of students in Theology once shared with me, "We're actually really good friends—besties—but we don't talk about it. If someone finds out that we're close and they get mad at one of us, they can report us to an officer, lie about something, and get one of us moved to another dorm or even shipped to another prison. We finally live in the same dorm, I don't want to mess that up, so we only talk this much on Fridays when we're in Theology." This confession highlights the fear and protective nature with which students treat their relationships. Re-created social networks in prison can be sources of good, but they can be fragile and used as a tool of control or punishment by a death-loving institution. The Theology classroom becomes one space of creating and maintaining social connection—an otherworld inside prison, a place to be otherwise, a place where it is safe to belong, a place to be missed.

Beyond establishing relationships *in* prison, life-affirming praxis may help restore relationships with people *outside* of prison as well. Remember CJ and Briar. Their participation in Theology encouraged them to reconnect with their religious family outside of prison (mother and grandfather, respectively). Students like Hope used theological study to connect with her incarcerated son at another institution, and several women used their involvement in Theology to encourage their younger children to do well in school. Both in how students re-create relationships inside and restore relationships outside, life-affirming praxis creates gracious communities where people can get to know one another, listen to one another, and miss one another.

In addition to maintaining opportunities to come together, life-affirming learning communities should focus on interpersonal skill development as part of its mission to redeem human relationships, such as conflict transformation, dealing with differences respectfully, and learning how to live with strangers. For many students, prison was the first time they met someone from a different religious background. For nearly all, it was the first time they had ever lived in such a diverse context across racial, religious, and sexual lines. "I never met anyone who wasn't Christian before I came to prison. Now my bunkmate is Muslim, and I want to know more about both Christianity and the Muslim faith," one student remarked when she described why she was interested in Theology. Not only do students come to theological study to learn about the God of their tradition, but they also come to learn about other religions and other ways of conceiving of divine relation in the world. Learning to listen to opinions that are radically different from your own, and do so with care and respect, could make the difference between living a decent life in a diverse and dynamic community and living a detrimental one.

If theological education seeks to be *more* life-affirming in prison, it should also address the human need for mental and emotional acuity and stimulation—dynamism. For many students, Theology is one place where they can experience the dynamism of living. Students testify to the joy and sense of accomplishment they feel when they learn new concepts such as Hebrew, ancient arithmetic, and hermeneutics. "I never knew I could write until I came to Theology," one student said. This student is now applying for her associate degree from a program offered at the prison. The writing, critical thinking, and analysis skills gained from the educational endeavor contribute to a sense of growth and accomplishment as much as they promote mental stimulation, a sense of self-esteem, and transferable skills. Intellectual pursuits build confidence and are a healthy way of coping with prison life and proving to oneself that their life indeed matters. A commitment to intellectual well-being involves learning the community's needs and providing means for each person to actualize their potential.

Finally, if theological education seeks to be more life-affirming in prison, it should equip students with a safe space to be critical, angry, and honest about the system that confines them. Whether freedom is defined as a mindset, a practice of moving forward, or the experience of physical liberation, students create ways of experiencing this freedom in Theology. Students in Theology use theological study to make sense of their past, present, and possibilities for the future. It gives them space to reflect on the religious and social language used to condemn or sustain them. For example, a recurring theme among students was either a total distrust or a growing disillusionment with the criminal justice system. "When I got locked up, I lost faith in the justice system," one student remarked. Another student said that everything she ever believed about fairness and justice was a lie—that everything she thought she knew about the type of people in prison was false. Students are suspicious of the claims made about them in the justice system. These claims often use religious language.

Educators embracing life-affirming practices in the prison classroom are conveners, relational leaders creating spaces and experiences for others to engage in liberating, soul-making, and futuring practices in a world that desperately needs them. These are practices we do with students, not for them. We cultivate classroom spaces where these practices can be explored, examined, critically engaged, and improved. Together, students and teachers participate in practices that are part of God's redeeming work to shape us, healing our alienation and brokenness. We are all students learning fresh with new grace and mercies each day what it means to do justice, love God, walk humbly, and love one another.

Theology and education are intertwined in practices, but the practices embraced in the prison Theology classroom are not necessarily Christian or religious practices.[53] Rather, they are pedagogical practices with theological meaning. Theologically speaking, these pedagogical practices are part of the liberating practice of God. In their contribution to practical theology, Craig Dykstra and Dorothy Bass define practices as corporately produced and shared actions that address "fundamental human needs and conditions."[54] Likewise, the liberating and life-affirming practices in the Theology classroom are not activities we do to make something spiritual happen, nor are they duties we undertake to be obedient to God. Rather, they are patterns of communal action that create openings in our lives where the grace, mercy, and presence of God may be made known to us. They are places where the power of God is experienced.[55]

Redemptive practices must be engaged again and again if they seek to have a positive, formative impact. In the words of Nancy Bedford, they are "little moves against destructiveness" that allow for the participant to experience an eschatological glimpse of a redeemed life in the here and now. Redemptive practices are an active, human way of participating in God's work of redeeming human life and the world. These practices involve a fluid, mysterious relationship between God and human action to bring about glimpses of hope amid a broken and imperfect reality.

Through intentional life-affirming and redemptive pedagogical practices, a learning community can create or encourage opportunities for participants to live into God's redemptive reality even while living and learning in contexts that attempt to deny it. A learning community can rehearse redemption as theo-pedagogical practice. In a social death institution, a learning community can help people come alive again. A learning community can become a redemptive and life-affirming community.

Evelyn Parker describes a redemptive community as one that

> symbolizes daily living that ushers in justice and peace for all humankind, all creatures, and the earth. It offers salvation and freedom from death-dealing acts of racism, classism, sexism, ageism, heterosexism, and all other sins that physically destroy and psychologically debilitate God's good creation. A redemptive community, as empowered by the Holy Spirit, rescues, reclaims, and restores all of creation to God's gift of life that flourishes.[56]

Furthermore, Débora Junker writes that redemptive communities are spaces for sharing experiences, weaving new narratives, communion, inclusion, dialogue, and hope—places for imagining together how dignity and divine love can be experienced.[57] Redemptive communities are in a perpetual state of learning. In the process of learning with and from one another, redemptive communities thus become prophetic communities according to Junker:

> The prophet's task, thus, can be rooted in the effort to promote an alternative consciousness for the people who have been convinced to accept their fate, the suffering and oppression imposed on them, by those who use an ideological discourse intended to justify their status quo. Such a task may help to re-envision realities that at first glance may seem doomed to suffering and brokenness.[58]

Learning communities that embrace and enact redemptive pedagogical practices, that locate its theological telos in a redemptive vision to diminish harm and participate in God's work to bring life to death-dealing contexts, hope to despair, and freedom to contexts of constraint, can conjure spaces within contexts of social death that can value and sustain human life. And wherever human pain and violence are diminished, there is the inbreaking of God's redemptive reality.

6
NURTURING LIFE-AFFIRMING FUTURES THROUGH THEOLOGICAL EDUCATION

> We in theological education have a special mandate to . . . develop and deploy our knowledge and the tools of our trade—beginning with an informed and active commitment to human well-being—to do what we can to eliminate (or where that is beyond our power, to diminish) human suffering. This allegiance is not simply something we prepare students to take into the world later. It must be the immediate basis of what we teach and learn and of how we teach and learn.[1]

Death-dealing educational spaces abound. What if the life-enhancing, humanizing experience of students in Theology *is* the first purpose of all theological education, not just in prisons? As a theological educator, my constructive concern in this project is how learning communities can better participate with God to bring about meaningful life in death-dealing educational spaces; how we might nurture life-affirming experiences and futures *through* theological education. While my summer was spent listening to students describe what it feels like to live in prison, their hopes for a good life, and how they make life meaningful in Theology, it was also spent reflecting on New Testament narratives of everyday restorations—times when Jesus calls people back to life from experiences with death. While restoring the believed-to-be-dead to life is miraculous, I was most interested in the role of the community in these stories, in what Jesus asks of those witnessing the restorations. In each of these stories, Jesus asks the community to participate in helping the once-dead live again. Affirming life is a communal project. These willing participants disrupted paths to the grave, restored relationships of care, believed in what was (im)possible, and removed constraints that hindered hope-filled futures. They demonstrate the theo-pedagogical goals of a life-affirming learning community. The interplay of student stories with biblical narrative provided me a theological lens with which to name life-affirming communal praxis as a theologically potent Christian responsibility, one that should direct the future of theological educational practice.

Disrupting Paths to the Grave; Restoring Relationships of Care

In Luke's Gospel, we learn of the death of a young man, the son of a widow from Nain (Luke 7:11–17). As Jesus enters Nain, he sees the mother weeping and a crowd lamenting as they carry the dead man on a stretcher. The gospel records that Jesus has compassion for the mother and tells her not to cry. He goes to the stretcher and touches the dead man. The crowd stands still. Jesus then says to the son, "Get up." Jesus calls the young man back to life, and he sits up and begins to speak, reclaiming his voice. Jesus returns a son to his mother. The bystanders are amazed and respond by praising God.

As I read this account, I was drawn to the partnership demonstrated between Jesus and the crowd. When Jesus touches the dead son, the crowd stands still. This act of pausing inhibits the progression toward the grave. By standing still, the crowd gives time for something new to occur. This momentary refusal of the inevitable gives time for transformation. The crowd participates in renewed life by refusing to complete the journey to the grave.

Any community that seeks to be life-affirming must recognize the pathways to graves and find ways to interrupt their progression. Pathways to the grave are the paths that social death paves, paths that disconnect people from themselves, their histories, communities, and senses of purpose. Pathways to the grave are educational paths that institutionalize disenfranchisement and indebt students with an impractical or inadequate education that does not provide them with tools to live better lives or enhance the lives of their communities.

A life-affirming community must believe in the redemptive possibility of someone once cast away as dead. They must create space, time, and opportunity for new life to emerge. They must create an in-breaking in what has been inevitable to give people a chance to respond to calls to live again. Like the crowd in the text, a life-affirming community will respond to new life with celebration.

The divine-human partnership demonstrated in raising the widow's son not only interrupts systems of death, but it also returns a son to his mother, thereby reconnecting and restoring meaningful relationships. Biblical scholars have written about the economic and social implications of this restoration. The son of a widow was likely the primary source of economic stability and social status. To lose her son is to lose not only a loved one but also her quality of life. There are many people in prison whose families and communities suffer because of their absence—who "watch as their family fills the gap their absence creates," to quote Cate once again. Life-affirming praxis recognizes the importance of restoring relationships as part of its commitment and connects the restoration of relationships to broader socio-economic concerns.

Believing in What Is (Im)possible

Each writer of the Synoptic Gospels tells the story of a religious leader named Jairus and his young daughter. In Luke's Gospel (Luke 8:40–56), we learn that as the leader begs Jesus to heal his sick daughter, the young girl dies. People close to Jairus advise him to give up his mission to seek Jesus' help, but Jesus intervenes. Jesus tells Jairus not to be afraid and to remain trustful. Jesus then goes to Jairus' home and takes only Peter, John, James, and the girl's parents into the house with him. In Mark's account (Mark 5:21–43), a large crowd is surrounding the house, wailing, and mourning. When Jesus tells the crowd that the child is not dead, they laugh at him. Jesus sends the skeptical crowd away. With a few select disciples and the girl's parents, Jesus enters the house and takes the young girl's hand. As he did with the widow's son, Jesus tells this daughter to arise or get up (*talitha cum*). The Gospel records that she got up at once when her life returned. In Mark's account, she walks around. Jesus tells the witnesses to give her something to eat, and her parents are filled with joy.

This story of a young girl restored to life has captured the imagination of biblical scholars like Musa Dube, who sees within it a hermeneutic of life that captures the essence of some African women's ways of living. In it, Dube finds a story that embodies the arts of hope, healing, resurrection, and liberation. According to Dube, "where one walks too close to death and cohabits with the dead . . . where one lives for too long in ill-health and suffering . . . one can actually be healed. One can resurrect from death and return to life."[2] For Dube, *talitha cum* refers to "the art of living in the resurrection space . . . the art of continually rising against the powers of death—the powers of patriarchy, the powers of colonial oppression and exploitation, the powers that produce and perpetuate poverty, disease, and all forms of exclusion and dehumanization. . . . African women's *talitha cum* hermeneutics are ways of living and insisting on staying alive, even when confronted with oppressive powers that crush, one dares to rise."[3] This is a bold text, demonstrating an audacity to live. Throughout the summer, I heard resonances between the perspectives of Theology students and the ideas of daring to rise and live in the resurrection space. Could there be a similar hermeneutic of life operating in this text and among the students in prison?

I was again drawn to the relationship between Jesus and the bystanders. This time, I was struck by how Jesus reorganized the crowd. In Mark's Gospel, we read that people are wailing and mourning at the dead girl's home. The crowd responds with laughter and skepticism when Jesus offers them an alternative word of life. Some biblical scholars suggest that these wailers were professional mourners, people whose economic livelihood was attached to the mechanisms and rituals of dying—people who profit from death. Jesus asks these people to leave, suggesting to me that there is no room in a life-affirming community for those who benefit from someone's improper death. Choosing instead to surround the young girl with people invested in her living, Jesus reorders the community.

As in the previous story, the crowd has responsibility to participate in restoring life. Jesus asks the community to believe in the possibility of life after death—to have faith that death is not final. For those who could not or would not believe in this possibility, those who laughed at the idea, Jesus asked them to leave. Again, a life-affirming community requires people who have faith in the redemptive possibility of others.

Like he did to the widow's son, Jesus invites the girl to get up, and once she exercises her agency and responds to the invitation to live, Jesus asks the bystanders to give her something to eat. Some scholars suggest that eating is proof of living, so the instruction for the community to provide food is more than a command to attend to physical needs. It is a charge to provide people with the means by which they will prove to themselves (and perhaps to others) that they are indeed alive. A life-affirming community provides resources and opportunities for people to live into their new life, affirming their aliveness first to themselves and then perhaps to others. It helps people *believe* in their living, in their possibility.

Removing Constraints from a Hope-Filled Life

The final story that journeyed with me throughout the summer was that of Jesus raising Lazarus from the dead, found only in the Gospel of John (11:1–44). In the writer's account, we learn that Jesus loved Lazarus and his sisters, Mary and Martha. We might presume it is this love that caused Jesus to ignore the disciples' fear that harm would come to them if they returned to Judea where people sought to kill him. When Jesus arrives, people are mourning the loss of his friend, who has been dead for four days. Jesus weeps along with the crowd. Unlike the widow's son or the religious leader's daughter, Lazarus has been wrapped and placed in a tomb sealed with a stone. He has already been placed in the grave—death feels final. When Jesus approaches the tomb, he asks the bystanders to remove the stone. Martha hesitates and declares that the stench of someone dead so long would be unbearable. Nevertheless, the bystanders remove the stone. After speaking aloud to God, Jesus speaks directly to Lazarus, saying, "Lazarus, come out." The gospel records that the dead man comes out of the tomb, his feet and hands tied, and his face covered with a cloth. Jesus instructs the witnesses to "unbind him and let him go." The next time we read about Lazarus, he is seated at a table with his sisters, Jesus, and friends, enjoying a dinner celebration before Passover.

As with the other restoration stories, Jesus asks the witnesses to participate in the restoration of life. In the story of Lazarus, Jesus asks the community to complete three tasks: the first to remove the stone from the tomb, the second to unbind Lazarus, and the third to let him go. Because Lazarus was entombed and dead for several days, there was more work for the community to do. As with the widow's son and religious leader's daughter, Lazarus responds to the call to live, but in this case, he remains entrapped by structures and linens of death. For Lazarus to live fully, he needs to be freed from the bindings of death: stones, ties, and linens. The community's task is to get close to Lazarus and remove the barriers to living so that Lazarus can make the most of his life.

A life-affirming community must be able to identify the death-dealing systems and structures that inhibit life, diagnose their impact on members of the community, and work alongside the socially devalued to remove them, especially for those whose experience with (social) death have been prolonged. This is intimate and messy work. This summer of research was one attempt to embody this commitment even as I continue to consider how prison and learning communities can better diagnose needs and alleviate suffering. A life-affirming future for theological education requires identifying and working to dismantle (or at minimum diminish) the systems and structures that inhibit more hope-filled futures for members of the learning community and beyond.

Toward a Life-Affirming Theological Education

The stories from students in Theology invite us to consider that the Spirit of God is still at work calling people from (social) death back to life through the practice of theological education. The communal praxis demonstrated through Jesus' instructions inspires theological classrooms to do the work of disrupting pathways to the grave, restoring relationships of care, meeting fundamental and more profound social and psychological needs, and liberating people from the limitations that hinder their ability to live lives of freedom, flourishing, and wholeness. Together, student narratives and biblical illustrations model a life-affirming commitment that stands in stark opposition to the death-dealing educational practices of the prison. I conclude by envisioning the characteristics and commitments of life-affirming theological educational practice that point us toward more hope-filled futures.

Life-affirming theological education is organic. It prioritizes experience and curiosity and values being and becoming over having. A life-affirming theological education recognizes that the community has shaping power over the form and function of education and must be agile and flexible in its design. Finally, life-affirming theological education views the learner as an active agent in the learning process, receiving and contributing to the learning experience. Whereas a death-dealing education is outcome-oriented, a life-affirming approach to education is commitment focused. Life-affirming praxis is more concerned with the process of nurturing life than with a preordained outcome of what that life will look like. As such, life-affirming theological education is committed to cultivating reflexivity, where a person's identity is reflected upon and (re)constructed; creative imagining, where a community can practice imagining alternative possibilities beyond those prescribed by a death-dealing reality; and meaningful relationships, where stories are the central educational material and the connecting of stories is a central feature of the educational journey. Life-affirming theological education is committed to the performance of dignity, where people are encouraged to demand and practice freedom. Finally, life-affirming theological education enlarges vocation to encompass all forms of living, from survival to flourishing and everything in between.

The fundamental goal of life-affirming theological education must be doing justice, diminishing, and when possible, liberating people from the power of structures of oppression. We must engage pedagogical practices concerned first and foremost with life, redeeming life, and creating spaces for the in-breaking of God's justice in the present. Our task is to help students discern this vision for themselves and create it to the best of their ability.

Life-affirming education is how religious educators nurture classrooms to participate with God to restore, nurture, and promote the fullness of life for all of God's people, especially for those who have experienced the disenfranchisement of dehumanization and domination. To center life-affirming praxis as the process and goal of (theological) education is to position education as a counter-response to the death-dealing realities, structures, and systems that distort and deny quality of life. The communal praxis outlined in the gospel narratives and the prison community provides a vision of the work that theological education must do to be and become life-affirming in its purpose.

Death-Dealing Education	Life-Affirming Education

Characteristics:
   Mechanical
   Prioritizes memorization and obedience
   Values having
   Governed by overwhelming control
   Learner is a receiving object
	Characteristics:
	   Organic
	   Prioritizes experience and curiosity
	   Values being
	   Community has shaping power; agile
	   Learner is a living agent

Outcome Oriented:
   Disidentification
   Disimagination
   Disconnection
   Dispossession of dignity
   Diminished sense of vocation
	Commitment Focused:
	   Reflexivity; identity ownership
	   Creative imagining; imagining alternative possibilities
	   Cultivating meaningful relationships; connecting stories
	   Performing dignity
	   Enlarging vocation

Doing theology in prison has taught me that, as educators, we are always confronted with the task of resisting pedagogies of domination. In prison, these practices are easier to acknowledge and resist. But dominator culture is everywhere "maintaining injustice, teaching fear and violence, teaching terrorism."[4] The intertwining of theology and education in prison produced different practices for theological education to consider, practices that shape and redeem life and participate in God's work to redeem human dignity in contexts of oppression and degradation.[5] Social death practices foreclose opportunities for growth and development and are not just operating in prison settings. We must embrace a redemptive, justice-oriented vision to embolden our work as theological educators both in prison and beyond, as we ask ourselves: What does God desire for theological education in this day and time?

This project left me asking, Where else in our formational and educational institutions do contexts of oppression need to be challenged and transformed? How might theological education better participate in God's work to redeem life from death-dealing constraint *in these places*? To teach and learn toward life in death-dealing institutions is how we live out our commitment to hoping beyond hope. By attending to the lived experiences of students engaged in theological education in prison, we begin to (re)consider the life-affirming responsibility of theological education in prison, and far beyond. I suspect the future of my scholarly work and practice will continue to wrestle with these questions and concerns, challenging what and for whom theological education will be in the future.

NOTES

Preface

1. Examples include Lora Bex Lempert, *Women Doing Life: Gender, Punishment and the Struggle for Identity* (New York: NYU Press, 2016); Tanya Erzen, *God in Captivity: The Rise of Faith-Based Prison Ministries in the Age of Mass Incarceration* (Boston: Beacon, 2017); Barbara A. Owen, Joycelyn M. Pollock, and James Wells, *In Search of Safety: Confronting Inequality in Women's Imprisonment*, Gender and Justice (Oakland: University of California Press, 2017); and Jill L. Snodgrass, *Women Leaving Prison: Justice-Seeking Spiritual Support for Female Returning Citizens* (Lanham, Md.: Lexington Books, 2018).

2. In her work to articulate core themes of Black feminine consciousness, Patricia Hill Collins argues for an alternative epistemology or way of producing and validating knowledge that includes alternative sites such as music, literature, daily conversations, and everyday behavior as important locations. Collins provides a book-length treatment of epistemological truth concerns among oppressed peoples in *Fighting Words: Black Women and the Search for Justice* (Minneapolis: University of Minnesota Press, 1998). Also, see Collins' chapter "Black Feminist Epistemology," in *Black Feminist Thought: Knowledge, Consciousness, and the Politics of Empowerment*, 2nd ed. (New York: Routledge, 2000).

3. To bring together multiple qualitative accounts, I followed the basic techniques of meta-ethnography as used by mujerista theologian Ada María Isasi-Díaz. Meta-ethnography provides a process for synthesizing multiple ethnographic data sources without collapsing differences. I use this inductive and interpretive method to connect qualitative data from multiple sources to identify similarities and differences. The meta-ethnography process has four basic moves. First, I gathered information from various accounts, as previously mentioned. Second, I read the data repeatedly to

identify commonalities and differences. Third, I identified key ideas that emerged. Fourth and finally, I joined the similarities to create generative themes of the critical ideas.

4   Paulo Freire, *Pedagogy of the Oppressed*, new rev. 20th anniversary ed. (New York: Continuum, 1993), 89.

5   Freire, *Pedagogy of the Oppressed*, 89–90.

6   bell hooks, *All about Love: New Visions* (New York: William Morrow Paperbacks, 2018), 14.

7   Freire, *Pedagogy of the Oppressed*, 90.

Introduction

1   The course, Pastoral Perspectives on Death and Dying, was designed and taught by then–Candler School of Theology MDiv student Hillary Taylor. Thank you, Hillary.

2   Sociologist Erving Goffman (1961) calls prisons a perfect and most sinister example of a total institution which he defines as "a place of residence and work where a large number of like-situated individuals, cut off from the wider society for an appreciable period of time, together lead an enclosed, formally administered round of life" (xiii). Through a process Goffman calls "mortification of the self," prisons strip incarcerated people of individual expression so that they might deeply embody the identity of "inmate." See Erving Goffman, *Asylums: Essays on the Social Situation of Mental Patients and Other Inmates* (New York: Doubleday, 1961). Sociologists have relied on Goffman's concept to describe prisons, though recent research puts the totality of prisons into question. Scholar of women's experiences of punishment, Rachel Ellis argues that a porous institution is a better term to describe prisons, suggesting that there are predefined openings in the structure of the prison institution (e.g., religion) through which outside influences may permeate. See "Prisons as Porous Institutions," *Theory and Society* 50, no. 2 (2021): 175–99, https://doi.org/10.1007/s11186-020-09426-w.

3   Ellison defines being unheard and unseen as muteness and invisibility. Muteness is related to silencing that occurs either by outside forces or by internal repression. Invisibility refers to that which is not an object of sight which he suggests is related to an unexamined life. Invisibility relates to the complicit acceptance of a limiting identity and the failure to risk the required self-scrutiny to know one's own humanity. See chapter 1 in Gregory C. Ellison, *Cut Dead but Still Alive: Caring for African American Young Men* (Nashville: Abingdon, 2013).

4   Lila Kazemian, *Positive Growth and Redemption in Prison: Finding Light behind Bars and Beyond*, International Series on Desistance and Rehabilitation (Abingdon: Routledge, 2020), 6.

5   According to a 2018 study by the Department of Justice, participating in a postsecondary education program while incarcerated lowers the likelihood that a person returns to prison by 48%. See Robert Bozick et al., "Does Providing Inmates with Education Improve Postrelease Outcomes? A Meta-analysis of Correctional Education Programs in the United States," *Journal of Experimental Criminology* 14, no. 3 (2018): 389–428, https://doi.org/10.1007/s11292-018-9334-6.

6   "Fact Sheet: Incarcerated Women and Girls," The Sentencing Project, November 2020, 1.

7   "Fact Sheet: Incarcerated Women and Girls," The Sentencing Project, April 2023, 1.

8   I use *women* here to refer to people sentenced to prisons and jails for women. This designation refers to people who are classified as female by the Department of Corrections. These statistics do not reflect people's self-identified gender designation. As of 2023, transgender and gender nonconforming people are sentenced according to their biological identification assigned at birth.

9   Sociologist Dana Britton, in *At Work in the Iron Cage: The Prison as Gendered Organization* (New York: NYU Press, 2003), argues that prisons, through their so-called gender-neutral structures, practices, and policies, presumes and reproduces gender and gender inequality. She explores prisons as masculine institutions and suggests that women's prisons, when seen at all, are often sexualized and gendered.

10 Barbara A. Owen, Joycelyn M. Pollock, and James Wells, *In Search of Safety: Confronting Inequality in Women's Imprisonment*, Gender and Justice (Oakland: University of California Press, 2017), 2.

11 Beth E. Richie, "Feminist Ethnographies of Women in Prison," *Feminist Studies* 30, no. 2 (2004): 438, https://doi.org/10.2307/20458973.

12 I am referring to Barbara Bloom, Meda Chesney-Lind, and Barbara Owen's 1994 report *Women in California Prisons: The Hidden Victims of the War on Drugs* published for the San Francisco Center of Juvenile and Criminal Justice.

13 For detailed treatment of intersectional concerns and challenges of nonconforming gender and sexual identities, see Eric A. Stanley and Nat Smith, *Captive Genders: Trans Embodiment and the Prison Industrial Complex*, expanded 2nd ed. (Oakland, Calif.; Edinburgh:

AK Press, 2015); Brenda V. Smith and Jamie M. Yarussi, *Breaking the Code of Silence: Correction Officers' Handbook on Identifying and Addressing Sexual Misconduct—Scholar's Choice Edition*, National Institute of Corrections, US Department of Justice (Scholar's Choice, 2015); Mary K. Stohr, "The Hundred Years' War: The Etiology and Status of Assaults on Transgender Women in Men's Prisons," *Women & Criminal Justice* 25, nos. 1–2 (2015): 120–29, https://doi.org/10.1080/08974454.2015.1026154.

14 Wendy Sawyer, "The Gender Divide: Tracking Women's State Prison Growth," Prison Policy Initiative, January 9, 2018, https://www.prisonpolicy.org/reports/women_overtime.html.

15 Green et al. make this claim in "Trauma Exposure, Mental Health Functioning, and Program Needs of Women in Jail," *Crime & Delinquency* 51, no. 1 (2005): 133–51, https://doi.org/10.1177/0011128704267477. For a comprehensive analysis of issues surrounding women's justice involvement and the pathways framework, see Joanne Belknap, *The Invisible Woman: Gender, Crime, and Justice*, 5th ed. (Los Angeles: SAGE, 2021); Joycelyn M. Pollock, *Women's Crimes, Criminology, and Corrections* (Long Grove, Ill.: Waveland, 2014); Susan F. Sharp, *Mean Lives, Mean Laws: Oklahoma's Women Prisoners*, Critical Issues in Crime and Society (New Brunswick, N.J.: Rutgers University Press, 2014). For an in-depth consideration of race and gender, see Beth E. Richie, *Arrested Justice Black Women, Violence, and America's Prison Nation* (New York: NYU Press, 2012); and *Compelled to Crime: The Gender Entrapment of Battered Black Women* (New York: Routledge, 1996).

16 For a full treatment of these concerns, see chapter 2 of Owen, Pollock, and Wells, *In Search of Safety*.

17 From the Georgia Department of Corrections 2018 Inmate Statistical Profile.

18 For an analysis of the history of prison religious education, see Charles Atkins et al., "'Using the Language of Christian Love and Charity': What Liberal Religion Offers Higher Education in Prison," *Religions* 10, no. 3 (2019): 169, https://doi.org/10.3390/rel10030169.

19 The first recorded program on record began before the Pell Grants in 1953 when Southern Illinois University launched the first degree-granting college-in-prison program when it enrolled twenty-five students at Menard State Prison. The decades to follow, however, saw a steady increase in secular and religious institutions offering similar higher education programs in prison made increasingly accessible by Pell spending.

20 "INFOGRAPHIC: A Second Chance at Education | Washington State Department of Corrections," accessed September 24, 2023, https://www.doc.wa.gov/docs/publications/infographics/100-PO034.htm.

21 The FAFSA Simplification Act (the Act), signed into law in December 2020, restored Pell Grant eligibility to confined or incarcerated individuals for the first time since 1994.

22 Lucius Couloute, "Getting Back on Course: Educational Exclusion and Attainment among Formerly Incarcerated People," Prison Policy Initiative, October 2018, https://www.prisonpolicy.org/reports/education.html.

23 See figure 3 in Couloute, "Getting Back on Course."

24 See Kaia Stern, *Voices from American Prisons: Faith, Education and Healing* (London: Routledge, 2014).

25 In 1995, New Orleans Baptist Theological Seminary (NOBTS) began a program offering a bachelor of arts degree in Christian ministry in Angola Prison in Louisiana. Designed to develop missionaries, the program claims to have helped reduce violence at Angola and alter its identity as one of America's bloodiest prisons. In 2009, NOBTS extended its program to Georgia in a men's facility. In 2017, it began offering an associate's program at Whitworth Prison for Women in Georgia. In 2007, Columbia International University (CIU) started its Prison Initiative, which offers an accredited associate of arts degree from CIU and trains inmates in the South Carolina Department of Corrections to serve as chaplains' assistants upon completion. They extended the program to women in 2012. In 2011, Southwestern Baptist Theological Seminary started a bachelor's degree program at Darrington Prison in Texas. Students graduate to become assistant chaplains, ministers, and mentors in the Texas correctional system. In 2015, Calvin Theological Seminary and Calvin College formed the Calvin Prison Initiative that provides a Christian liberal arts education to inmates at Handlon Prison in Michigan. The five-year program results in a bachelor of arts degree from Calvin College. In 2014, Appalachian Bible College partnered with the correctional department to start Mount Olive Bible College inside the Mount Olive Correctional Complex in West Virginia. It offers inmates the opportunity to receive a bachelor's degree in Bible/theology and pastoral ministry. In 2017, Southeastern Baptist Theological Seminary began offering a bachelor of arts degree in pastoral ministry in Nash Correctional Institution in Nashville, North Carolina to train students to minister in the context of the North Carolina prison system.

26 In addition to working with incarcerated students, the Certificate in Theological Studies Program was designed to provide doctoral students with "unique" teaching opportunities and MDiv students with formative experiences for congregational leadership. Class offerings over the years include The Gospel of Mark, Biblical Perspectives on Criminal Justice, Reading the Bible from a Woman's Perspective, World Religions, Bonhoeffer, and Restorative Justice, each taught by doctoral or seminary MDiv students.

27 For works written by incarcerated women that more explicitly describe pathways to and experiences of crime, see Ayelet Waldman and Robin Levi, eds., *Inside This Place, Not of It: Narratives from Women's Prisons* (London: Verso, 2017). Also, for stories that center Black women's experiences, see Richie, *Compelled to Crime*.

28 The racial makeup among men in Georgia prisons is 61% Black, 34% white, 3.85% Hispanic, with the remaining 1.15% being a combination of Asian, Native American, Native Hawaiian, and other or unknown categories. Based on Georgia Department of Corrections 2018 Inmate Profile.

29 This statistic is in line with national averages that further emphasize that incarceration is not indiscriminate among women. According to the 2018 Prison Policy Report on Women's Mass Incarceration, incarcerated women are 53% white, 29% Black, 14% Hispanic, 2.5% American Indian and Alaskan Native, 0.9% Asian, and 0.4% Native Hawaiian and Pacific Islander, nationally. This does not include women housed in immigration centers. In Georgia, Hispanic women comprise 1.4% of the prison population, the remaining 0.6% being a combination of Asian, Native American, Native Hawaiian, and other or unknown categories.

30 According to the 2019 US census, 60% of Hispanics in Georgia self-identify as white, and the Georgia Department of Corrections does not designate white non-Hispanic as a separate category. Georgia's white non-Hispanic population is just shy of 52%, and Hispanic-Latinx population is 9.8%.

31 The statistics used to construct the profile of a Georgia incarcerated woman are based on the January 2015 and February 2018 Inmate Statistical profiles provided by the Georgia Department of Corrections in their Inmate Facts factsheets.

32 The average age of admission is thirty-four, but the most frequent is twenty-four.

33 According to the Prison Policy's report on Mass Incarceration 2018, 80% does reflect the national statistic on women who are mothers in the US jail population.

34 It is not in this project's scope to explore the full intersectional impacts of sexuality and ethnicity on women's incarceration. Sexual fluidity and gender "nonconformity" are frequent expressions among students in the Theology program. Due to the openness of the Theology program toward self-expression and self-naming, the program has seen a rise in students applying who openly identify as gay, lesbian, queer, and transgender. These categories are fluid and changing in women's carceral contexts, and more work is needed to understand better the experiences of LGBTQ+ persons in women's confinement. For information that does exist on national statistics, see the Prison Policy report on Women's Mass Incarceration 2018 and the article "Incarceration Rates and Traits of Sexual Minorities in the United States: National Inmate Survey, 2011–2012," *American Journal of Public Health* 107, no. 2 (February 2017): 267–73.

35 Lisa Marie Cacho, *Social Death: Racialized Rightlessness and the Criminalization of the Unprotected*, Nation of Newcomers: Immigrant History as American History (New York: NYU Press, 2012), 33.

36 In scholarship, the term "carceral pedagogy" is used in two ways: to describe the teaching strategies used in carceral spaces like prisons and jails and to diagnose a broader problem in educational spaces, many of which are becoming increasingly prison-like in their purpose, nature, and ends. I am using carceral pedagogy in its problematic sense, to refer to the oppressive nature of the methods and techniques used in learning spaces including but not limited to prisons and jails. For example, explore Ilana Horn's 2020 #EndCarceralPedagogy campaign.

1 Learning in a Place that Feels like Dying

1 Taken from focus group transcriptions.

2 The activity reflects a desire to begin by valuing popular knowledge, the self-reflexive activity of naming one's relationship to and view of the Bible. We value this knowledge as the starting point for doing biblical exploration. For more on valuing popular knowledge as a starting point, see Freire, *Pedagogy of the Oppressed*.

3 One of the pedagogical commitments in the Theology classroom is to practice multiple ways of learning. By acting out instead of merely reading the text, we engage the bodily kinesthetics learning style which acknowledges and promotes a person's ability to process information physically through bodily movement and expression; see Howard Gardner, *Frames of Mind: The Theory of Multiple Intelligences* (New York: Basic Books, 1983). The activity described is Bibliodrama, a form of interpretive play used in Christian educa-

tion where the biblical text is used as a platform for investigation; see Peter Pitzele, *Scripture Windows: Towards a Practice of Bibliodrama* (Los Angeles: Alef Design Group, 1998).

4   The feeling of creation here is a liberating act. The theatrical performance of the biblical text allows for students to be what Augusto Boal calls receptors of the production, where they are active participants in the production, individually and communally. Boal asserts that this embodied dramaturgy moves the oppressed from silent receivers to protagonists asserting agency. He labels this practice the poetics of the oppressed. See chapter 4 in *Theatre of the Oppressed* (New York: Theatre Communications Group, 1985). Furthermore, practical theologians describe play as embodied theology. Courtney T. Goto asserts that there is realized knowledge and wisdom that is discerned through bodily play. In addition, Jaco Hamman argues that play fosters and enriches faith, deepens hope, and can help us to love our neighbors and ourselves by minimizing conflict and opening new possibilities for being in relationship. See Courtney T. Goto, *The Grace of Playing: Pedagogies for Learning into God's New Creation* (Eugene, Ore.: Pickwick, 2016); Jaco J. Hamman, *A Play-Full Life: Slowing Down and Seeking Peace* (Cleveland: Pilgrim, 2011).

5   These three ways of thinking about the text come from the three worlds of the text, a contextual approach to reading scripture where students explore the world behind the text (historical context), the world of the text (literary context), and the world in front of the text (contemporary context). The world behind the text includes the context in which a text arose—historical situations, the world of the authors and their communities. The world of the text includes the structures of narrative, characterization, and use of language. The world in front of the text is that imaginative dialogue in which the reader interacts with the text in the effort to understand it. All three worlds are intimately interconnected, but it is a helpful model for understanding the different aspects and, thus, different approaches of each dimension (129). For more on the worlds of the text, see D. Andrew Kille, "Psychology and the Bible: Three Worlds of the Text," *Pastoral Psychology* 51, no. 2 (2002): 125–34, https://doi.org/10.1023/A:1020054613578.

6   There are fewer programming resources in jails than in prisons. However, there are many religious volunteers (predominantly Christian) who come to jails to lead Bible studies, prayer groups, and pass out religious tracts.

7	bell hooks, *Teaching to Transgress: Education as the Practice of Freedom* (New York: Routledge, 1994), 207.
8	I share Claira's essay as an offering of Art and Public Narrative from a woman serving a life sentence in prison. I hope it will be as impactful for you as it continues to be for me. I also share it because Claira's story illustrates the complicated process of trying to create a meaningful life in and against death-dealing systems. Claira's story illuminates a collective experience of long-term incarcerated women as they attempt to construct a life of meaning inside an institution that feels like dying.
9	Kazemian, *Positive Growth and Redemption in Prison*, 7.
10	Kazemian, *Positive Growth and Redemption in Prison*, 7.
11	Kazemian, *Positive Growth and Redemption in Prison*, 7.
12	Kazemian, *Positive Growth and Redemption in Prison*, 8.
13	Mika'il DeVeaux, "The Trauma of the Incarceration Experience," *Harvard Civil Rights—Civil Liberties Law Review* 48 (2013): 257–77.
14	M. Dyan McGuire, "Doing the Life: An Exploration of the Connection between the Inmate Code and Violence among Female Inmates," *Journal of the Institute of Justice and International Studies* 11 (2011): 154, original emphasis.
15	David J. Rothman, *The Discovery of the Asylum: Social Order and Disorder in the New Republic* (Boston: Little, Brown, 1971), 95.
16	When scholars of prison studies and practitioners of prison education utilize the concept of social death, they often do so by using the work of sociologist Orlando Patterson. See Fiona Greenland and George Steinmetz, "Orlando Patterson, His Work, and His Legacy: A Special Issue in Celebration of the Republication of Slavery and Social Death," *Theory and Society* 48 (2019): 788, https://doi.org/10.1007/s11186-019-09371-3.
17	Orlando Patterson, *Slavery and Social Death: A Comparative Study* (Cambridge, Mass.: Harvard University Press, 1982), 13, defines slavery as "the permanent, violent domination of natally alienated and generally dishonored persons."
18	Patterson, *Slavery and Social Death*, 5.
19	To explore social death in the context of theological education in men's prisons, see Stern, *Voices from American Prisons*.
20	As Henry Giroux maintains, pedagogy is a form of ideological and cultural production that implies the construction and organization of knowledge, values, and social relations. For more on Giroux's politicized understanding of pedagogy and his efforts to broaden

the discussion of public pedagogy into broader social discourse, see Henry A. Giroux, *Border Crossings: Cultural Workers and the Politics of Education* (London: Routledge, 1992).

21   Kimberley Benedict, "Writing-about-Writing Pedagogies in Prison," in *Prison Pedagogies: Learning and Teaching with Imprisoned Writers*, ed. Joe Lockard (Syracuse, N.Y.: Syracuse University Press, 2018), 224.

22   For Mbembe, these small doses are inflicted one day at a time, using an implacable logic of separation. See Achille Mbembe, *Necropolitics* (Durham, N.C.: Duke University Press, 2019), 36–38.

23   Lora Bex Lempert's description, in *Women Doing Life*, 49, of carceral erosion illuminates the impact of small doses of death. Lempert defines carceral erosion as "a damaging experience . . . resulting from the continuous process of erosion—the slow wearing away of self, of social value, of autonomy, and of agency through the daily assaults of institutional policies." The image of erosion holds together the dimensions of time and practice. Erosion happens slowly through repetitive action and requires both substantial time and prolonged replication. The consequences of persistent small doses of death are numerous, ranging from depression and other forms of mental illness to physical illness and even physical death.

24   Lempert, *Women Doing Life*, 242–43.

25   Though people use Mbembe to talk about social death in a general way, Patterson shows how social death is used in institutional formation. Christophe Ringer makes this point in his book *Necropolitics* (2021) and why he prefers Mbembe necropolitics to Foucault's biopolitics. For Ringer, Foucault's ideas are driven by ideas of a monarchy and do not take into account a racist popularized sovereignty. Foucault does not quite capture the images and realities of social death. See *Necropolitics: The Religious Crisis of Mass Incarceration in America* (Lanham, Md.: Lexington Books, 2021).

26   Erica Bryant, "Words Matter: Don't Call People Felons, Convicts, or Inmates," Vera Institute of Justice, March 31, 2021, https://www.vera.org/news/words-matter-dont-call-people-felons-convicts-or-inmates.

27   Timothy J. Flanagan, "Dealing with Long-Term Confinement: Adaptive Strategies and Perspectives among Long-Term Prisoners," *Criminal Justice and Behavior* 8, no. 2 (1981): 215.

28   I am referencing James Fowler's essay titled "An Experience of the Contemporary Personally Guided Spiritual Exercises" in *An Ignatian Spirituality Reader* (2008).

29 Mai-Anh Le Tran, *Reset the Heart: Unlearning Violence, Relearning Hope* (Nashville: Abingdon, 2017), 32.

30 Henry A. Giroux, "The Disimagination Machine and the Pathologies of Power," *Symplokē* 21, nos. 1–2 (2013): 263, https://doi.org/10.5250/symploke.21.1-2.0257.

31 Giroux, "Disimagination Machine," 263.

32 Marieke Liem and Maarten Kunst, "Is There a Recognizable Post-incarceration Syndrome among Released 'Lifers'?" *International Journal of Law and Psychiatry* 36, nos. 3–4 (2013): 336.

33 For an in-depth treatment of Kipling's argument, see Kipling D. Williams, Joseph P. Forgas, and William von Hippel, eds., *The Social Outcast: Ostracism, Social Exclusion, Rejection, and Bullying* (New York: Psychology Press, 2005).

34 Alison Liebling and Helen Arnold, *Prisons and Their Moral Performance: A Study of Values, Quality, and Prison Life*, Clarendon Studies in Criminology (Oxford: Oxford University Press, 2004), 530.

35 Vincent Lloyd, "Black Dignity," *CrossCurrents* 68, no. 1 (2018): 77, https://doi.org/10.1111/cros.12301.

36 Lloyd, "Black Dignity," 81.

37 Lloyd, "Black Dignity," 79.

38 Patrick B. Reyes, *Nobody Cries When We Die: God, Community, and Surviving to Adulthood* (Saint Louis: Chalice Press, 2016), 172.

2 Imagining Your Good Life

1 Katie G. Cannon and Mud Flower Collective, *God's Fierce Whimsy: Christian Feminism and Theological Education* (New York: Pilgrim, 1985), 158.

2 Cacho, *Social Death*, 33.

3 The use of images and their collaborative interpretation are themselves a theological practice. According to the scholars of the Mud Flower Collective, in *God's Fierce Whimsy*, "images, rather than conceptual discourse or linear logic, are the roots of feminist theology, our primary language. Images are not simply the first mode of our expression, the one we employ before we get down to serious business, but the most basic—and usually the most substantive—language of feminist theology. To image is to portray what is experienced in word pictures, stories and narrative, sound, movement, art. It is a nonexpository form of communication that mobilizes our imaginative faculties" (158). Moreover, "images are

intensely participatory, calling for connections with the experience of others if they are to be received meaningfully and powerfully" (158–59). Imaging follows a "transformational logic" rather than a static or linear one. "The value of imaging, as a mode of theological teaching and learning, is that it creates relationship—concrete bonds—among those engaged in the process" (160).

4   Susan Starr Sered and Maureen Norton-Hawk, *Can't Catch a Break: Gender, Jail, Drugs and the Limits of Personal Responsibility* (Oakland: University of California Press, 2014).

5   Elizabeth M. Bounds, "What Must I Do to Be Saved? Punishment and Redemption under Incarceration," *Political Theology* 23, no. 4 (2022): 298–316, https://doi.org/10.1080/1462317X.2022.2039345.

6   Joni Hersch and Erin E. Meyers, "The Gendered Burdens of Conviction and Collateral Consequences on Employment," *Journal of Legislation* 45, no. 2 (2018): 183.

7   Owen, Pollock, and Wells, *In Search of Safety*, 39.

8   Kazemian, *Positive Growth and Redemption in Prison*, 112.

9   See Shadd Maruna, Louise Wilson, and Kathryn Curran, "Why God Is Often Found behind Bars: Prison Conversions and the Crisis of Self-Narrative," *Research in Human Development* 3, no. 2 (2006): 161–84, https://doi.org/10.1207/s15427617rhd0302&3_6.

10 Kazemian, *Positive Growth and Redemption in Prison*, 141. Other studies that make similar observations include Tharina Guse and Daphne Hudson, "Psychological Strengths and Posttraumatic Growth in the Successful Reintegration of South African Ex-Offenders," *International Journal of Offender Therapy and Comparative Criminology* 58, no. 12 (2014): 1449–65, https://doi.org/10.1177/0306624X13502299; Siebrecht Vanhooren, Mia Leijssen, and Jessie Dezutter, "Loss of Meaning as a Predictor of Distress in Prison," *International Journal of Offender Therapy and Comparative Criminology* 61, no. 13 (2017): 1411–32; Siebrecht Vanhooren, Mia Leijssen, and Jessie Dezutter, "Ten Prisoners on a Search for Meaning: A Qualitative Study of Loss and Growth during Incarceration," *The Humanistic Psychologist* 45, no. 2 (2017): 162–78, https://doi.org/10.1037/hum0000055; Esther F. J. C. Van Ginneken, "Making Sense of Imprisonment: Narratives of Posttraumatic Growth among Female Prisoners," *International Journal of Offender Therapy and Comparative Criminology* 60, no. 2 (2016): 208–27; Wilfried Rasch, "The Effects of Indeterminate Detention," *International Journal of Law and Psychiatry* 4, no. 3–4 (1981): 417–31; Ian O'Donnell, ed., *Prisoners, Solitude*

and Time, Clarendon Studies in Criminology (Oxford: Oxford University Press, 2014).

11 Criminological reports suggest that the most significant benefit gained from incarceration pertain to the vast reflection time that occurs with long sentencing. Crewe et al. (2017) found that many study participants viewed their sentence as a chance to work on themselves and to better understand themselves. See "The Gendered Pains of Life Imprisonment," *British Journal of Criminology*, January 12, 2017, https://doi.org/10.1093/bjc/azw088. Still, scholars argue that "narratives of thriving" in prison should be read with caution. Megan Comfort, "'It Was Basically College to Us': Poverty, Prison, and Emerging Adulthood," *Journal of Poverty* 16, no. 3 (2012): 308–22, https://doi.org/10.1080/10875549.2012.695923, builds on the work of K. M. Blankenship (1998) and argues that stories about positive change do not reflect thriving but rather Bourdieu's (1984) amor fati or "forced choice"— produced by conditions of existence which rule out all alternatives as mere daydreams and leave no choice but the taste for the necessary.

12 According to the Georgia Department of Corrections (GADOC), the Faith and Character Based Initiative began in 2004 to provide the state of Georgia and its citizens with a model for positive change by allowing offenders to strengthen their mind, body, and spirit in an environment that promotes positive change. GADOC reports that the Faith and Character Based programs have been shown to have a treatment effect of 10; meaning someone is ten times less likely to return to prison after completing a Faith and Character Based program. The program consists of Faith and Character Based prison and Faith and Character Based dorm programs throughout the state. The program operates on a holistic approach, secular in nature, which involves our stakeholders and community volunteers in the process of the offenders learning to change their attitudes, beliefs, and behaviors. For more, see http://www.dcor.state.ga.us/Divisions/Facilities/Transitional/FCBI.

13 Spicey's path to imprisonment mirrors in many ways the gender entrapment model that Beth Richie describes in *Compelled to Crime*. Richie presents narratives and experiences of Black women who were vulnerable to intimate partner violence and lured into compromising acts that led them to prison. The model "illustrates how gender, race/ethnicity, and violence can intersect to create a subtle yet profoundly effective system of organizing women's behavior into patterns that leave women vulnerable to private and

public subordination, to violence and their intimate relationships and, in turn, to participation in illegal activities" (4).

14 Lempert, *Women Doing Life*, 7.

15 The Harvard Study of Adult Development reveals that the strength of our connections with others can predict the health of both our bodies and our brains as we go through life. Relationships in all their forms contribute to a happier, healthier life. The study reveals that positive relationships, not career achievement, money, exercise, or a healthy diet, keep people happier, healthier, and help us live longer. See https://www.adultdevelopmentstudy.org/.

3 Is Your Good Life Possible Here?

1 Kazemian, *Positive Growth and Redemption in Prison*, 212.

2 Patricia Hill Collins, "Piecing Together a Genealogical Puzzle: Intersectionality and American Pragmatism," *European Journal of Pragmatism and American Philosophy* 3, no. 2 (2011): 20.

3 Collins, *Fighting Words*, 188, describes the work of Black women's visionary pragmatism as pragmatic choices that reflect the principled stances that people take in response to the constraints and opportunities associated with specific social contexts.

4 The data on PREA comes from the Georgia Department of Corrections 2018 Annual PREA Report, accessible at http://www.dcor.state.ga.us/sites/default/files/GDC-Annual-PREA%20Report-CY2018.pdf.

5 Scholars argue that agency is critical to understanding women's carceral experiences. See Owen, Pollock, and Wells, *In Search of Safety*; Lempert, *Women Doing Life*; and Susan Batchelor, "'Prove Me the Bam!' Victimization and Agency in the Lives of Young Women Who Commit Violent Offences," *Probation Journal* 52, no. 4 (2005): 358–75, https://doi.org/10.1177/0264550505058034. Owen et al., for instance, offer the idea of constrained choice to refer to the limited options available to many marginalized women (*In Search of Safety*, 5).

6 Data on women, prisons, and drugs can be found at https://drugpolicy.org/issues/women-drug-war.

7 For more on drug addiction and criminal punishment, see Allison McKim, *Addicted to Rehab: Race, Gender, and Drugs in the Era of Mass Incarceration* (New Brunswick, N.J.: Rutgers University Press, 2017).

8 Lempert, *Women Doing Life*, 291.

9 Lempert, *Women Doing Life*, 139.

10   Claira and Ilillana are referencing programs at Angola Prison, and possibly the Angola Prison Seminary where incarcerated persons serve in key roles across the compound including as "Inmate Ministers." For more on Angola, see Michael Hallet, *The Angola Prison Seminary: Effects of Faith-Based Ministry on Identity Transformation, Desistance, and Rehabilitation*, Routledge Innovations in Corrections LCNAMES (New York: Routledge, 2017).

11   Owen, *In Search of Safety*, 59. See also Elaine Rizzo and Margaret Hayes, "Struggling for Healthcare in the Inside," *Correctional Healthcare Report*, 2011, 3–14.

12   Georgia Department of Corrections, "Education: Why to Provide Academic Education to Offenders?" n.d., https://gdc.georgia.gov/organization/about-gdc/divisions-and-org-chart/inmate-services-division/education, accessed June 2022.

13   Owen et al. note that because relationships among incarcerated people and staff contain the possibility for conflict and violence, "prison culture may require women to resort to forms of aggression to protect themselves and their reputations as they do their time" (*In Search of Safety*, 3).

14   In desistance narratives, finagling or conning is referred to as "rule-breaking behavior" and is viewed as purposeful and used as a means to "advance positive self-development, desistance efforts, or preparation for release." See Kazemian, *Positive Growth and Redemption in Prison*, 176.

15   Definitions of finagle used here are derived from various uses according to the *Merriam-Webster Dictionary* (2019).

16   Chi Wai Chan, "The Ultimate Trickster in the Story of Tamar from a Feminist Perspective," *Feminist Theology* 24, no. 1 (2015): 93.

17   To live fully is what theologian Ada María Isasi-Díaz contends is the hope of humanity, particularly among those facing struggle and oppression. True liberation and salvation include the ability to live fully as human beings in the world. See *En La Lucha = In the Struggle: A Hispanic Women's Liberation Theology* (Minneapolis: Fortress, 1993). Likewise, ethicist Emilie Townes suggests that it is in the relational matrix where wholeness can be found. See *Womanist Ethics and the Cultural Production of Evil* (New York: Palgrave Macmillan, 2006).

18   Charles Vogl, *The Art of Community: Seven Principles for Belonging* (Oakland, Calif.: Berrett-Koehler, 2016), 47.

19   Erzen, *God in Captivity*, 13.

20	Evelyn L. Parker, *Between Sisters: Emancipatory Hope out of Tragic Relationships* (Eugene, Ore.: Cascade, 2017), 80.
21	Parker, *Between Sisters*, 83.
22	Parker, *Between Sisters*, 80.

4 What Theology Makes Possible

1	bell hooks, *Teaching Community: A Pedagogy of Hope* (New York: Routledge, 2003), 2.
2	See Lauren E. Glaze and Laura M. Maruschak, "Parents in Prison and Their Minor Children," Special Report, Bureau of Justice Statistics (US Department of Justice, 2010).
3	HB's description of the dorm experience is similar to accounts from other carceral institutions. Owen et al. refer to dorms as "good and bad neighborhoods" and offers a comparative account of a good neighborhood (*In Search of Safety*, 53). That study also contends that older women in prison feel highly vulnerable to exploitation by younger ones (59).
4	The belief of rampant proselytizing in prison is expressed by Erzen, *God in Captivity*. Erzen writes that "faith-based programs allow massive numbers of Christians to enter and proselytize to those desperate for a lifeline" (5), and "faith-based ministers flock to prisons to convert, pray, teach, and proselytize, but they neglect why people end up there in the first place" (8). While proselytizing is likely one objective of faith-based ministry, it is not the only reason why faith-based practitioners volunteer in prisons, nor is it students' experience of Theology.
5	"Compassionate Integrity Training," The Center for Compassion, Integrity, and Secular Ethics at Life University, https://www.compassionateintegrity.org/about-the-program/.
6	"Alternatives to Violence Project," Alternatives to Violence Project-USA, https://avpusa.org/.
7	https://gdc.georgia.gov/press-releases/2020-01-27/faith-character-based-program-participants-graduate.

5 Fostering Life-Affirming Praxis in Theology

1	Jack L. Seymour et al., *Educating for Redemptive Community: Essays in Honor of Jack Seymour and Margaret Ann Crain* (Eugene, Ore.: Wipf & Stock, 2015), xiv.
2	Débora B. A. Junker, "Embodied Redemption: Implications for a Transforming Community," in *Educating for Redemptive*

Community: Essays in Honor of Jack Seymour and Margaret Ann Crain, ed. Denise Janssen (Eugene, Ore.: Wipf & Stock, 2015), 91.

3   In the New Testament, two distinct shifts occur in conceptions of redemption: one was from a social definition to an individualistic, otherworldly definition; the second was from an egalitarian definition to one reinforcing gender hierarchy. See Rosemary Radford Ruether, *Introducing Redemption in Christian Feminism*, Introductions in Feminist Theology 1 (Sheffield, England: Sheffield Academic, 1998), 11–13.

4   For more on this relationship, see Olin P. Moyd, *Redemption in Black Theology* (Valley Forge, Pa.: Judson, 1979).

5   For Womanist perspectives on redemption, liberation, and social salvation, see Emilie Maureen Townes, *Womanist Justice, Womanist Hope*, American Academy of Religion 79 (Atlanta: Scholars, 1993) and Delores S. Williams, *Sisters in the Wilderness: The Challenge of Womanist God-Talk* (Maryknoll, N.Y.: Orbis Books, 1993).

6   Junker, "Embodied Redemption," argues that embodied redemptive communities are sites of resistance and protest against all that diminishes us as human beings. They have the responsibility of teaching how to critically read the world, seeking to understand it from the perspective of excluded groups.

7   See the discussions of the significance of humanizing relational pedagogies in Nancy Lynne Westfield, ed., *Being Black, Teaching Black: Politics and Pedagogy in Religious Studies* (Nashville: Abingdon, 2008).

8   Maxine Greene, *Landscapes of Learning* (New York: Teachers College Press, 1978), 3–4.

9   The concept of emancipatory education has been popular among liberative pedagogues and educators. Scholarly contributions can be found from Greene, *Landscapes of Learning*; Jack Mezirow, *Fostering Critical Reflection in Adulthood: A Guide to Transformative and Emancipatory Learning* (San Francisco: Jossey-Bass, 1990); Westfield, *Being Black, Teaching Black*.

10 Townes, *Womanist Justice, Womanist Hope*, 198.

11 Townes, *Womanist Justice, Womanist Hope*, 200.

12 In slavery, enslaved peoples gathered in secret to practice religious traditions free from the constraints and demands of the dominators. They were able to mix their African traditions with Christianity, to interpret Christianity for themselves, to name their experiences, and to imagine freedom beyond enslavement. Likewise, students in Theology gather in broad daylight to mix and interpret their

religious experiences, to interpret the system that confines them, and to imagine a freedom from the oppression of social death. The classroom becomes a sanctuary, or a place set apart, where these experiences can happen free from the observation and surveillance of officers and administrators.

13　Mary McClintock Fulkerson argues that it is not accurate theological speech but rather altered social conditions, diminishing brokenness, that testify to God's redeeming presence. See "Ethnography: A Gift to Theology and Ethics," *Practical Matters Journal*, March 1, 2013, http://practicalmattersjournal.org/2013/03/01/ethnography-gift/.

14　By considering the practices of theological education instead of the content of theological education, the goal of theological study becomes more than an intellectual product in which students demonstrate mastery. Focusing on the practices engaged in theological study suggests that theological education is a process that students and teachers engage and embody to shape life. Theological study in prison must first attend to the life and social well-being of all experiencing the sin of social death practices.

15　Peter Block, *Community: The Structure of Belonging* (San Francisco: Berrett-Koehler, 2009), 10.

16　Block, *Community*, 9.

17　Block, *Community*, 14.

18　A community of practice is a group of people who share a craft or a profession. The concept was first proposed by cognitive anthropologist Jean Lave and educational theorist Etienne Wenger (1991). Wenger significantly expanded on the concept in his book *Communities of Practice: Learning, Meaning, and Identity* (Cambridge: Cambridge University Press, 1998).

19　hooks, *Teaching Community*, 36.

20　John Swinton, "From Inclusion to Belonging: A Practical Theology of Community, Disability and Humanness," *Journal of Religion, Disability & Health* 16, no. 2 (2012): 183, https://doi.org/10.1080/15228967.2012.676243.

21　Swinton, "From Inclusion to Belonging," 184.

22　Freire's concept of "naming the world" (*Pedagogy of the Oppressed*, 1993, chapter 3) influenced scholars such as Greene (*Dialectic of Freedom*, 1988) who draw connections between naming and becoming.

23　Katie G. Cannon, *Katie's Canon: Womanism and the Soul of the Black Community* (New York: Continuum, 1995), 7.

24 hooks, *Teaching Community*, 44, argues that conversation is the central practice of democratic educators who seek to resist the devaluation of vernacular speech and popular knowledge.

25 Paulo Freire, *Pedagogy of Hope: Reliving Pedagogy of the Oppressed* (New York: Continuum, 1994), 110.

26 Paulo Freire, *Education for Critical Consciousness*, 1st US paperback ed., Continuum (New York: Seabury, 1973), 45.

27 Cannon and Mud Flower Collective, *God's Fierce Whimsy*, 134.

28 Cannon and Mud Flower Collective, *God's Fierce Whimsy*, 141–42.

29 Freire uses the phrase "reading of the world" to denote the initial content of education. The role of the progressive educator, accordingly, is to share their own readings of the world and to bring out the fact that there are other readings of the world different from the ones being offered. At times, the role of the educator is to antagonize the readings to deepen understanding and increase reflective awareness. For more, see Freire, *Pedagogy of Hope*, 102–3.

30 Freire, *Education for Critical Consciousness*, 45.

31 Freire, *Pedagogy of Hope*, 88.

32 Greene, *Landscapes of Learning*, 14.

33 For more on wide-awakeness, see Greene, *Landscapes of Learning*; and *The Dialectic of Freedom*, John Dewey Lecture (New York: Teachers College Press, 1988).

34 Greene, *Landscapes of Learning*, 19.

35 Alfred Schutz, *The Problem of Social Reality* (The Hague: Martinus Nijhoff, 1962), 213.

36 hooks, *Teaching Community*, 2.

37 Block, *Community*, 105.

38 Nancy Lynne Westfield, "'Mama Why . . . ?' A Womanist Epistemology of Hope," in *Deeper Shades of Purple: Womanism in Religion and Society*, ed. Stacey M. Floyd-Thomas (New York: NYU Press, 2006), 138.

39 Block, *Community*, 101.

40 Greene, *Landscapes of Learning*, also argues that, in addition to critical awareness, self-understanding and social commitment are fundamental to emancipatory education. These three together are reflective of redemptive practices commitments to cultivating contexts where meaning-making and community/belonging might be possible.

41 James H. Cone, *Said I Wasn't Gonna Tell Nobody: The Making of a Black Theologian* (Maryknoll, N.Y.: Orbis Books, 2018), 91.

42 Cone, *Said I Wasn't Gonna Tell Nobody*, 114.

43 Here I am suggesting that merely receiving theological information is a form of banking education, from the banking model of learning that Freire and critical pedagogues argue is a pedagogy of domination. See Freire, *Pedagogy of the Oppressed*.

44 Freire, *Pedagogy of Hope*, 30.

45 Cannon and Mud Flower Collective, *God's Fierce Whimsy*, 140–41.

46 Courtney T. Goto, "Asian American Practical Theologies," in *Opening the Field of Practical Theology: An Introduction*, ed. Kathleen A. Cahalan and Gordon S. Mikoski (Lanham, Md.: Rowman & Littlefield, 2014), 32.

47 Goto, "Asian American Practical Theologies," 44.

48 Angie Titchen and Brendan McCormack, "Dancing with Stones: Critical Creativity as Methodology for Human Flourishing," *Educational Action Research* 18, no. 4 (2010): 532.

49 Titchen and McCormack, "Dancing with Stones," 532.

50 Willie James Jennings, "Gathering Joy," Yale Center for Faith & Culture, Yale Divinity School, July 31, 2018, https://faith.yale.edu/media/gathering-joy.

51 Jennings, "Gathering Joy."

52 Seymour et al., *Educating for Redemptive Community*, 116–17.

53 If Christian practices are practices that Christian people do over time, and the Theology classroom is comprised of students across the religious spectrum, then it would be inaccurate to use the term "Christian" to refer to their practices. Practices in and of themselves are not religious. Human beings are religious. Dykstra and Bass expanded the notion of Christian practice to mean things Christian people do together over time to address fundamental human needs in response to and in the light of God's active presence for the life of the world. See Miroslav Volf and Dorothy C. Bass, *Practicing Theology: Beliefs and Practices in Christian Life* (Grand Rapids: Eerdmans, 2002). For a broad list of Christian practices that suggest a way of life, see Dorothy C. Bass, ed., *Practicing Our Faith: A Way of Life for a Searching People*, 2nd ed. (San Francisco: Jossey-Bass, 2010).

54 In the prison, it is less helpful to make a distinction in this multi-religious context between Christian and non-Christian practices; the definition is allusive and not necessary. What is more important

and helpful is that people of all faith traditions or no faith tradition can embrace and enact these practices from their standpoint. For these reasons, I refer to these as pedagogical practices and not Christian practices.

55 Craig R. Dykstra, "What Are Christian Practices?" Practicing Our Faith, February 6, 2013, https://practicingourfaith.org/practices/.
56 Evelyn Parker, "A Pedagogy of Redemption with Incarcerated Girls," in *Educating for Redemptive Community*, ed. Jack L. Seymour et al. (Eugene, Ore.: Wipf & Stock, 2015), 111.
57 Junker, "Embodied Redemption," 91.
58 Junker, "Embodied Redemption," 79.

6 Nurturing Life-Affirming Futures through Theological Education

1 Cannon and Mud Flower Collective, *God's Fierce Whimsy*, 34.
2 Musa W. Dube, "Talitha Cum Hermeneutics of Liberation: Some African Women's Ways of Reading the Bible," in *The Bible and the Hermeneutics of Liberation*, ed. Alejandro F. Botta and Pablo R. Andinach (Atlanta: Society of Biblical Literature, 2009), 139.
3 Dube, "Talitha Cum Hermeneutics of Liberation," 137–38.
4 hooks, *Teaching Community*, 8.
5 Rebecca Chopp urges readers to think of theological education as a process of intertwining theology and education in and through practices, within which different voices reflect and construct practices of theological education. See *Saving Work: Feminist Practices of Theological Education* (Louisville: Westminster John Knox, 1995), 113.

BIBLIOGRAPHY

Atkins, Charles, Joshua Dubler, Vincent Lloyd, and Mel Webb. "'Using the Language of Christian Love and Charity': What Liberal Religion Offers Higher Education in Prison." *Religions* 10, no. 3 (2019): 169. https://doi.org/10.3390/rel10030169.
Bass, Dorothy C., ed. *Practicing Our Faith: A Way of Life for a Searching People*. 2nd ed. San Francisco: Jossey-Bass, 2010.
Batchelor, Susan. "'Prove Me the Bam!': Victimization and Agency in the Lives of Young Women Who Commit Violent Offences." *Probation Journal* 52, no. 4 (2005): 358–75. https://doi.org/10.1177/0264550505058034.
Belknap, Joanne. *The Invisible Woman: Gender, Crime, and Justice*. 5th ed. Los Angeles: SAGE, 2021.
Benedict, Kimberley. "Writing-about-Writing Pedagogies in Prison." In *Prison Pedagogies: Learning and Teaching with Imprisoned Writers*, edited by Joe Lockard, 224–45. Syracuse, N.Y.: Syracuse University Press, 2018.
Blankenship, Kim M. "A Race, Class, and Gender Analysis of Thriving." *Journal of Social Issues* 54, no. 2 (1998): 393–404.
Block, Peter. *Community: The Structure of Belonging*. San Francisco: Berrett-Koehler, 2009.
Bloom, Barbara, Meda Chesney-Lind, and Barbara Owen. *Women in California Prisons: The Hidden Victims of the War on Drugs*. San Francisco: Center of Juvenile and Criminal Justice, 1994.
Boal, Augusto. *Theatre of the Oppressed*. New York: Theatre Communications Group, 1985.
Bounds, Elizabeth M. "What Must I Do to Be Saved? Punishment and Redemption under Incarceration." *Political Theology* 23, no. 4 (2022): 298–316. https://doi.org/10.1080/1462317X.2022.2039345.
Bozick, Robert, Jennifer Steele, Lois Davis, and Susan Turner. "Does Providing Inmates with Education Improve Postrelease Outcomes? A Meta-analysis of Correctional Education Programs in the United States." *Journal of Experimental Criminology* 14, no. 3 (2018): 389–428. https://doi.org/10.1007/s11292-018-9334-6.

Britton, Dana M. *At Work in the Iron Cage: The Prison as Gendered Organization*. New York: NYU Press, 2003.

Cacho, Lisa Marie. *Social Death: Racialized Rightlessness and the Criminalization of the Unprotected*. Nation of Newcomers: Immigrant History as American History. New York: NYU Press, 2012.

Cannon, Katie G. *Katie's Canon: Womanism and the Soul of the Black Community*. New York: Continuum, 1995.

Cannon, Katie G., and Mud Flower Collective. *God's Fierce Whimsy: Christian Feminism and Theological Education*. New York: Pilgrim, 1985.

Chan, Chi Wai. "The Ultimate Trickster in the Story of Tamar from a Feminist Perspective." *Feminist Theology* 24, no. 1 (2015): 93.

Chopp, Rebecca S. *Saving Work: Feminist Practices of Theological Education*. Louisville: Westminster John Knox, 1995.

Comfort, Megan. "'It Was Basically College to Us': Poverty, Prison, and Emerging Adulthood." *Journal of Poverty* 16, no. 3 (2012): 308–22. https://doi.org/10.1080/10875549.2012.695923.

Cone, James H. *Said I Wasn't Gonna Tell Nobody: The Making of a Black Theologian*. Maryknoll, N.Y.: Orbis Books, 2018.

Couloute, Lucius. "Getting Back on Course: Educational Exclusion and Attainment among Formerly Incarcerated People." Prison Policy Initiative, October 2018. https://www.prisonpolicy.org/reports/education.html.

Crewe, Ben, Susie Hulley, and Serena Wright. "The Gendered Pains of Life Imprisonment." *British Journal of Criminology*, January 12, 2017. https://doi.org/10.1093/bjc/azw088.

DeVeaux, Mika'il. "The Trauma of the Incarceration Experience." *Harvard Civil Rights—Civil Liberties Law Review* 48 (2013): 257–77.

Dube, Musa W. "Talitha Cum Hermeneutics of Liberation: Some African Women's Ways of Reading the Bible." In *The Bible and the Hermeneutics of Liberation*, edited by Alejandro F. Botta and Pablo R. Andinach, 133–46. Atlanta: Society of Biblical Literature, 2009.

Dykstra, Craig R. "What Are Christian Practices?" Practicing Our Faith, February 6, 2013. https://practicingourfaith.org/practices/.

Ellis, Rachel. "Prisons as Porous Institutions." *Theory and Society* 50, no. 2 (2021): 175–99. https://doi.org/10.1007/s11186-020-09426-w.

Ellison, Gregory C. *Cut Dead but Still Alive: Caring for African American Young Men*. Nashville: Abingdon, 2013.

Erzen, Tanya. *God in Captivity: The Rise of Faith-Based Prison Ministries in the Age of Mass Incarceration*. Boston: Beacon, 2017.

Flanagan, Timothy J. "Dealing with Long-Term Confinement: Adaptive Strategies and Perspectives among Long-Term Prisoners." *Criminal Justice and Behavior* 8, no. 2 (1981): 201–22.

Fowler, James W. "An Experience of the Contemporary Personally Guided Spiritual Exercises." In *An Ignatian Spirituality Reader*, edited by George W. Traub, 136–39. Chicago: Loyola Press, 2008.

Freire, Paulo. *Education for Critical Consciousness*. 1st US paperback ed. Continuum. New York: Seabury, 1973.
———. *Pedagogy of Hope: Reliving Pedagogy of the Oppressed*. New York: Continuum, 1994.
———. *Pedagogy of the Oppressed*. New rev. 20th anniversary ed. New York: Continuum, 1993.
Fulkerson, Mary McClintock. "Ethnography: A Gift to Theology and Ethics." *Practical Matters Journal*, March 1, 2013. http://practicalmattersjournal.org/2013/03/01/ethnography-gift/.
Gardner, Howard. *Frames of Mind: The Theory of Multiple Intelligences*. New York: Basic Books, 1983.
Giroux, Henry A. *Border Crossings: Cultural Workers and the Politics of Education*. London: Routledge, 1992.
———. "The Disimagination Machine and the Pathologies of Power." *Symplokē* 21, nos. 1–2 (2013): 257–68. https://doi.org/10.5250/symploke.21.1-2.0257.
Glaze, Lauren E., and Laura M. Maruschak. "Parents in Prison and Their Minor Children." Special Report, Bureau of Justice Statistics. US Department of Justice, 2010.
Goffman, Erving. *Asylums: Essays on the Social Situation of Mental Patients and Other Inmates*. New York: Doubleday, 1961.
Goto, Courtney T. "Asian American Practical Theologies." In *Opening the Field of Practical Theology: An Introduction*, edited by Kathleen A. Cahalan and Gordon S. Mikoski, 31–44. Lanham, Md.: Rowman & Littlefield, 2014.
———. *The Grace of Playing: Pedagogies for Learning into God's New Creation*. Eugene, Ore.: Pickwick, 2016.
Green, Bonnie L., Jeanne Miranda, Anahita Daroowalla, and Juned Siddique. "Trauma Exposure, Mental Health Functioning, and Program Needs of Women in Jail." *Crime & Delinquency* 51, no. 1 (2005): 133–51. https://doi.org/10.1177/0011128704267477.
Greene, Maxine. *Landscapes of Learning*. New York: Teachers College Press, 1978.
———. *The Dialectic of Freedom*. John Dewey Lecture. New York: Teachers College Press, 1988.
Greenland, Fiona, and George Steinmetz. "Orlando Patterson, His Work, and His Legacy: A Special Issue in Celebration of the Republication of Slavery and Social Death." *Theory and Society* 48 (2019): 785–97. https://doi.org/10.1007/s11186-019-09371-3.
Guse, Tharina, and Daphne Hudson. "Psychological Strengths and Posttraumatic Growth in the Successful Reintegration of South African Ex-Offenders." *International Journal of Offender Therapy and Comparative Criminology* 58, no. 12 (2014): 1449–65. https://doi.org/10.1177/0306624X13502299.

Hallet, Michael. *The Angola Prison Seminary: Effects of Faith-Based Ministry on Identity Transformation, Desistance, and Rehabilitation*. Routledge Innovations in Corrections LCNAMES. New York: Routledge, 2017.

Hamman, Jaco J. *A Play-Full Life: Slowing Down and Seeking Peace*. Cleveland: Pilgrim, 2011.

Hersch, Joni, and Erin E. Meyers. "The Gendered Burdens of Conviction and Collateral Consequences on Employment." *Journal of Legislation* 45, no. 2 (2018): 171–93.

Hill Collins, Patricia. *Black Feminist Thought: Knowledge, Consciousness, and the Politics of Empowerment*. 2nd ed. New York: Routledge, 2000.

———. *Fighting Words: Black Women and the Search for Justice*. Minneapolis: University of Minnesota Press, 1998.

———. "Piecing Together a Genealogical Puzzle: Intersectionality and American Pragmatism." *European Journal of Pragmatism and American Philosophy* 3, no. 2 (2011): 1–27.

hooks, bell. *All about Love: New Visions*. New York: William Morrow Paperbacks, 2018.

———. *Teaching Community: A Pedagogy of Hope*. New York: Routledge, 2003.

———. *Teaching to Transgress: Education as the Practice of Freedom*. New York: Routledge, 1994.

Isasi-Díaz, Ada María. *En La Lucha = In the Struggle: A Hispanic Women's Liberation Theology*. Minneapolis: Fortress, 1993.

Jennings, Willie James. "Gathering Joy." Presented at the Yale Center for Faith & Culture, Yale Divinity School, July 31, 2018. https://faith.yale.edu/media/gathering-joy.

Junker, Débora B. A. "Embodied Redemption: Implications for a Transforming Community." In *Educating for Redemptive Community: Essays in Honor of Jack Seymour and Margaret Ann Crain*, edited by Denise Janssen, 78–94. Eugene, Ore.: Wipf & Stock, 2015.

Kazemian, Lila. *Positive Growth and Redemption in Prison: Finding Light behind Bars and Beyond*. International Series on Desistance and Rehabilitation. Abingdon: Routledge, 2020.

Kille, D. Andrew. "Psychology and the Bible: Three Worlds of the Text." *Pastoral Psychology* 51, no. 2 (2002): 125–34. https://doi.org/10.1023/A:1020054613578.

Lave, Jean, and Etienne Wenger. *Situated Learning: Legitimate Peripheral Participation*. Cambridge: Cambridge University Press, 1991.

Lempert, Lora Bex. *Women Doing Life: Gender, Punishment and the Struggle for Identity*. New York: NYU Press, 2016.

Liebling, Alison, and Helen Arnold. *Prisons and Their Moral Performance: A Study of Values, Quality, and Prison Life*. Clarendon Studies in Criminology. Oxford: Oxford University Press, 2004.

Liem, Marieke, and Maarten Kunst. "Is There a Recognizable Post-incarceration Syndrome among Released 'Lifers'?" *International Journal of Law and Psychiatry* 36, nos. 3–4 (2013): 333–37.

Lloyd, Vincent. "Black Dignity." *CrossCurrents* 68, no. 1 (2018): 73–92. https://doi.org/10.1111/cros.12301.

Maruna, Shadd, Louise Wilson, and Kathryn Curran. "Why God Is Often Found behind Bars: Prison Conversions and the Crisis of Self-Narrative." *Research in Human Development* 3, no. 2 (2006): 161–84. https://doi.org/10.1207/s15427617rhd0302&3_6.

Mbembe, Achille. *Necropolitics*. Durham, N.C.: Duke University Press, 2019.

McGuire, M. Dyan. "Doing the Life: An Exploration of the Connection between the Inmate Code and Violence among Female Inmates." *Journal of the Institute of Justice and International Studies* 11 (2011): 145–58.

McKim, Allison. *Addicted to Rehab: Race, Gender, and Drugs in the Era of Mass Incarceration*. New Brunswick, N.J.: Rutgers University Press, 2017.

Mezirow, Jack. *Fostering Critical Reflection in Adulthood: A Guide to Transformative and Emancipatory Learning*. San Francisco: Jossey-Bass, 1990.

Moyd, Olin P. *Redemption in Black Theology*. Valley Forge, Pa.: Judson, 1979.

O'Donnell, Ian, ed. *Prisoners, Solitude and Time*. Clarendon Studies in Criminology. Oxford: Oxford University Press, 2014.

Owen, Barbara A., Joycelyn M. Pollock, and James Wells. *In Search of Safety: Confronting Inequality in Women's Imprisonment*. Gender and Justice. Oakland: University of California Press, 2017.

Parker, Evelyn. "A Pedagogy of Redemption with Incarcerated Girls." In *Educating for Redemptive Community*, edited by Jack L. Seymour, Margaret Ann Crain, Denise Janssen, and Mary Elizabeth Moore, 111–23. Eugene, Ore.: Wipf & Stock, 2015.

Parker, Evelyn L. *Between Sisters: Emancipatory Hope out of Tragic Relationships*. Eugene, Ore.: Cascade, 2017.

Patterson, Orlando. *Slavery and Social Death: A Comparative Study*. Cambridge, Mass.: Harvard University Press, 1982.

Pitzele, Peter. *Scripture Windows: Towards a Practice of Bibliodrama*. Los Angeles: Alef Design Group, 1998.

Pollock, Joycelyn M. *Women's Crimes, Criminology, and Corrections*. Long Grove, Ill.: Waveland, 2014.

Rasch, Wilfried. "The Effects of Indeterminate Detention." *International Journal of Law and Psychiatry* 4, nos. 3–4 (1981): 417–31.

Reyes, Patrick B. *Nobody Cries When We Die: God, Community, and Surviving to Adulthood*. Saint Louis: Chalice Press, 2016.

Richie, Beth E. *Arrested Justice Black Women, Violence, and America's Prison Nation*. New York: NYU Press, 2012.

———. *Compelled to Crime: The Gender Entrapment of Battered Black Women*. New York: Routledge, 1996.

———. "Feminist Ethnographies of Women in Prison." *Feminist Studies* 30, no. 2 (2004): 438–50. https://doi.org/10.2307/20458973.

Ringer, Christophe D. *Necropolitics: The Religious Crisis of Mass Incarceration in America*. Lanham, Md.: Lexington Books, 2021.

Rizzo, Elaine, and Margaret Hayes. "Struggling for Healthcare in the Inside." *Correctional Healthcare Report*, 2011, 3–14.

Rothman, David J. *The Discovery of the Asylum: Social Order and Disorder in the New Republic*. Boston: Little, Brown, 1971.

Ruether, Rosemary Radford. *Introducing Redemption in Christian Feminism*. Introductions in Feminist Theology 1. Sheffield, England: Sheffield Academic, 1998.

Schutz, Alfred. *The Problem of Social Reality*. The Hague: Martinus Nijhoff, 1962.

Sered, Susan Starr, and Maureen Norton-Hawk. *Can't Catch a Break: Gender, Jail, Drugs and the Limits of Personal Responsibility*. Oakland: University of California Press, 2014.

Seymour, Jack L., Margaret Ann Crain, Denise Janssen, and Mary Elizabeth Moore. *Educating for Redemptive Community: Essays in Honor of Jack Seymour and Margaret Ann Crain*. Eugene, Ore.: Wipf & Stock, 2015.

Sharp, Susan F. *Mean Lives, Mean Laws: Oklahoma's Women Prisoners*. Critical Issues in Crime and Society. New Brunswick, N.J.: Rutgers University Press, 2014.

Smith, Brenda V., and Jamie M. Yarussi. *Breaking the Code of Silence: Correction Officers' Handbook on Identifying and Addressing Sexual Misconduct—Scholar's Choice Edition*. National Institute of Corrections, US Department of Justice. Scholar's Choice, 2015.

Snodgrass, Jill L. *Women Leaving Prison: Justice-Seeking Spiritual Support for Female Returning Citizens*. Lanham, Md.: Lexington Books, 2018.

Stanley, Eric A., and Nat Smith. *Captive Genders: Trans Embodiment and the Prison Industrial Complex*. Expanded 2nd ed. Oakland, Calif.; Edinburgh, Scotland: AK Press, 2015.

Stern, Kaia. *Voices from American Prisons: Faith, Education and Healing*. London: Routledge, 2014.

Stohr, Mary K. "The Hundred Years' War: The Etiology and Status of Assaults on Transgender Women in Men's Prisons." *Women & Criminal Justice* 25, nos. 1–2 (2015): 120–29. https://doi.org/10.1080/08974454.2015.1026154.

Swinton, John. "From Inclusion to Belonging: A Practical Theology of Community, Disability and Humanness." *Journal of Religion, Disability*

& *Health* 16, no. 2 (2012): 172–90. https://doi.org/10.1080/15228967.2012.676243.

Titchen, Angie, and Brendan McCormack. "Dancing with Stones: Critical Creativity as Methodology for Human Flourishing." *Educational Action Research* 18, no. 4 (2010): 531–54.

Townes, Emilie Maureen. *Womanist Ethics and the Cultural Production of Evil*. New York: Palgrave Macmillan, 2006.

———. *Womanist Justice, Womanist Hope*. American Academy of Religion 79. Atlanta: Scholars, 1993.

Tran, Mai-Anh Le. *Reset the Heart: Unlearning Violence, Relearning Hope*. Nashville: Abingdon, 2017.

Van Ginneken, Esther F. J. C. "Making Sense of Imprisonment: Narratives of Posttraumatic Growth among Female Prisoners." *International Journal of Offender Therapy and Comparative Criminology* 60, no. 2 (2016): 208–27.

Vanhooren, Siebrecht, Mia Leijssen, and Jessie Dezutter. "Loss of Meaning as a Predictor of Distress in Prison." *International Journal of Offender Therapy and Comparative Criminology* 61, no. 13 (2017): 1411–32.

———. "Ten Prisoners on a Search for Meaning: A Qualitative Study of Loss and Growth during Incarceration." *The Humanistic Psychologist* 45, no. 2 (2017): 162–78. https://doi.org/10.1037/hum0000055.

Vogl, Charles. *The Art of Community: Seven Principles for Belonging*. Oakland, Calif.: Berrett-Koehler, 2016.

Volf, Miroslav, and Dorothy C. Bass. *Practicing Theology: Beliefs and Practices in Christian Life*. Grand Rapids: Eerdmans, 2002.

Waldman, Ayelet, and Robin Levi, eds. *Inside This Place, Not of It: Narratives from Women's Prisons*. London: Verso, 2017.

Wenger, Etienne. *Communities of Practice: Learning, Meaning, and Identity*. Cambridge: Cambridge University Press, 1998.

Westfield, Nancy Lynne. *Being Black, Teaching Black: Politics and Pedagogy in Religious Studies*. Nashville: Abingdon, 2008.

———. "'Mama Why . . . ?' A Womanist Epistemology of Hope." In *Deeper Shades of Purple: Womanism in Religion and Society*, edited by Stacey M. Floyd-Thomas, 128–42. New York: NYU Press, 2006.

Williams, Delores S. *Sisters in the Wilderness: The Challenge of Womanist God-Talk*. Maryknoll, N.Y.: Orbis Books, 1993.

Williams, Kipling D., Joseph P. Forgas, and William von Hippel, eds. *The Social Outcast: Ostracism, Social Exclusion, Rejection, and Bullying*. New York: Psychology Press, 2005.

INDEX

abuse: physical, sexual, 7, 8, 97; substance, 8, 105
addiction, 14, 30, 104–6, 220n7
Advanced Certificate in Theological Studies, 11–12, 50–51, 64, 65, 79, 155, 169
adversarial growth, 31
Alcoholics Anonymous, 57, 105, 145, 163
Alternatives to Violence Project, 143–44, 160, 222n6
Althaus-Reid, Marcella, 21
Amari, 50–51, 57, 59, 61, 62, 92–93
Aminah, 99–100, 102–3, 108–10, 117, 119, 122, 151, 164–65, 167, 168, 170
Ancient Math, 142–44, 160, 192
Angola prison, 115, 211n25, 221n10
Arabella, 81–82, 85–86, 89, 92, 110–13, 115–17, 170–71

Baptist, 11, 20, 124, 145, 149, 161, 162, 163, 211n25
bathroom, 29–30, 32, 38–39, 41, 43
Bedford Hills Correctional Facility for Women, 11
belonging, 2, 4, 16, 17, 33, 41–43, 70, 92–93, 119–20, 123, 171, 174, 178–80, 188, 190–91, 225n40
Bible, 11, 12, 23–26, 60, 65, 68, 69–71, 77, 106, 125, 131, 134–36, 145, 148, 151, 158, 166, 183–84, 211n25, 213n2, 214n6

Biblical Foundations, x, 22, 58, 60–61, 70, 181, 183
Block, Peter, 178, 186
Bounds, Elizabeth, xv, 54–55
Braley, 50, 52–53, 59, 60–61, 62
Briar, 50–55, 58, 60–61, 62, 91, 123, 146, 183–84, 191
Brouhaha, 99–101, 103–4, 108, 110, 165–68

Cacho, Lisa Marie: *see* social death
Cannon, Katie, 182
carceral feminism, 7–8
carceral pedagogy: *see* pedagogy
Cat, 64–66, 72, 73
Cate, 1–4, 16, 34, 64–67, 72, 74, 80, 146, 169, 177, 199
Catholic, 124–25, 129–30, 145, 161
celebrating life, 15, 189
Certificate in Theological Studies/Theology: courses, 11, 141–44; graduation, 11; origin, 5–11, 212n26
chaplain, 5, 8–11, 14, 33, 124, 125, 155, 156
charter school, 63, 145, 171
children, 14, 20, 52, 56, 57, 59, 67, 81, 85, 90, 102, 108, 110, 120, 124, 127–28, 136, 139, 150–51, 154–55, 162, 191
choosing names, 17, 178, 181–82, 190
church, 18, 20, 23, 25, 52, 57, 60, 67, 76–78, 124–26, 136–37, 153, 158–59, 161–62, 185, 189

Claira, 15, 32, 34–35, 37, 81–90, 110–15, 117–19, 170–71, 221n10; homework, 29–32, 38–47, 215n8
Clarisse, 50–53, 57–62, 123
Clear, Todd, 106
coercive power, 33
college-in-prison, 9–10, 164, 210n19
coming together, 17, 178–79, 190
community capacity, 57
Compassionate Integrity Training, 71, 143–44, 222n5
Cone, James, 186–87
conning, 117–18, 221n14
considering one another, 17, 178, 182–84, 190
correctional officers, xvi, 20–22, 26, 27, 29, 40, 60, 61–63, 71–72, 76, 78, 97–98, 107, 113, 116, 131, 139, 153, 159, 164, 180, 191, 224n12
count, 27, 49, 98, 112; emergency, 26–27
court, 28, 42, 150, 152
creating theology, 17, 178, 186–88, 190
Creative Justice (CJ), 126–28, 132–41, 149, 184, 191
critical creativity, 187–88
critical questioning, 17, 178, 184–86, 188, 190

dance, 66, 169, 185, 187, 188
Darla, 181
death: in Gospel narratives, 198–202; near-death experiences, 112; of loved ones, 1, 152, 157; saving from, 104, 114; small doses of, 36, 216n23; theme of incarceration, xi, 1–2, 74, 190; *see also* social death
dignity, 2, 30, 33, 36, 37, 38, 40, 43–46, 95, 118, 121, 175, 187, 194, 203–5
disconnection, 41, 43, 92, 204
dishonor, 33, 43, 215n17
disidentification, 38, 204
disimagination, 39–41, 187, 204
domestic violence, 7, 152, 219n13

domination: bell hooks, 123, 179, 186; contexts, institutions, or systems of, 4, 16–17, 37, 44–45, 123; gender, 6; in research, xiii; in social death, 33; logic of, xi, 32; pedagogies of, 5, 176, 205, 226n43; practices of, 5, 176; relationship to dignity, 44–45, 121
dorm, 21–23, 26, 43, 49, 61, 63, 72, 76, 106, 108, 115, 124, 131, 138–41, 146, 155, 160, 164, 179, 191, 219n12, 222n3
dreams, xv, 39–40, 86, 112–13, 151
drug treatment, 105
drugs, 7, 14, 22, 54, 69, 79, 105, 113, 130, 138, 157, 163, 220n6
Dube, Musa, 200
dynamism, 16, 17, 92–93, 96, 119–21, 123, 133, 171, 173–74, 192

education, prison, 2, 54, 59–60, 101, 102, 116, 123, 133–34, 139, 142–45, 155; as practice of freedom, 27; attainment among incarcerated students, 14, 80, 102; death-dealing, 18, 37–38, 40, 45–46, 203–4; emancipatory, 176, 186, 223n9, 225n40; for extinction, 36; importance of, 101, 123, 133, 162; life-affirming, 104–5; post-secondary/higher education in prison, 5–10, 209n5, 210n19; process of, 173; redemptive, 175; *see also* theological education
Ellison, Gregory, 2, 208n3

family, 1, 11, 23, 43, 52–53, 57, 59, 60, 63, 65, 67–70, 74–75, 76, 81, 86, 89–91, 95, 101–2, 104, 105–6, 111, 120, 124, 127–28, 130, 136–37, 139, 140, 149–52, 161, 163, 169, 170, 189, 191, 199
felon, 35, 38–39, 56, 171; conviction, 55–56; felony, 55–56, 126; record, 55–57

felony: *see* felon
finagle, finagling, 117–19, 221n14, 221n15; *see also* conning
Flanagan, Timothy, 39
flourishing, 61–62, 80–81, 109–10, 140, 143, 164, 177, 188, 203
freedom, xiii–xiv, 4, 15–17, 27, 33, 59, 62–64, 80–81, 84–89, 93, 96, 102, 103–5, 109, 111, 114, 118–21, 123, 140, 164, 167, 171, 173–75, 180, 181, 186–88, 190, 193–95, 203, 223–24n12
Freire, Paulo, xiii, 181, 184, 225n29, 226n43
futuring, 175–76, 186, 193

GED, 9–10, 14, 63, 116, 134, 145, 152, 155, 170, 171
God, xvii, 3–4, 12, 17–18, 24–25, 44–46, 58–59, 65–71, 76–79, 85, 114, 125–28, 130, 134, 136–38, 140, 148, 151–53, 162, 166, 173–77, 180, 187–95, 197–98, 201–5, 224n13, 226n53
good day, 71–73, 190
good life: definition, 16, 89–93; descriptions of, 51–68, 80–81, 84–87, 89, 101–2, 106, 127–29, 138, 140, 150; drawings, 87–89, 90–91; possibilities in prison, 73–76, 95–96, 102–4, 110–12, 119, 132
Goto, Courtney, 187, 214n4
Greene, Maxine, 176, 181, 184–86, 223n9, 224n22, 225n40

Handsome, 64–67, 72, 74–75
Harold, 81–82, 84–89, 93, 110, 112, 114–15, 117, 121–22, 171
Higher Education Act of 1965, 8–9
Hill Collins, Patricia, 95–96, 207n2, 220n3
Honey Bee II (HB II), 9, 126–31, 133, 135, 140–41
hooks, bell, xiv, 26–27, 123, 179, 182, 186, 225n24
Hope, 149–53, 158–64, 191

hope, x–xiv, 3, 5, 16–18, 22–24, 26, 36, 39, 40, 42–43, 46, 55, 57, 59, 66, 77, 80–83, 85–93, 96, 100, 102, 105–7, 111, 112, 119, 120–22, 123–24, 127, 128, 133, 150–52, 153, 156, 171, 173, 174, 175, 181, 182, 186–88, 194–95, 197–98, 200–205, 214n4, 221n17,

Ilillana, 81–82, 85–86, 89, 110–15, 117, 119, 170, 171, 220n10
incarcerated women, 6, 8, 10, 14, 212n27, 212n29, 212n31, 215n8
inmate, 8, 27, 30, 32, 33, 38–43, 97, 109, 153, 181, 208n2, 210n17, 211n25, 212n28, 212n31, 213n34, 220n10
inspection, 22, 27, 36, 47, 71–73
institutional circuit, 54
integrity, 69, 71, 121; *see also* Compassionate Integrity Training

jail, 24, 25, 104, 113, 124, 148, 162, 163, 165, 209n8, 212n33, 213n36, 214n6,
Jairus, daughter, 199
Jehovah's Witness, 14, 65, 67, 68, 76
Jennings, Willie, 189
Jesus, 4, 17, 70, 73, 76–77, 141, 153, 159, 163, 168, 169, 197–202
Joan, 123–28, 132–35, 140–42
Jordan, 99–101, 104–6, 110, 168
joy, ix, xv, 17, 37, 62, 80, 85, 90, 105, 109, 140, 152, 164, 189–90, 192, 200
Jum'ah, 63, 99, 145, 153–54
Junker, Debora, 173, 194–95, 223n6
juveniles, 108

Kairos, 10, 123, 130, 145–46
Karisma, 99–103, 107, 110, 148, 165, 167–68
Kazemian, Lila, 31, 75

Lazarus, 210–12
Le Tran, Mai-Anh, 40

240 | Index

Lempert, Lora Bex, 81–82, 216n23
lessons in dying, 35–36, 39–40, 42, 47
liberating practices: see practices
life sentence, 28, 64–65, 82, 84, 85, 100, 107, 115, 124, 126, 127, 132, 150–52, 164, 215n8
life-affirming practices: see practices
lifers, 81–82, 100, 110, 114–17, 126, 140, 147, 149, 151, 155, 164, 171,
Lloyd, Vincent, 44–45

Malcolm X, 136, 153–54
Master of Professional Studies (MPS), 11
Mbembe, Achille, 36, 216n22, 216n25
McGuire, Dyan, 32
medical, 23, 115
Mena, 64–75, 147–48
mental health, 8, 106, 125, 163
Methodist, 124
Mickey, 158–59
Moon, 126–29, 132–36, 140–41
Morgen, 90, 92, 149–52, 156–57, 159, 160, 164, 166, 191
Mud Flower Collective, 187, 217n3

Narcotics Anonymous, 57, 105–6, 125, 145
natal alienation, 33, 215n17
necropedagogy, 36
New Orleans Baptist Theological Seminary, 11, 211n25
New York Theological Seminary (NYTS), 11
Nikki, 65–67, 147

occupational collateral consequences, 56
offender, 8, 22, 26, 38–39, 57, 83, 98, 106, 116, 138, 219n12
Owen, Barbara, 6, 209n12, 210n16

Parker, Evelyn, 121, 190, 194
parole, 59, 64, 85, 93, 100, 126–29, 140, 147, 152; life without, 9, 100, 151

pathways, 5, 6, 8, 198, 203, 210n15, 212n27
Patterson, Orlando: see social death
pedagogy, 3, 5, 17, 34, 215–16n20; carceral, 18, 213n36; critical, 181; embodied, 34, 160; necropedagogy, 36; practice and, 193, 204, 226–27n54; redemptive, 190, 194; relational, 175, 182, 223n7; see also social death, 160, 175–76, 178, 181, 182, 184, 188, 190, 193–95, 198, 204–5, 213n3, 215–16n20, 223n7, 223n9, 226n43, 226–27n54
Pell Grant, 8–9, 210n19, 211n21
Pellauer, Mary, 183
Pentecostal, 153, 159, 161
practices, ethnographic, xi; carceral, 18, 38, 44, 189; in social death, 15, 33–37, 43, 205; liberating, 176, 181; life-affirming, 17, 173–78, 193–94; pedagogical, 5, 204; redemptive, 17, 190, 195, 225n40; religious, 125, 135, 154, 168; survival, 122
praxis, 17, 181, 183, 191, 198, 199, 202–4
Prison Fellowship, 10
Prison Policy Initiative, 10, 13, 212n29
Prison Rape Elimination Act (PREA), 96
prisons for women: ministry in, xii, 10–11; mothering in, 56, 100, 120, 212n33; statistics, 6–8, 13–15, 100, 105, 208n2, 209n9, 212nn29–32; see also Kairos

redemptive, 4, 164, 174–75, 177, 189, 194–95, 199, 201, 205; community, 173, 190, 194–95, 223n6; see also pedagogy; practices
relationships, 41, 43, 54, 74, 89–92, 108, 111, 120, 122, 128, 146, 157,

158, 176, 179, 190–92, 198–99, 203, 204, 220n15, 221n13
release: *see* parole
Residential Substance Abuse Treatment (RSAT), 105–6
responsibility, xiv, 4, 28, 38, 54–55, 67, 128–29, 136, 138, 149, 198, 201, 205, 223n6
restorative justice, 70, 152–53, 212n26
Reyes, Patrick, 45–46
Richie, Beth, 6–7, 219n13
Ruether, Rosemary Radford, 174
Rylee, 50, 52, 57–61, 95, 132, 145

Scott, 149–50, 152, 158–59
Sing Sing Prison, 11, 33
Sister, 149–56, 158
slavery, 33–34, 37, 215n17, 223n12
social death: education, 15, 34–47, 92, 189; institution, 16, 34, 49, 92–93, 111, 122, 171, 173, 187, 194, 216n25; and Lisa Marie Cacho, 16, 49; and Orlando Patterson, 15, 33–34, 215n16, 215n17, 216n25; theory, 15–17, 33–35, 37, 173, 175, 177, 180, 186, 188, 195, 198, 205, 215n16, 216n25; *see also* practices
Spicey, 64–67, 72, 73, 75–80, 91, 219–20n13
Spirit, 149–52, 157–58, 160, 164
spirituality, 99, 130, 137, 142–43, 145–46, 155, 156, 170, 177, 186, 194
Stern, Kaia, 2
suicide, 42, 96, 108, 125
support groups, 63, 107, 125, 135–36, 145–46
survival: criminalization of, 7–8; mode, 73; needs, 62, 100, 117, 175; strategies and practices, 60, 118–19, 122, 181, 187; as vocation, 46
Swinton, John, 119, 179–80

talitha cum: *see* Dube, Musa; Jairus, daughter
theological education, in prison, 4–5, 10–12, 14–19, 190–95, 215n19; life-affirming, 202–5; purposes, xi, 3, 176, 197, 224n14, 227n5; *see also* Certificate in Theological Studies
Theological Foundations, 21, 60, 84, 144
Theology: *see* Certificate in Theological Studies
theology, 45, 168, 183, 205, 227n5; embedded, 162–63; embodied, 214n4; feminist, 217n3; liberation, 175; practical, x, xii, 5, 45, 121, 193; *see also* creating theology
thirty-year rule, 126, 127, 149–50
Townes, Emilie, 110, 176, 221n17
transition center, 64
trauma, 8, 31–32, 38, 46, 113, 135–36, 145
trickster, 118–19
turning points, 31, 157

Violent Crime and Law Enforcement Act, 9
vocation, xiv, 38, 45–46, 203, 204
vocational-technical, 63, 135, 145
voodoo, 136–37

War on Drugs, 7
Westfield, Lynne, 175, 186
wholeness, 61, 80, 109–10, 119, 140–41, 164, 203, 221n17
wide-awakeness, 184–85
widow from Nain, 198–99
Williams, Kipling, 41–43

youth detention center, 86

Zakkiyah, 99–102, 104, 107–8, 110, 165, 167–70

www.ingramcontent.com/pod-product-compliance
Lightning Source LLC
Chambersburg PA
CBHW041310240426
43661CB00064B/2886